React and React Native

Fifth Edition

Build cross-platform JavaScript and TypeScript apps for the web, desktop, and mobile

Mikhail Sakhniuk

Adam Boduch

React and React Native
Fifth Edition

Publishing Product Manager: Lucy Wan
Acquisition Editor – Peer Reviews: Gaurav Gavas
Senior Project Editor: Rianna Rodrigues
Senior Content Development Editor: Matthew Davies
Content Development Editor: Shazeen Iqbal
Copy Editor: Safis Editing
Technical Editor: Simanta Rajbangshi
Proofreader: Safis Editing
Indexer: Pratik Shirodkar
Presentation Designer: Rajesh Shirsath
Senior Developer Relations Marketing Executive: Priyadarshini Sharma

First published: February 2017
Second edition: September 2018
Third edition: April 2020
Fourth edition: May 2022
Fifth edition: April 2024

Production reference: 1230424

Published by Packt Publishing Ltd.
Grosvenor House
11 St Paul's Square
Birmingham
B3 1RB, UK.

ISBN 978-1-80512-730-7

www.packt.com

Contributors

About the authors

Mikhail Sakhniuk is a seasoned software engineer specializing in TypeScript, React, and React Native. With extensive experience in developing web and mobile applications, he has worked for start-ups, fintech companies, and product companies serving millions of users. Currently, Mikhail holds a Principal Frontend Engineer position at KappaPay. In addition to his professional work, he actively contributes to the developer community by maintaining several open-source projects and sharing his knowledge through books and articles.

Adam Boduch has been involved in large-scale JavaScript development for nearly 15 years. Before moving to the frontend, he worked on several large-scale cloud computing products using Python and Linux. No stranger to complexity, Adam has practical experience with real-world software systems and the scaling challenges they pose.

About the reviewers

Jonathan Reeves is a software engineer specializing in React and TypeScript programming. He has implemented React with TypeScript at companies such as Home Depot, Toyota, and Walmart. He is currently working on implementing internal tools within the gaming industry, making use of React for the UI. Additionally, he was one of the reviewers for *React 18: Design Patterns and Best Practices*.

I would like to thank my wife, Sondra, as well as my children, Ava and Grayson, for their continued support in what I do and believing in me to always finish what I start. I love you all.

Slava Knyazev has been writing software since he was 12 and has been advancing his mastery of the craft ever since. He has worked for well-known companies, including theScore, Amazon Web Services, Airbnb, and the Government of Canada. His favorite part of work is the opportunity to solve challenging problems and discover the "Aha!" moment in them. When he isn't writing code, he often shares his latest thoughts on his blog, "Building Better Software Slower."

Join us on Discord!

Read this book alongside other users and the authors themselves. Ask questions, provide solutions to other readers, chat with the authors, and more. Scan the QR code or visit the link to join the community.

https://packt.link/ReactAndReactNative5e

Table of Contents

Chapter 4: Event Handling in the React Way · 57

Chapter 5: Crafting Reusable Components · 67

Chapter 8: Code Splitting Using Lazy Components and Suspense   121

Chapter 9: User Interface Framework Components   133

Chapter 19: Navigating Between Screens   301

Chapter 20: Rendering Item Lists   325

Chapter 21: Geolocation and Maps   345

Chapter 28: Going Offline   449

Other Books You May Enjoy   467

Index   471

Preface

Over the years, **React** and **React Native** have proven themselves among JavaScript developers as popular choices for a comprehensive and practical guide to the React ecosystem. This fifth edition comes with the latest features, enhancements, and fixes of React, while also being compatible with React Native. It includes new chapters covering critical features and concepts in modern cross-platform app development with React and **TypeScript**.

From the basics of React to popular features such as **Hooks**, server rendering, and unit testing, this definitive guide will help you become a professional React developer in a step-by-step manner.

You'll begin by learning about the essential building blocks of React components. Next, you'll learn how to improve the stability of your components using TypeScript. As you advance through the chapters, you'll work with higher-level functionalities in application development and then put your knowledge to work by developing user interface components for the web and native platforms.

By the end of this book, you'll be able to build React applications for the web and React Native applications for multiple platforms: web, mobile, and desktop: with confidence.

Who this book is for

This book is for any JavaScript developer who wants to start learning how to use React and React Native for mobile and web application development. No prior knowledge of React is required; however, working knowledge of JavaScript, HTML and CSS is necessary to be able to follow along with the content covered.

What this book covers

Chapter 1, Why React?, describes what React is and why you want to use it to build your application.

Chapter 2, Rendering with JSX, teaches the basics of JSX, the markup language used by React components.

Chapter 3, Understanding React Components and Hooks, introduces the core mechanisms of components and Hooks in React application.

Chapter 4, Event Handling, the React Way, gives an overview of how events are handled by React components.

Chapter 5, Crafting Reusable Components, guides you through the process of refactoring components by example.

Chapter 6, Type Checking and Validation with TypeScript, describes the various phases that React components go through and why it's important for React developers.

Chapter 7, Handling Navigations with Routes, provides plenty of examples of how to set up routing for your React web app.

Chapter 8, Code Splitting Using Lazy Components and Suspense, introduces code-splitting techniques that result in performant, more efficient applications.

Chapter 9, User Interface Framework Components, gives an overview of how to get started with MUI, a React component library for building UIs.

Chapter 10, High-Performance State Updates, goes into depth on the new features in React that allow for efficient state updates and a high-performing application.

Chapter 11, Fetching Data from a Server, discusses how we can retrieve the data from servers using various ways.

Chapter 12, State Management in React, covers managing state in the app with popular solutions like Redux and Mobx.

Chapter 13, Server-Side Rendering, teaches you how to use Next.js to build large-scale React applications that render content on a server and a client.

Chapter 14, Unit Testing in React, gives an overview of testing software with focus on unit testing using Vittest.

Chapter 15, Why React Native?, describes what the React Native library is and the differences between native mobile development.

Chapter 16, React Native under the Hood, gives an overview of the architecture of React Native.

Chapter 17, Kick-Starting React Native Projects, teaches you how to start a new React Native project.

Chapter 18, Building Responsive Layouts with Flexbox, describes how to create a layout and add styles.

Chapter 19, Navigating between Screens, shows the approaches to switching between screens in an app.

Chapter 20, Rendering Item Lists, describes how to implement lists of data in an application.

Chapter 21, Geolocation and Maps, explains on how to track geolocation and add a map to an app.

Chapter 22, Collecting User Input, teaches you how to create forms.

Chapter 23, Responding to User Gestures, provides examples of how to handle user gestures.

Chapter 24, Showing Progress, shows you how to handle process indications and progress bars.

Chapter 25, Displaying Modal Screens, teaches you how to create dialog modals.

Chapter 26, Using Animations, describes how to implement animations in an app.

Chapter 27, Controlling Image Display, gives an overview of how to render images in a React Native app.

Chapter 28, Going Offline, shows how to deal with an app when a mobile phone doesn't have an internet connection.

To get the most out of this book

This book assumes you have a basic understanding of the JavaScript programming language. It also assumes that you'll be following along with the examples, which require a command-line terminal, a code editor, and a web browser. You'll learn how to set up a React project in *Chapter 1, Why React?*.

The requirements for learning React Native are the same as for React development, but to run an app on a real device, you will need an Android or iOS smartphone. In order to run iOS apps in the simulator, you will need a Mac computer. To work with Android simulator, you can use any kind of PC.

Download the example code files

The code bundle for the book is hosted on GitHub at https://github.com/PacktPublishing/React-and-React-Native-5E. We also have other code bundles from our rich catalog of books and videos available at https://github.com/PacktPublishing/. Check them out!

Download the color images

We also provide a PDF file that has color images of the screenshots/diagrams used in this book. You can download it here: https://packt.link/gbp/9781805127307.

Conventions used

There are a number of text conventions used throughout this book.

CodeInText: Indicates code words in text, database table names, folder names, filenames, file extensions, pathnames, dummy URLs, user input, and Twitter handles. For example: "You have the actual routes declared as <Route> elements."

A block of code is set as follows:

```
export default function First() {
  return <p>Feature 1, page 1</p>;
}
```

When we wish to draw your attention to a particular part of a code block, the relevant lines or items are set in bold:

```
export default function List({ data, fetchItems, refreshItems,
isRefreshing }) {
  return (
    <FlatList
data={data}
      renderItem={({ item }) => <Text style={styles.
item}>{item.value}</Text>}
onEndReached={fetchItems} onRefresh={refreshItems}
refreshing={isRefreshing}
/> );
}
```

Any command-line input or output is written as follows:

```
npm install @react-navigation/bottom-tabs @react-navigation/
drawer
```

Bold: Indicates a new term, an important word, or words that you see on the screen. For instance, words in menus or dialog boxes appear in the text like this. For example: "Select **System info** from the **Administration** panel."

 Warnings or important notes appear like this.

 Tips and tricks appear like this.

Get in touch

Feedback from our readers is always welcome.

General feedback: Email feedback@packtpub.com and mention the book's title in the subject of your message. If you have questions about any aspect of this book, please email us at questions@packtpub.com.

Errata: Although we have taken every care to ensure the accuracy of our content, mistakes do happen. If you have found a mistake in this book, we would be grateful if you reported this to us. Please visit http://www.packtpub.com/submit-errata, click **Submit Errata**, and fill in the form.

Piracy: If you come across any illegal copies of our works in any form on the internet, we would be grateful if you would provide us with the location address or website name. Please contact us at copyright@packtpub.com with a link to the material.

If you are interested in becoming an author: If there is a topic that you have expertise in and you are interested in either writing or contributing to a book, please visit http://authors.packtpub.com.

Share your thoughts

Once you've read *React and React Native, Fifth Edition,* we'd love to hear your thoughts! Scan the QR code below to go straight to the Amazon review page for this book and share your feedback.

https://packt.link/r/1805127306

Your review is important to us and the tech community and will help us make sure we're delivering excellent quality content.

Download a free PDF copy of this book

Thanks for purchasing this book!

Do you like to read on the go but are unable to carry your print books everywhere?

Is your eBook purchase not compatible with the device of your choice?

Don't worry, now with every Packt book you get a DRM-free PDF version of that book at no cost.

Read anywhere, any place, on any device. Search, copy, and paste code from your favorite technical books directly into your application.

The perks don't stop there, you can get exclusive access to discounts, newsletters, and great free content in your inbox daily.

Follow these simple steps to get the benefits:

1. Scan the QR code or visit the link below:

https://packt.link/free-ebook/9781805127307

2. Submit your proof of purchase.
3. That's it! We'll send your free PDF and other benefits to your email directly.

Part 1

React

In this part, we will cover the fundamentals of React tools and concepts, applying them to build high-performance web apps.

In this part, we will cover the following chapters:

- *Chapter 1, Why React?*
- *Chapter 2, Rendering with JSX*
- *Chapter 3, Understanding React Components and Hooks*
- *Chapter 4, Event Handling in the React Way*
- *Chapter 5, Crafting Reusable Components*
- *Chapter 6, Type-Checking and Validation with TypeScript*
- *Chapter 7, Handling Navigations with Routes*
- *Chapter 8, Code Splitting Using Lazy Components and Suspense*
- *Chapter 9, User Interface Framework Components*
- *Chapter 10, High-Performance State Updates*
- *Chapter 11, Fetching Data from a Server*
- *Chapter 12, State Management in React*
- *Chapter 13, Server-Side Rendering*
- *Chapter 14, Unit Testing in React*

1

Why React?

If you're reading this book, you probably are already familiar with **React**. But if you're not, don't worry. I'll do my best to keep philosophical definitions to a minimum. However, this is a long book with a lot of content, so I feel that setting the tone is an appropriate first step. Our goal is to learn React and **React Native**, but it's also to build a scalable and adaptive architecture that can handle everything we want to build with React today and in the future. In other words, we want to create a foundation around React, with a set of additional tools and approaches that can withstand the test of time. This book will guide you through the process of using tools like routing, TypeScript typing, testing, and many more.

This chapter starts with a brief explanation of why React exists. Then, we'll think about the simplicity of React and how it is able to handle many of the typical performance issues faced by web developers. Next, we'll go over the declarative philosophy of React and the level of abstraction that React programmers can expect to work with. Then, we'll touch on some of the major features of React. And finally, we will explore how we can set up a project to start to work with React.

Once you have a conceptual understanding of React and how it solves problems with UI development, you'll be better equipped to tackle the remainder of the book. This chapter will cover the following topics:

- What is React?
- What's new in React?
- Setting up a new React project

What is React?

I think the one-line description of React on its home page (`https://react.dev/`) is concise and accurate:

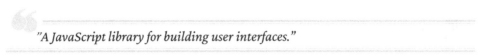

> *"A JavaScript library for building user interfaces."*

This is perfect because, as it turns out, this is all we want most of the time. I think the best part about this description is everything that it leaves out. It's not a mega-framework. It's not a full-stack solution that's going to handle everything, from the database to real-time updates over **WebSocket** connections. We might not actually want most of these prepackaged solutions. If React isn't a framework, then what is it exactly?

React is just the view layer

React is generally thought of as the *view layer* in an application. Applications are typically divided into different layers, such as the view layer, the logic layer, and the data layer. React, in this context, primarily handles the view layer, which involves rendering and updating the UI based on changes in data and application state. React components change what the user sees. The following diagram illustrates where React fits in our frontend code:

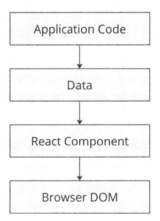

Figure 1.1: The layers of a React application

This is all there is to React – the core concept. Of course, there will be subtle variations to this theme as we make our way through the book, but the flow is more or less the same:

1. **Application logic**: Start with some application logic that generates data.
2. **Rendering data to the UI**: The next step is to render this data to the UI.
3. **React component**: To accomplish this, you pass the data to a React component.
4. **Component's role**: The React component takes on the responsibility of getting the HTML onto the page.

You may wonder what the big deal is; React appears to be yet another rendering technology. We'll touch on some of the key areas where React can simplify application development in the remaining sections of the chapter.

Simplicity is good

React doesn't have many moving parts to learn about and understand. While React boasts a relatively simple API, it's important to note that beneath the surface, React operates with a degree of complexity. Throughout this book, we will delve into these internal workings, exploring various aspects of React's architecture and mechanisms to provide you with a comprehensive understanding. The advantage of having a small API to work with is that you can spend more time familiarizing yourself with it, experimenting with it, and so on. The opposite is true of large frameworks, where all of your time is devoted to figuring out how everything works. The following diagram gives you a rough idea of the APIs that we have to think about when programming with React:

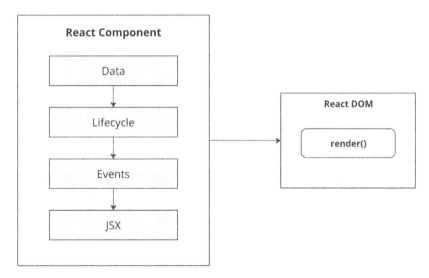

Figure 1.2: The simplicity of the React API

React is divided into two major APIs:

- **The React Component API**: These are the parts of the page that are rendered by the **React DOM**.
- **React DOM**: This is the API that's used to perform the rendering on a web page.

Within a React component, we have the following areas to think about:

- **Data**: This is data that comes from somewhere (the component doesn't care where) and is rendered by the component.
- **Lifecycle**: For example, one phase of the lifecycle is when the component is about to be rendered. Within a React component, methods or hooks respond to the component's entering and exiting phases of the React rendering process as they happen over time.
- **Events**: These are the code that we write to respond to user interactions.
- **JSX**: This is the syntax commonly used for describing UI structures in React components. Even though JSX is closely associated with React, it can also be used alongside other **JavaScript** frameworks and libraries.

Don't fixate on what these different areas of the React API represent just yet. The takeaway here is that React, by nature, is simple. Just look at how little there is to figure out! This means that we don't have to spend a ton of time going through API details here. Instead, once you pick up on the basics, we can spend more time on nuanced React usage patterns that fit in nicely with declarative UI structures.

Declarative UI structures

React newcomers have a hard time getting to grips with the idea that components mix in markup with their JavaScript in order to declare UI structures. If you've looked at React examples and had the same adverse reaction, don't worry. Initially, we can be skeptical of this approach, and I think the reason is that we've been conditioned for decades by the *separation of concerns* principle. This principle states that different concerns, such as logic and presentation, should be separate from one another. Now, whenever we see things combined, we automatically assume that this is bad and shouldn't happen.

The syntax used by React components is called **JSX** (short for **JavaScript XML**, also known as **JavaScript Syntax Extension**). A component renders content by returning some JSX. The JSX itself is usually HTML markup, mixed with custom tags for React components. The specifics don't matter at this point; we'll go into detail in the coming chapters.

What's groundbreaking about the declarative JSX approach is that we don't have to manually perform intricate operations to change the content of a component. Instead, we describe how the UI should look in different states, and React efficiently updates the actual DOM to match. As a result, React UIs become easier and more efficient to work with, resulting in better performance.

For example, think about using something such as jQuery to build your application. You have a page with some content on it, and you want to add a class to a paragraph when a button is clicked:

```
$(document).ready(function() {
  $('#my-button').click(function() {
    $('#my-paragraph').addClass('highlight');
  });
});
```

Performing these steps is easy enough. This is called imperative programming, and it's problematic for UI development. The problem with imperative programming in UI development is that it can lead to code that is difficult to maintain and modify. This is because imperative code is often tightly coupled, meaning that changes to one part of the code can have unintended consequences elsewhere. Additionally, imperative code can be difficult to reason about, as it can be hard to understand the flow of control and the state of an application at any given time. While this example of changing the class of an element is simple, real applications tend to involve more than three or four steps to make something happen.

React components don't require you to execute steps in an imperative way. This is why JSX is central to React components. The XML-style syntax makes it easy to describe what the UI should look like – that is, what are the HTML elements that component is going to render?

```
export const App = () => {
  const [isHighlighted, setIsHighlighted] = useState(false);
  return (
    <div>
      <button onClick={() => setIsHighlighted(true)}>Add Class</button>
      <p className={isHighlighted && "highlight"}>This is paragraph</p>
    </div>
  );
};
```

In this example, we're not just writing the imperative procedure that the browser should execute. This is more like an instruction, where we say how the UI should look and what user interaction should happen on it. This is called declarative programming and is very well suited for UI development. Once you've declared your UI structure, you need to specify how it changes over time.

Data changes over time

Another area that's difficult for React newcomers to grasp is the idea that JSX is like a static string, representing a chunk of rendered output. This is where data and the passage of time come into play. React components rely on data being passed into them. This data represents the dynamic parts of the UI – for example, a UI element that's rendered based on a Boolean value could change the next time the component is rendered. Here's a diagram illustrating the idea:

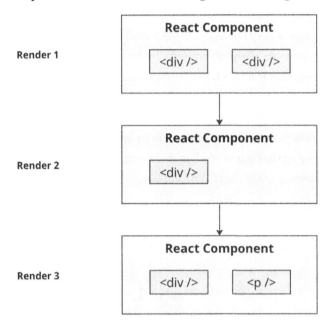

Figure 1.3: React components changing over time

Each time the React component is rendered, it's like taking a snapshot of the JSX at that exact moment in time. As your application moves forward through time, you have an ordered collection of rendered UI components. In addition to declaratively describing what a UI should be, re-rendering the same JSX content makes things much easier for developers. The challenge is making sure that React can handle the performance demands of this approach.

Performance matters

Using React to build UIs means that we can declare the structure of the UI with JSX. This is less error-prone than the imperative approach of assembling the UI piece by piece. However, the declarative approach does present a challenge with performance.

For example, having a declarative UI structure is fine for the initial rendering because there's nothing on the page yet. So the React renderer can look at the structure declared in JSX and render it in the DOM browser.

 The Document Object Model (DOM) represents HTML in the browser after it has been rendered. The DOM API is how JavaScript is able to change content on a page.

This concept is illustrated in the following diagram:

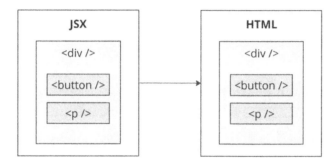

Figure 1.4: How JSX syntax translates to HTML in the browser DOM

On the initial render, React components and their JSX are no different from other template libraries. For instance, there is a templating library called **Handlebars** used for server-side rendering, which will render a template to HTML markup as a string that is then inserted into the browser DOM. Where React is different from libraries such as Handlebars is that React can accommodate when data changes and we need to re-render the component, whereas Handlebars will just re-build the entire HTML string, the same way it did on the initial render. Since this is problematic for performance, we often end up implementing imperative workarounds that manually update tiny bits of the DOM. We end up with a tangled mess of declarative templates and imperative code to handle the dynamic aspects of the UI.

We don't do this in React. This is what sets React apart from other view libraries. Components are declarative for the initial render, and they stay this way even as they're re-rendered. It's what React does under the hood that makes re-rendering declarative UI structures possible.

In React, however, when we create a component, we describe what it should look like clearly and straightforwardly. Even as we update our components, React handles the changes smoothly behind the scenes. In other words, components are declarative for the initial render, and they stay this way even as they're re-rendered. This is possible because React employs the virtual DOM, which is used to keep a representation of the real DOM elements in memory. It does this so that each time we re-render a component, it can compare the new content to the content that's already displayed on the page. Based on the difference, the virtual DOM can execute the imperative steps necessary to make the changes. So not only do we get to keep our declarative code when we need to update the UI but React will also make sure that it's done in a performant way. Here's what this process looks like:

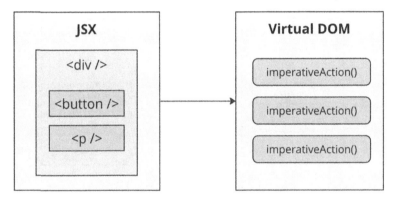

Figure 1.5: React transpiles JSX syntax into imperative DOM API calls

When you read about React, you'll often see words such as **diffing** and **patching**. Diffing means comparing *old content* (the previous state of the UI) with *new content* (the updated state) to identify the differences, much like comparing two versions of a document to see what's changed. Patching means executing the necessary DOM operations to render the new content, ensuring that only the specific changes are made, which is crucial for performance.

As with any other JavaScript library, React is constrained by the *run-to-completion* nature of the main thread. For example, if the React virtual DOM logic is busy diffing content and patching the real DOM, the browser can't respond to user input such as clicks or interactions.

As you'll see in the next section of this chapter, changes were made to the internal rendering algorithms in React to mitigate these performance pitfalls. With performance concerns addressed, we need to make sure that we're confident that React is flexible enough to adapt to the different platforms that we might want to deploy our apps to in the future.

The right level of abstraction

Another topic I want to cover at a high level before we dive into React code is **abstraction**.

In the preceding section, you saw how JSX syntax translates to low-level operations that update our UI. A better way to look at how React translates our declarative UI components is via the fact that we don't necessarily care what the render target is. The render target happens to be the browser DOM with React, but, as we will see, it isn't restricted to the browser DOM.

React has the potential to be used for any UI we want to create, on any conceivable device. We're only just starting to see this with React Native, but the possibilities are endless. I would not be surprised if *React Toast*, which is totally not a thing, suddenly becomes relevant, where React targets toasters that can singe the rendered output of JSX onto bread. React's abstraction level strikes a balance that allows for versatility and adaptability while maintaining a practical and efficient approach to UI development.

The following diagram gives you an idea of how React can target more than just the browser:

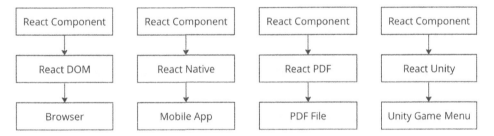

Figure 1.6: React abstracts the target rendering environment from the components that we implement

From left to right, we have **React DOM, React Native, React PDF**, and **React Unity**. All of these React Renderer libraries accept the React component and return a platform-specific result. As you can see, to target something new, the same pattern applies:

- Implement components specific to the target.
- Implement a React renderer that can perform the platform-specific operations under the hood.

This is, obviously, an oversimplification of what's actually implemented for any given React environment. But the details aren't so important to us. What's important is that we can use our React knowledge to focus on describing the structure of our UI on any platform.

Now that you understand the role of abstractions in React, let's see what's new in React.

What's new in React?

React is a continuously evolving library in the ever-changing web development landscape. As you embark on your journey to learn and master React, it's important to understand the evolution of the library and its updates over time.

One of the advantages of React is that its core API has remained relatively stable in recent years. This provides a sense of continuity and allows developers to leverage their knowledge from previous versions. The conceptual foundation of React has remained intact, meaning that the skills acquired three or five years ago can still be applied today. Let's take a step back and trace the history of React from its early versions to the recent ones. From **React 0.x** to **React 18**, numerous pivotal changes and enhancements have been made as follows:

- **React 0.14**: In this version, the introduction of functional components allowed developers to utilize functions as components, simplifying the creation of basic UI elements. At that time, no one knew that now we would write only functional components and almost completely abandon class-based components.
- **React 15**: With a new versioning scheme, the next update of React 15 brought a complete overhaul of the internal architecture, resulting in improved performance and stability.
- **React 16**: This version, however, stands as one of the most notable releases in React's history. It introduced hooks, a revolutionary concept that enables developers to use state and other React features without the need for class components. Hooks make code simpler and more readable, transforming the way developers write components. We will explore a lot of hooks in this book. Additionally, React 16 introduced **Fiber**, a new reconciliation mechanism that significantly improved performance, especially when dealing with animations and complex UI structures.
- **React 17**: This version focused on updating and maintaining compatibility with previous versions. It introduced a new JSX transform system.

- **React 18**: This release continues the trajectory of improvement and emphasizes performance enhancements and additional features, such as the automatic batching of renders, state transitions, server components, and streaming server-side rendering. Most of the important updates related to performance will be explored in *Chapter 12, High-Performance State Updates*. More details about server rendering will be covered in *Chapter 14, Server Rendering and Static Site Generation with React Frameworks*.

- **React 19**: Introduces several major features and improvements. The **React Compiler** is a new compiler that enables automatic memoization and optimizes re-rendering, eliminating the need for manual useMemo, useCallback, and memo optimizations. Enhanced **Hooks** like use(promise) for data fetching, useFormStatus() and useFormState() for form handling, and useOptimistic() for optimistic UI simplify common tasks. React 19 also brings simplified APIs, such as ref becoming a regular prop, React.lazy being replaced, and Context.Provider becoming just Context. Asynchronous rendering allows fetching data asynchronously during rendering without blocking the UI, while error handling improvements provide better mechanisms to diagnose and fix issues in applications.

React's stability and compatibility make it a reliable library for long-term use, while the continuous updates ensure that it remains at the forefront of web and mobile development. Throughout this book, all examples will utilize the latest React API, ensuring that they remain functional and relevant in future versions.

Now that we have explored the evolution and updates in React, we can delve deeper into React and examine how to get set up with the new React project.

Setting up a new React project

There are several ways to create a React project when you are getting started. In this section, we will explore three common approaches:

- Using web bundlers
- Using frameworks
- Using online code editors

 To start developing and previewing your React applications, you will first need to have **Node.js** installed on your computer. Node.js is a runtime environment for executing JavaScript code.

Let's dive into each approach in the following subsections.

Using web bundlers

Using a web bundler is an efficient way to create React projects, especially if you are building a **single-page application (SPA)**. For all of the examples in this book, we will use **Vite** as our web bundler. Vite is known for its remarkable speed and ease of setup and use.

To set up your project using Vite, you will need to take the following steps:

1. Ensure that you have Node.js installed on your computer by visiting the official *Node.js* website (https://nodejs.org/) and downloading the appropriate version for your operating system.

2. Open your terminal or command prompt and navigate to the directory where you want to create your project:

    ```
    mkdir react-projects
    cd react-projects
    ```

3. Run the following command to create a new React project with Vite:

    ```
    npm create vite@latest my-react-app -- --template react
    ```

    This command creates a new directory called my-react-app and sets up a React project using the Vite template.

4. Once the project is created, your terminal should look like this:

    ```
    Scaffolding project in react-projects/my-react-app...
    Done. Now run:

      cd my-react-app
      npm install
        npm run dev
    ```

5. Navigate into the project directory and install dependencies. The result in the terminal should look like:

    ```
    added 279 packages, and audited 280 packages in 21s

    103 packages are looking for funding
    ```

```
    run 'npm fund' for details

    found 0 vulnerabilities
```

Finally, start the development server by running the following command: `npm run dev`

This command launches the development server, and you can view your React application by opening your browser and visiting `http://localhost:3000`.

By now, you will have successfully set up your React project using Vite as the web bundler. For more information about Vite and its possible configurations, visit the official website at `https://vitejs.dev/`.

Using frameworks

For real-world and commercial projects, it is recommended to use frameworks built on top of React. These frameworks provide additional features out of the box, such as routing and asset management (images, SVG files, fonts, etc.). They also guide you in organizing your project structure effectively, as frameworks often enforce specific file organization rules. Some popular React frameworks include **Next.js**, **Gatsby**, and **Remix**.

In *Chapter 13*, *Server-Side Rendering*, we will explore setting up Next.js and some differences between that and using a plain web bundler.

Online code editors

Online code editors combine the advantages of web bundlers and frameworks but allow you to set up your React development environment in the cloud or right inside of the browser. This eliminates the need to install anything on your machine and lets you write and explore React code directly in your browser.

While there are various online code editors available, some of the most popular options include **CodeSandbox**, **StackBlitz**, and **Replit**. These platforms provide a user-friendly interface and allow you to create, share, and collaborate on React projects without any local setup.

To get started with an online code editor, you don't even need an account. Simply follow this link on your browser: `https://react.new`. In a few seconds, you will see that CodeSandbox is ready to work with a template project, and a live preview of the editor is available directly in the browser tab. If you want to save your changes, then you need to create an account.

Using online code editors is a convenient way to learn and experiment with React, especially if you prefer a browser-based development environment.

In this section, we explored different methods to set up your React project. Whether you choose web bundlers, frameworks, or online code editors, each approach offers its unique advantages. Select the method that you prefer and suits your project requirements. Now, we are ready to dive into the world of React development!

Summary

In this chapter, you were introduced to React comprehensively so that you have an idea of what it is and the necessary aspects of it, setting the tone for the rest of the book. React is a library with a small API used to build UIs. Then, you were introduced to some of the key concepts of React. We discussed the fact that React is simple because it doesn't have a lot of moving parts.

Afterward, we explored the declarative nature of React components and JSX. Following that, you learned that React enables effective performance by writing declarative code that can be re-rendered repeatedly.

You also gained insight into the idea of render targets and how React can easily become the UI tool of choice for various platforms. We then provided you with a brief overview of React's history and introduced the latest developments. Finally, we delved into how to set up a new React project and initiate the learning process.

That's sufficient introductory and conceptual content for now. As we progress through the book's journey, we'll revisit these concepts. Next, let's take a step back and nail down the basics, starting with rendering with JSX in the next chapter.

Join us on Discord!

Read this book alongside other users and the authors themselves. Ask questions, provide solutions to other readers, chat with the authors, and more. Scan the QR code or visit the link to join the community.

```
https://packt.link/ReactAndReactNative5e
```

2

Rendering with JSX

This chapter will introduce you to **JSX**, which is the XML/HTML markup syntax that's embedded in your JavaScript code and used to declare your React components. At the lowest level, you'll use HTML markup to describe the pieces of your UI. Building React applications involves organizing these pieces of HTML markup into components. In React, creating a component allows you to define custom elements that extend beyond basic HTML markup. These custom elements, or components, are defined using JSX, which then translates them into standard HTML elements for the browser. This ability to create and reuse custom components is a core feature of React, enabling more dynamic and complex UIs. This is where React gets interesting – having your own JSX tags that can use JavaScript expressions to bring your components to life. JSX is the language used to describe UIs built using React.

In this chapter, we'll cover the following:

- Your first JSX content
- Rendering HTML
- Creating your own JSX elements
- Using JavaScript expressions
- Building fragments of JSX

Technical requirements

The code for this chapter can be found in the following directory of the accompanying GitHub repository: https://github.com/PacktPublishing/React-and-React-Native-5E/tree/main/Chapter02.

Your first JSX content

In this section, we'll implement the obligatory `Hello World` JSX application. This initial dive is just the beginning – it's a simple yet effective way to get acquainted with the syntax and its capabilities. As we progress, we'll delve into more complex and nuanced examples, demonstrating the power and flexibility of JSX in building React applications. We'll also discuss what makes this syntax work well for declarative UI structures.

Hello JSX

Without further ado, here's your first JSX application:

```
import * as ReactDOM from "react-dom";

const root = ReactDOM.createRoot(document.getElementById("root"));

root.render(
  <p>
    Hello, <strong>JSX</strong>
  </p>
);
```

Let's walk through what's happening here.

The `render()` function takes JSX as an argument and renders it to the DOM node passed to `ReactDOM.createRoot()`.

The actual JSX content in this example renders a paragraph with some bold text inside. There's nothing fancy going on here, so we could have just inserted this markup into the DOM directly as a plain string. However, the aim of this example is to show the basic steps involved in getting JSX rendered onto the page.

Under the hood, JSX is not directly understood by web browsers and needs to be transformed into standard JavaScript code that browsers can execute. This transformation is typically done using a tool like **Vite** or **Babel**. When Vite processes JSX code, it compiles the JSX down to `React.createElement()` calls. These calls create JavaScript objects that represent the virtual DOM elements. For example, the JSX expression in the example above is compiled into this:

```
import * as ReactDOM from "react-dom";

const root = ReactDOM.createRoot(document.getElementById("root"));
```

```
root.render(
  React.createElement(
    "p",
    null,
    "Hello, ",
    React.createElement("strong", null, "JSX")
  )
);
```

The first argument to `React.createElement` is the type of the element (such as a string like `div` or `p` for DOM elements, or a React component for composite components). The second argument is an object containing the props for this element, and any subsequent arguments are the children of this element. This transformation is done by Vite under the hood, and you never write such code.

These objects created by `React.createElement()`, known as **React elements**, describe the structure and properties of a UI component in an object format that React can work with. React then uses these objects to construct the actual DOM and keep it up to date. This process involves a reconciliation algorithm that efficiently updates the DOM to match the React elements. When the state of a component changes, React calculates the minimal set of changes required to update the DOM, rather than re-rendering the entire component. This makes updates much more efficient and is one of the key advantages of using React.

Before we move forward with more in-depth code examples, let's take a moment to reflect on our `Hello World` example. The JSX content was short and simple. It was also declarative because it described *what* to render, not *how* to render it. Specifically, by looking at the JSX, you can see that this component will render a paragraph and some bold text within it. If this were done imperatively, there would probably be some more steps involved, and they would probably need to be performed in a specific order.

The example we just implemented should give you a feel for what declarative React is all about. As we move forward in this chapter and throughout the book, the JSX markup will grow more elaborate. However, it's always going to describe what is in the UI.

The `render()` function tells React to take your JSX markup and update the UI in the most efficient way possible. This is how React enables you to declare the structure of your UI without having to think about carrying out ordered steps to update elements on the screen, an approach that often leads to bugs. Out of the box, React supports the standard HTML tags that you would find on any HTML page, such as `div`, `p`, `h1`, `ul`, `li`, and others.

Now that we have discovered what JSX is, how it works, and what declarative idea it follows, let's explore how we can render plain HTML markup and what conventions we should follow.

Rendering HTML

At the end of the day, the job of a React component is to render HTML in the DOM browser. This is why JSX has support for HTML tags out of the box. In this section, we'll look at some code that renders a few of the available HTML tags. Then, we'll cover some of the conventions that are typically followed in React projects when HTML tags are used.

Built-in HTML tags

When we render JSX, element tags reference React components. Since it would be tedious to have to create components for HTML elements, React comes with HTML components. We can render any HTML tag in our JSX, and the output will be just as we'd expect.

Now, let's try rendering some of these tags:

```
import * as ReactDOM from "react-dom";

const root = ReactDOM.createRoot(document.getElementById("root"));

root.render(
  <div>
    <button />
    <code />
    <input />
    <label />
    <p />
    <pre />
    <select />
    <table />
    <ul />
  </div>
);
```

Don't worry about the formatting of the rendered output for this example. We're making sure that we can render arbitrary HTML tags, and they render as expected, without any special definitions and imports.

You may have noticed the surrounding <div> tag, grouping together all of the other tags as its children. This is because React needs a root element to render. Later in the chapter, you'll learn how to render adjacent elements without wrapping them in a parent element.

HTML elements rendered using JSX closely follow regular HTML element syntax, with a few subtle differences regarding case-sensitivity and attributes.

HTML tag conventions

When you render HTML tags in JSX markup, the expectation is that you'll use lowercase for the tag name. In fact, capitalizing the name of an HTML tag will fail. Tag names are case-sensitive and non-HTML elements are capitalized. This way, it's easy to scan the markup and spot the built-in HTML elements versus everything else.

You can also pass HTML elements any of their standard properties. When you pass them something unexpected, a warning about the unknown property is logged. Here's an example that illustrates these ideas:

```
import * as ReactDOM from "react-dom";

const root = ReactDOM.createRoot(document.getElementById("root"));

root.render(
  <button title="My Button" foo="bar">
    My Button
  </button>
);

root.render(<Button />);
```

When you run this example, it will fail to compile because React doesn't know about the <Button> element; it only knows about <button>.

You can use any valid HTML tags as JSX tags, as long as you remember that they're case-sensitive and that you need to pass the correct attribute names. In addition to simple HTML tags that only have attribute values, you can use more semantic HTML tags to describe the structure of your page content.

Describing UI structures

JSX is capable of describing screen elements in a way that ties them together to form a complete UI structure. Let's look at some JSX markup that declares a more elaborate structure than a single paragraph:

```
import * as ReactDOM from "react-dom";

const root = ReactDOM.createRoot(document.getElementById("root"));

root.render(
  <section>
    <header>
      <h1>A Header</h1>
    </header>
    <nav>
      <a href="item">Nav Item</a>
    </nav>
    <main>
      <p>The main content...</p>
    </main>
    <footer>
      <small>&copy; 2024</small>
    </footer>
  </section>
);
```

This JSX markup describes a fairly sophisticated UI structure. Yet, it's easier to read than imperative code because it's HTML, and HTML is good for concisely expressing a hierarchical structure. This is how we want to think of our UI when it needs to change – not as an individual element or property but the UI as a whole.

Here is what the rendered content looks like:

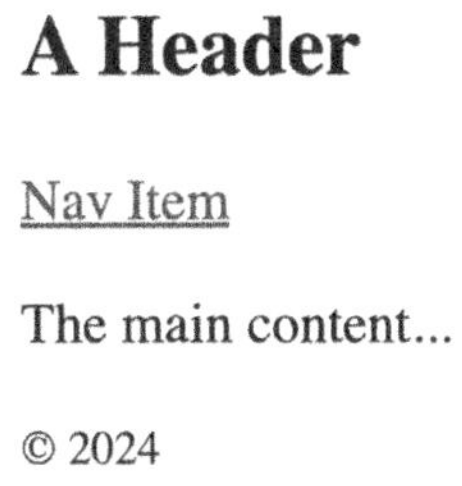

A Header

Nav Item

The main content...

© 2024

Figure 2.1: Describing HTML tag structures using JSX syntax

There are a lot of semantic elements in this markup describing the structure of the UI. For example, the `<header>` element describes the top part of the page where the title is, and the `<main>` element describes where the main page content goes. This type of complex structure makes it clearer for developers to reason about. But before we start implementing dynamic JSX markup, let's create some of our own JSX components.

Creating your own JSX elements

Components are the fundamental building blocks of React. In fact, they can be thought of as the vocabulary of JSX markup, allowing you to create complex interfaces through reusable, encapsulated elements. In this section, we'll delve into how to create your own components and encapsulate HTML markup within them.

Encapsulating HTML

We create new JSX elements so that we can encapsulate larger structures. This means that instead of having to type out complex markup, you can use your custom tag. The React component returns the JSX that goes where the tag is used. Let's look at the following example:

```
import * as ReactDOM from "react-dom";

function MyComponent() {
  return (
    <section>
      <h1>My Component</h1>
```

```
        <p>Content in my component...</p>
    </section>
  );
}


const root = ReactDOM.createRoot(document.getElementById("root"));
root.render(<MyComponent />);
```

Here's what the rendered output looks like:

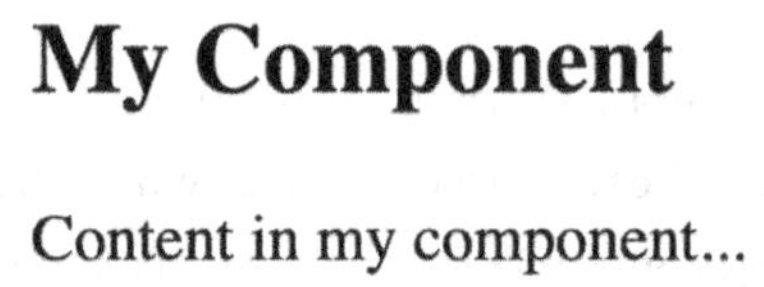

My Component

Content in my component...

Figure 2.2: A component rendering encapsulated HTML markup

This is the first React component that we've implemented, so let's take a moment to dissect what's going on here. We created a function called MyComponent, in the return statement of which we put our HTML tags. This is how we create a React component that is used as a new JSX element. As you can see in the call to render(), you're rendering a <MyComponent> element.

The HTML that this component encapsulates is returned from the function we created. In this case, when the JSX is rendered by react-dom, it's replaced by a <section> element and everything within it.

 When React renders JSX, any custom elements that you use must have their corresponding React component within the same scope. In the preceding example, the MyComponent function was declared in the same scope as the call to render(), so everything worked as expected. Usually, you'll import components, adding them to the appropriate scope. You'll see more of this as you progress through the book.

HTML elements such as <div> often take nested child elements. Let's see whether we can do the same with JSX elements, which we create by implementing components.

Nested elements

Using JSX markup is useful for describing UI structures that have parent-child relationships. Child elements are created by nesting them within another component: the parent.

For example, a `<li>` tag is only valid as the child of a `<ul>` tag or a `<ol>` tag – you're probably going to make similar nested structures with your own React components. For this, you need to use the `children` property. Let's see how this works. Here's the JSX markup:

```
import * as ReactDOM from "react-dom";

import MySection from "./MySection";
import MyButton from "./MyButton";

const root = ReactDOM.createRoot(document.getElementById("root"));

root.render(
  <MySection>
    <MyButton>My Button Text</MyButton>
  </MySection>
);
```

You're importing two of your own React components: `MySection` and `MyButton`.

Now, if you look at the JSX markup, you'll notice that `<MyButton>` is a child of `<MySection>`. You'll also notice that the `MyButton` component accepts text as its child, instead of more JSX elements.

Let's see how these components work, starting with `MySection`:

```
export default function MySection(props) {
  return (
    <section>
      <h2>My Section</h2>
      {props.children}
    </section>
  );
}
```

This component renders a standard `<section>` HTML element, a heading, and then `{props.children}`. It's this last piece that allows components to access nested elements or text and render them.

 The two braces used in the preceding example are used for JavaScript expressions. I'll touch on more details of the JavaScript expression syntax found in JSX markup in the following section.

Now, let's look at the MyButton component:

```
export default function MyButton(props) {
  return <button>{props.children}</button>;
}
```

This component uses the exact same pattern as MySection; it takes the {props.children} value and surrounds it with markup. React handles the details for you. In this example, the button text is a child of MyButton, which is, in turn, a child of MySection. However, the button text is transparently passed through MySection. In other words, we didn't have to write any code in MySection to make sure that MyButton got its text. *Pretty cool, right?* Here's what the rendered output looks like:

My Section

My Button Text

Figure 2.3: A button element rendered using child JSX values

You now know how to build your own React components that introduce new JSX tags in your markup. The components that we've looked at so far in this chapter have been static. That is, once we rendered them, they were never updated. JavaScript expressions are the dynamic pieces of JSX that give different output based on conditions.

Using JavaScript expressions

As you saw in the preceding section, JSX has a special syntax that allows you to embed JavaScript expressions. Any time React renders JSX content, expressions in the markup are evaluated. This feature is at the heart of JSX's dynamism; it enables the content and attributes of your components to change in response to different data or state conditions. Each time React renders or re-renders JSX content, these embedded expressions are evaluated, allowing the displayed UI to reflect current data and state. You'll also learn how to map collections of data to JSX elements.

Dynamic property values and text

Some HTML property or text values are static, meaning that they don't change as JSX markup is re-rendered. Other values, the values of properties or text, are based on data that is found elsewhere in the application. Remember, React is just the view layer. Let's look at an example so that you can get a feel for what the JavaScript expression syntax looks like in JSX markup:

```
import * as ReactDOM from "react-dom";
```

```
const enabled = false;
const text = "A Button";
const placeholder = "input value...";
const size = 50;


const root = ReactDOM.createRoot(document.getElementById("root"));


root.render(
  <section>
    <button disabled={!enabled}>{text}</button>
    <input placeholder={placeholder} size={size} />
  </section>
);
```

Anything that is a valid JavaScript expression, including nested JSX, can go in between the curly braces: {}. For properties and text, this is often a variable name or object property. Notice, in this example, that the !enabled expression computes a Boolean value. Here's what the rendered output looks like:

A Button input value...

Figure 2.4: Dynamically changing the property value of a button

If you're following along with the downloadable companion code, which I strongly recommend doing, try playing around with these values and seeing how the rendered HTML changes: https://github.com/PacktPublishing/React-and-React-Native-5E/tree/main/Chapter02

Primitive JavaScript values are straightforward to use in JSX syntax. Obviously, we can use more complex values such as objects and arrays in the JSX, as well as functions to handle events. Let's explore this.

Handling events

In React, you can easily pass functions to components' properties to handle user interactions such as button clicks, form submissions, and mouse movements. This allows you to create interactive and responsive UIs. React provides a convenient way to attach event handlers directly to components using a syntax, similar to how you would use the addEventListener and removeEventListener methods in traditional JavaScript.

To illustrate this, let's consider an example where we want to handle a button-click event in a React component:

```
import * as ReactDOM from "react-dom";

const handleClick = () => {
  console.log("Button clicked!");
};

const root = ReactDOM.createRoot(document.getElementById("root"));

root.render(
  <section>
    <button onClick={handleClick}>Click me</button>
  </section>
);
```

In this example, we define a function called `handleClick` that will be called when the button is clicked. We then attach this function as an event handler to the `onClick` property of the `<button>` component. Whenever the button is clicked, React will invoke the `handleClick` function.

Compared to using `addEventListener` and `removeEventListener` in traditional JavaScript, React abstracts away some of the complexities. With React's event handling, you don't have to worry about manually attaching and detaching event listeners to/from DOM elements. React manages the **event delegation** and provides a more **declarative** approach to handling events within components.

React implements event delegation by default to optimize performance. Instead of attaching event handlers to each individual element, React attaches a single event handler to the root of the application (or a parent component). When an event is triggered on a child element, it bubbles up the component tree until it reaches the parent with the event handler. React's synthetic event system then determines which component should handle the event based on the target property of the event object. This allows React to efficiently manage events without needing to attach handlers to every single element.

By using this approach, you can easily pass events to child components, handle them in parent components, or even propagate events through multiple levels of nested components. This helps in building a modular and reusable component architecture. We'll get to see this in action in the next chapter.

 In addition to the onClick event, React supports a wide range of other events, such as onChange, onSubmit, onMouseOver, and all standard events. You can attach event handlers to various elements like buttons, input fields, checkboxes, and so on.

Note that React promotes a unidirectional data flow, which means that data flows from parent components to child components. To pass data or information from child components back to the parent component, you can define callbacks as props and invoke them with the necessary data. In the upcoming chapters of this book, we will delve deeper into event handling in React and how to create custom callbacks.

Mapping collections to elements

Sometimes, you need to write JavaScript expressions that change the structure of your markup. In the preceding section, you learned how to use JavaScript expression syntax to dynamically change the property values of JSX elements. What about when you need to add or remove elements based on JavaScript collections?

 Throughout the book, when I refer to a JavaScript collection, I'm referring to both plain objects and arrays, or, more generally, anything that's *iterable*.

The best way to dynamically control JSX elements is to map them from a collection. Let's look at an example of how this is done:

```
import * as ReactDOM from "react-dom";

const array = ["First", "Second", "Third"];

const object = {
  first: 1,
  second: 2,
  third: 3,
};
```

```
const root = ReactDOM.createRoot(document.getElementById("root"));

root.render(
  <section>
    <h1>Array</h1>
    <ul>
      {array.map((i) => (
        <li key={i}>{i}</li>
      ))}
    </ul>

    <h1>Object</h1>
    <ul>
      {Object.keys(object).map((i) => (
        <li key={i}>
          <strong>{i}: </strong>
          {object[i]}
        </li>
      ))}
    </ul>
  </section>
);
```

The first collection is an array called array, populated with string values. Moving down to the JSX markup, you can see the call to array.map(), which returns a new array. The mapping function actually returns a JSX element (<li>), meaning that each item in the array is now represented in the markup.

 The result of evaluating this expression is an array. Don't worry – JSX knows how to render arrays of elements. For enhanced performance, it is crucial to assign a unique key prop to each component within the array, enabling React to efficiently manage updates during subsequent re-renders.

The object collection uses the same technique, except that you have to call Object.keys() and then map this array. What's nice about mapping collections to JSX elements on the page is that you can control the structure of React components based on the collected data.

This means that you don't have to rely on imperative logic to control the UI.

Here's what the rendered output looks like:

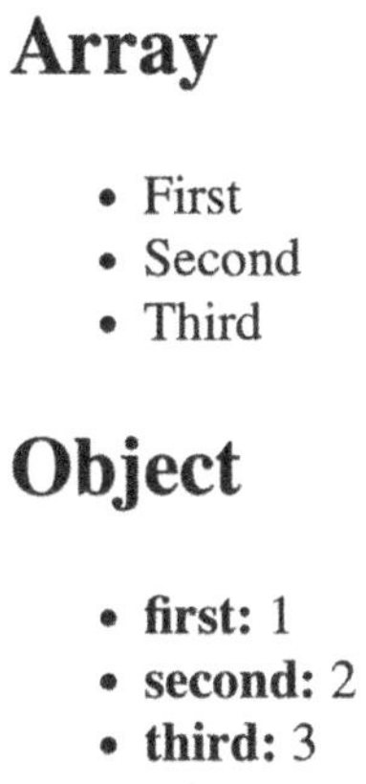

Array

- First
- Second
- Third

Object

- **first:** 1
- **second:** 2
- **third:** 3

Figure 2.5: The result of mapping JavaScript collections to HTML elements

JavaScript expressions bring JSX content to life. React evaluates expressions and updates the HTML content based on what has already been rendered and what has changed. Understanding how to utilize these expressions is important because it's one of the most common day-to-day activities of any React developer.

Now, it's time to learn how to group together JSX markup without relying on HTML tags to do so.

Building fragments of JSX

Fragments are a way to group together chunks of markup without having to add unnecessary structure to your page. For example, a common approach is to have a React component return content wrapped in a `<div>` element. This element serves no real purpose and adds clutter to the DOM.

Let's look at an example. Here are two versions of a component. One uses a wrapper element, and the other uses the new fragment feature:

```
import * as ReactDOM from "react-dom";

import WithoutFragments from "./WithoutFragments";
import WithFragments from "./WithFragments";

const root = ReactDOM.createRoot(document.getElementById("root"));

root.render(
```

```
  <div>
    <WithoutFragments />
    <WithFragments />
  </div>
);
```

The two elements rendered are `<WithoutFragments>` and `<WithFragments>`. Here's what they look like when rendered:

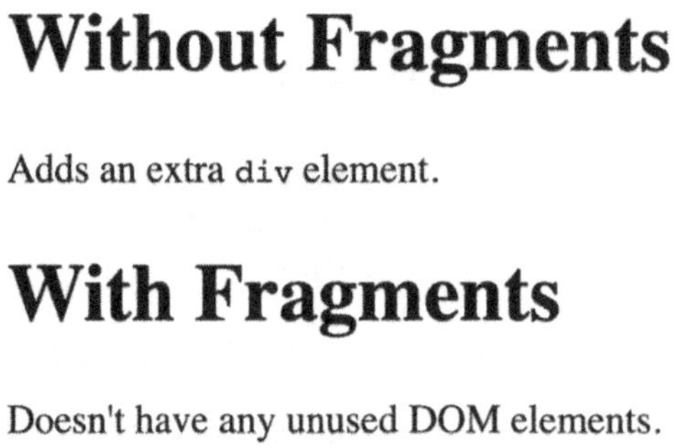

Without Fragments

Adds an extra `div` element.

With Fragments

Doesn't have any unused DOM elements.

Figure 2.6: Fragments help render fewer HTML tags without any visual difference

Let's compare the two approaches now.

Using wrapper elements

The first approach is to wrap sibling elements in `<div>`. Here's what the source looks like:

```
export default function WithoutFragments() {
  return (
    <div>
      <h1>Without Fragments</h1>
      <p>
        Adds an extra <code>div</code> element.
      </p>
    </div>
  );
}
```

The essence of this component is the `<h1>` and `<p>` tags. Yet, in order to return them from `render()`, you have to wrap them with `<div>`. Indeed, inspecting the DOM using your browser dev tools reveals that `<div>` does nothing but add another level of structure:

```
▼<div>
    <h1>Without Fragments</h1>
    ▼<p>
        "Adds an extra "
        <code>div</code>
        " element."
    </p>
</div>
```

Figure 2.7: Another level of structure in the DOM

Now, imagine an app with lots of these components—that's a lot of pointless elements! Let's see how to use fragments to avoid unnecessary tags.

Using fragments

Let's take a look at the WithFragments component, where we have avoided using unnecessary tags:

```
export default function WithFragments() {
  return (
    <>
      <h1>With Fragments</h1>
      <p>Doesn't have any unused DOM elements.</p>
    </>
  );
}
```

Instead of wrapping the component content in <div>, the <> element is used. This is a special type of element that indicates that only its children need to be rendered. The <> is a shorthand for React. Fragment component. If you need to pass a key property to the fragment, you can't use <> syntax.

You can see the difference compared to the WithoutFragments component if you inspect the DOM:

```
<h1>With Fragments</h1>
<p>Doesn't have any unused DOM elements.</p>
```

Figure 2.8: Less HTML in the fragment

With the advent of fragments in JSX markup, we have less HTML rendered on the page because we don't have to use tags such as <div> for the sole purpose of grouping elements together. Instead, when a component renders a fragment, React knows to render the fragment's child element wherever the component is used.

So fragments enable React components to render only the essential elements; no more will elements that serve no purpose appear on the rendered page.

Summary

In this chapter, you learned about the basics of JSX, including its declarative structure, which leads to more maintainable code. Then, you wrote some code to render some basic HTML and learned about describing complex structures using JSX; every React application has at least some structure.

Then, you spent some time learning about extending the vocabulary of JSX markup by implementing your own React components, which is how you design your UI as a series of smaller pieces and glue them together to form the whole. Then, you learned how to bring dynamic content into JSX element properties and how to map JavaScript collections to JSX elements, eliminating the need for imperative logic to control the UI display. Finally, you learned how to render fragments of JSX content, which prevents unnecessary HTML elements from being used.

Now that you have a feel for what it's like to render UIs by embedding declarative XML in your JavaScript modules, it's time to move on to the next chapter, where we'll take a deeper look at components, properties, and state.

3

Understanding React Components and Hooks

In this chapter, we will delve into the React components and their fundamental aspects and introduce you to the power of **Hooks**.

We will explore the essential concept of component data and how it shapes the structure of your React applications. We will discuss two primary types of component data: **properties** and **state**. Properties allow us to pass data to components, while state enables components to manage and update their internal data dynamically. We will examine how these concepts apply to function components and illustrate the mechanics of setting component state and passing properties.

In this chapter, we'll cover the following topics:

- Introduction to React components
- What are component properties?
- What is component state?
- React Hooks
- Maintaining state using Hooks
- Performing initialization and cleanup actions
- Sharing data using context Hooks
- Memoization with Hooks

Technical requirements

The code for this chapter can be found here: `https://github.com/PacktPublishing/React-and-React-Native-5E/tree/main/Chapter03`

Introduction to React components

React components are the building blocks of modern web and mobile applications. They encapsulate reusable sections of code that define the structure, behavior, and appearance of different parts of a user interface. By breaking down the UI into smaller, self-contained components, React enables developers to create scalable, maintainable, and interactive applications.

At its core, a React component is a JavaScript function or class that returns JSX syntax, which resembles HTML markup. In this book, we will focus mostly on function components, as they have become the preferred approach for building components in recent years. Function components are simpler, more concise, and easier to understand compared to class components. They leverage the power of JavaScript functions and utilize React Hooks to manage state and perform side effects.

One of the primary advantages of using components in React is their reusability. Components can be reused across multiple parts of an application, reducing code duplication and increasing development efficiency. Moreover, components promote a modular approach to development, allowing developers to break down complex UIs into smaller, manageable pieces.

What are component properties?

In React, **component properties**, commonly known as **props**, allow us to pass data from a parent component to its child components. Props provide a way to customize and configure components, making them flexible and reusable. Props are read-only, meaning that the child component should not modify them directly. Instead, the parent component can update the props value and trigger a re-render of the child component with the updated data.

When defining a function component, you can access the props passed to it as a parameter:

```
const MyComponent = (props) => {
  return (
    <div>
      <h1>{props.title}</h1>
      <p>{props.description}</p>
    </div>
  );
};
```

In the above example, the MyComponent function component receives the props object as a parameter. We can access the individual props by using dot notation, such as props.title and props.description, to render the data within the component's JSX markup. It is also possible to access props using destructuring:

```
const MyComponent = ({ title, description }) => {
  return (
    <div>
      <h1>{title}</h1>
      <p>{description}</p>
    </div>
  );
};
```

As you can see, this approach is even cleaner and also allows us to use another destructuring feature, default values, which we will discuss in this chapter.

Passing property values

React component properties are set by passing JSX attributes to the component when it is rendered. In *Chapter 7, Type Checking and Validation with TypeScript*, I'll go into more detail about how to validate the property values that are passed to components. Now let's create a couple of components in addition to MyComponent that expect different types of property values:

```
const MyButton = ({ disabled, text }) => {
  return <button disabled={disabled}>{text}</button>;
};
```

This simple button component expects a Boolean disabled property and a string text property. While we create components to show how we can pass the following props, you will notice how we already pass these properties to the button HTML element:

- **disabled property**: we put into the button attribute with the name disabled
- **text property**: we pass to the button as a child attribute

It's also important to know that any JavaScript expression you want to pass to the component should be wrapped with curly braces.

Let's create one more component that expects an array property value:

```
const MyList = ({ items }) => (
```

```
    <ul>
      {items.map((i) => (
        <li key={i}>{i}</li>
      ))}
    </ul>
  );
```

You can pass just about anything you want as a property value via JSX, just as long as it's a valid JavaScript expression. The MyList component accepts an items property, an array that is mapped to <li> elements.

Now, let's write some code to set these property values:

```
import * as ReactDOM from "react-dom";
import MyButton from "./MyButton";
import MyList from "./MyList";
import MyComponent from "./MyComponent";

const root = ReactDOM.createRoot(document.getElementById("root"));

const appState = {
  text: "My Button",
  disabled: true,
  items: ["First", "Second", "Third"],
};

function render(props) {
  root.render(
    <main>
      <MyComponent
        title="Welcome to My App"
        description="This is a sample component."
      />
      <MyButton text={props.text} disabled={props.disabled} />
      <MyButton text="Another Button" disabled />
      <MyList items={props.items} />
    </main>
  );
}
```

```
  render(appState);

setTimeout(() => {
  appState.disabled = false;
  appState.items.push("Fourth");

  render(appState);
}, 1000);
```

The render function looks like it's creating new React component instances every time it's called. React is smart enough to figure out that these components already exist, and that it only needs to figure out what the difference in output will be with the new property values. In this example, the call to setTimeout causes a delay of 1 second. Then, the appState.disabled value is changed to false and the appState.items array has a new value added to the end of it. The call to render will re-render the components with new property values.

Another takeaway from this example is that you have an appState object that holds onto the state of the application. Pieces of this state are then passed into components as properties when the components are rendered. The state has to live somewhere and, in this case, it's outside of the component. We'll explore this approach in depth, and why it's important, in *Chapter 12*, *State Management in React*.

I hope you noticed we've rendered another button where we passed props in a different way:

```
<MyButton text="Another Button" disabled />
```

This is a valid JSX expression and in case we want to pass constant values to the components, we can pass strings without curly braces and pass the Boolean value true, just leaving the attribute name in the component.

Default property values

In addition to passing data, we can also specify default values for props using the defaultProps property. This is helpful when a prop is not provided, ensuring that the component still behaves correctly:

```
const MyButton = ({ disabled, text }) => (
  <button disabled={disabled}>{text}</button>
);
```

```
MyButton.defaultProps = {
  disabled: false,
  text: "My Button",
};
```

In this case, if the parent component does not provide the text or disabled props, the component will fall back to the default values specified in defaultProps.

As I mentioned before, with destructuring, we have a more convenient way to set up default props.

Let's take a look at the updated example of the MyButton component:

```
const MyButton = ({ disabled = false, text = "My Button" }) => (
  <button disabled={disabled}>{text}</button>
);
```

Using destructuring, we can define props and set the default value right inside the function. It's cleaner and easy to see in cases when we have a big component with a lot of props.

In the upcoming sections, we will further dive into component state with Hooks, and other key concepts.

What is component state?

In React, component state refers to the internal data held by a component. It represents the mutable values that can be used within the component and can be updated over time. State allows components to keep track of information that can change, such as user input, API responses, or any other data that needs to be dynamic and responsive.

State is a feature provided by React that enables components to manage and update their own data. It allows components to re-render when the state changes, ensuring that the user interface reflects the latest data.

To define state in a React component, you should use the useState hook inside of the component. You can then access and modify the state within the component's methods or JSX code. When the state is updated, React will automatically re-render the component and its child components to reflect the changes.

Before jumping to examples of using state in components, let's briefly explore what a React hook is.

React Hooks

React Hooks are a feature introduced in **React 16.8** that allows you to use state and other React features in functional components. Before Hooks, state management and lifecycle methods were primarily used in class components. Hooks provide a way to achieve similar functionality in functional components, making them more powerful and easier to write and understand.

Hooks are functions that enable you to "hook into" React's internal features, such as state management, context, effects, and more. They are prefixed with the use keyword (such as useState, useEffect, useContext, and so on). React provides several built-in Hooks, and you can also create custom Hooks to encapsulate reusable stateful logic.

The most commonly used built-in Hooks are:

- useState: This hook allows you to add state to a functional component. It returns an array with two elements: the current state value and a function to update the state.
- useEffect: This hook lets you perform side effects in your components, such as fetching data, subscribing to events, or manually manipulating the DOM. It runs after every render by default and can be used to handle component lifecycle events like when the component is mounted, updated, or unmounted.
- useContext: This hook allows you to consume values from a React context. It provides a way to access context values without nesting multiple components.
- useCallback and useMemo: These Hooks are used for performance optimization. useCallback memoizes a function, preventing it from being recreated on every render, while useMemo memoizes a value, recomputing it only when its dependencies change.

We will examine all these Hooks in this chapter and will use them throughout the book. Let's continue with state and explore how we can manage it with the useState Hook.

Maintaining state using Hooks

The first React Hook API that we'll look at is called useState, which enables your functional React components to be stateful. In this section, you'll learn how to initialize state values and change the state of a component using Hooks.

Initial state values

When our components are first rendered, they probably expect some state values to be set. This is called the initial state of the component, and we can use the useState hook to set the initial state.

Let's take a look at an example:

```
export default function App() {
  const [name] = React.useState("Mike");
  const [age] = React.useState(32);

  return (
    <>
      <p>My name is {name}</p>
      <p>My age is {age}</p>
    </>
  );
}
```

The App component is a functional React component that returns JSX markup. But it's also now a stateful component, thanks to the useState hook. This example initializes two pieces of state, name and age. This is why there are two calls to useState, one for each state value.

You can have as many pieces of state in your component as you need. The best practice is to have one call to useState per state value. You could always define an object as the state of your component using only one call to useState, but this complicates things because you have to access state values through an object instead of directly. Updating state values is also more complicated using this approach. When in doubt, use one useState hook per state value.

When we call useState, we get an array returned to us. The first value of this array is the state value itself. Since we've used array-destructuring syntax here, we can call the value whatever we want; in this case, it is name and age. Both of these constants have values when the component is first rendered because we passed the initial state values for each of them to useState. Here's what the page looks like when it's rendered:

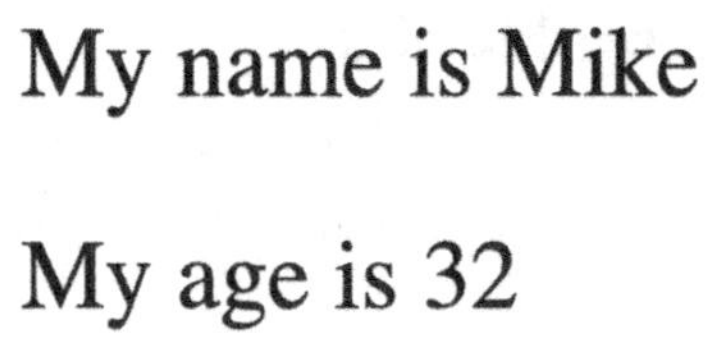

My name is Mike

My age is 32

Figure 3.1: Rendered output using values from state Hooks

Now that you've seen how to set the initial state values of your components, let's learn about updating these values.

Updating state values

React components use state for values that change over time. The state values used by components start off in one state, as we saw in the previous section, and then change in response to some event: for example, the server responds to an API request with new data, or the user has clicked a button or changed a form field.

To update the state, the useState hook provides an individual function for every piece of state, which we can access from the returned array from the useState hook. The first item is the state value and the second is the function used to update the value. Let's take a look at an example:

```
function App() {
  const [name, setName] = React.useState("Mike");
  const [age, setAge] = React.useState(32);

  return (
    <>
      <section>
        <input value={name} onChange={(e) => setName(e.target.value)} />
        <p>My name is {name}</p>
      </section>
      <section>
        <input
          type="number"
          value={age}
          onChange={(e) => setAge(e.target.value)}
        />
        <p>My age is {age}</p>
      </section>
    </>
  );
}
```

Just like the example from the initial state values section, the App component in this example has two pieces of state: name and age. Unlike the previous example, this component uses two functions to update each piece of state. These are returned from the call to useState. Let's take a closer look:

```
const [name, setName] = React.useState("Mike");
const [age, setAge] = React.useState(32);
```

Now, we have two functions: setName and setAge: that can be used to update the state of our component. Let's take a look at the text input field that updates the name state:

```
<section>
  <input value={name} onChange={(e) => setName(e.target.value)} />
  <p>My name is {name}</p>
</section>
```

Whenever the user changes the text in the <input> field, the onChange event is triggered. The handler for this event calls setName, passing it e.target.value as an argument. The argument passed to setName is the new state value of name. The succeeding paragraph shows that the text input is also updated with the new name value every time the user changes the text input.

Next, let's look at the age number input field and how this value is passed to setAge:

```
<section>
  <input
    type="number"
    value={age}
    onChange={(e) => setAge(e.target.value)}
  />
  <p>My age is {age}</p>
</section>
```

The age field follows the exact same pattern as the name field. The only difference is that we've made the input a number type. Any time the number changes, setAge is called with the updated value in response to the onChange event. The following paragraph shows that the number input is also updated with every change that is made to the age state.

Here is what the two inputs and their two corresponding paragraphs look like when they're rendered on the screen:

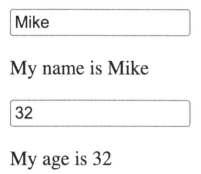

Figure 3.2: Using Hooks to change state values

In this section, you learned about the useState hook, which is used to add state to functional React components. Each piece of state uses its own hook and has its own value variable and its own setter function. This greatly simplifies accessing and updating state in your components. Any given state value should have an initial value so that the component can render correctly the first time. To re-render functional components that use state Hooks, you can use the setter functions that useState returns to update your state values as needed.

The next hook that you'll learn about is used to perform initialization and cleanup actions.

Performing initialization and cleanup actions

Often, our React components need to perform actions when the component is created. For example, a common initialization action is to fetch the API data that the component needs. Another common action is to make sure that any pending API requests are canceled when the component is removed. In this section, you'll learn about the useEffect hook and how it can help you with these two scenarios. You'll also learn how to make sure that the initialization code doesn't run too often.

Fetching component data

The useEffect hook is used to run "side effects" in your component. Another way to think about side-effect code is that functional components have only one job: returning JSX content to render. If the component needs to do something else, such as fetching API data, this should be done in a useEffect hook. For example, if you were to just make the API call as part of your component function, you would likely introduce race conditions and other difficult-to-fix buggy behavior.

Let's take a look at an example that fetches API data using Hooks:

```
function App() {
  const [id, setId] = React.useState("loading...");
  const [name, setName] = React.useState("loading...");

  const fetchUser = React.useCallback(() => {
    return new Promise((resolve) => {
      setTimeout(() => {
        resolve({ id: 1, name: "Mike" });
      }, 1000);
    });
  }, []);

  React.useEffect(() => {
    fetchUser().then((user) => {
      setId(user.id);
      setName(user.name);
    });
  });

  return (
    <>
      <p>ID: {id}</p>
      <p>Name: {name}</p>
    </>
  );
}
```

The useEffect hook expects a function as an argument. This function is called after the component finishes rendering, in a safe way that doesn't interfere with anything else that React is doing with the component under the covers. Let's look at the pieces of this example more closely, starting with the mock API function:

```
const fetchUser = React.useCallback(() => {
  return new Promise((resolve) => {
    setTimeout(() => {
```

```
      resolve({ id: 1, name: "Mike" });
    }, 1000);
  });
}, []);
```

The `fetchUser` function is defined using the `useCallback` hook. This hook is used to memoize the function, meaning that it will only be created once and will not be recreated on subsequent renders unless the dependencies change. The `useCallback` accepts two arguments: the first is the function we want to memorize and the second is the list of dependencies that will be used to identify when React should re-create this function instead of using the memorized version. The `fetchUser` function is passed an empty array (`[]`) as the dependency list. This means that the function will only be created once during the initial render and won't be recreated on subsequent renders.

The `fetchUser` function returns a promise. The promise resolves a simple object with two properties, `id` and `name`. The `setTimeout` function delays the promise resolution for 1 second, so this function is asynchronous, just as a normal `fetch` call would be.

Next, let's look at the Hooks used by the `App` component:

```
const [id, setId] = React.useState("loading...");
const [name, setName] = React.useState("loading...");

React.useEffect(() => {
  fetchUser().then((user) => {
    setId(user.id);
    setName(user.name);
  });
});
```

As you can see, in addition to `useCallback`, we're using two Hooks in this component: `useState` and `useEffect`. Combining hook functionality like this is powerful and encouraged. First, we set up the `id` and `name` states of the component. Then, `useEffect` is used to set up a function that calls `fetchUser` and sets the state of our component when the promise resolves.

Here is what the App component looks like when it's first rendered, using the initial state of id and name:

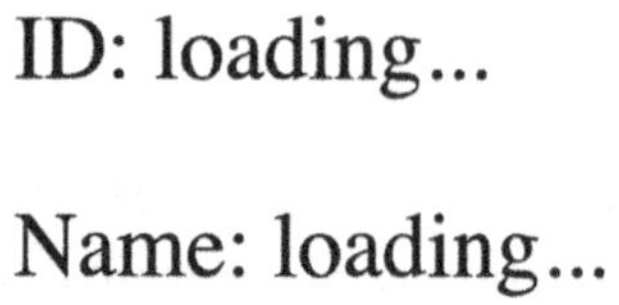

ID: loading...

Name: loading...

Figure 3.3: Displaying the loading text until the data arrives

After 1 second, the promise returned from fetchUser is resolved with data from the API, which is then used to update the ID and name states. This results in App being rerendered:

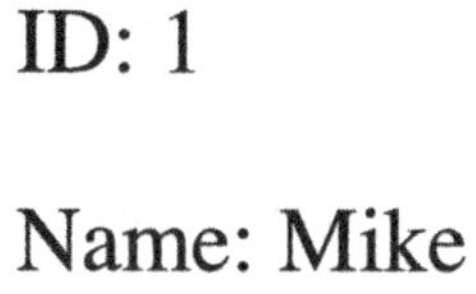

ID: 1

Name: Mike

Figure 3.4: The state changes, removing the loading text and displaying returned values

There is a good chance that your users will navigate around your application while an API request is still pending. The useEffect hook can be used to deal with canceling these requests.

Canceling actions and resetting state

There's a good chance that, at some point, your users will navigate your app and cause components to unmount before responses to their API requests arrive. Sometimes your component can listen for some events and you should delete all listeners before unmounting the component to avoid memory leaks. In general, it's important to stop performing any background actions when a related component is deleted from the screen.

Thankfully, the useEffect hook has a mechanism to clean up effects such as pending setInterval when the component is removed. Let's take a look at an example of this in action:

```
import * as React from "react";

function Timer() {
  const [timer, setTimer] = React.useState(100);

  React.useEffect(() => {
    const interval = setInterval(() => {
      setTimer((prevTimer) => (prevTimer === 0 ? 0 : prevTimer - 1));
```

```
    }, 1000);

    return () => {
      clearInterval(interval);
    };
  }, []);

  return <p>Timer: {timer}</p>;
}


export default Timer;
```

This is a simple `Timer` component. It has the state `timer`, it sets up interval callback to update `timer` inside `useEffect()`, and it renders the output with the current `timer` value. Let's take a closer look at the `useEffect()` hook:

```
React.useEffect(() => {
  const interval = setInterval(() => {
    setTimer((prevTimer) => (prevTimer === 0 ? 0 : prevTimer - 1));
  }, 1000);

  return () => {
    clearInterval(interval);
  };
}, []);
```

This effect creates an interval timer by calling the `setInterval` function with a callback, which updates our `timer` state. The interesting thing you will notice here is that to the `setTimer` function, we are passing a callback instead of a number. It's a valid React API: when we need the previous state value to use to calculate a new one, we can pass a callback where the first argument is the current or 'previous' state value and we should return the new state value from this callback to update our state.

Inside `useEffect`, we are also returning a function, which React runs when the component is removed. In this example, the interval that is created by calling `setInterval` is cleared by calling the function that we returned from `useEffect`, where we call `clearInterval`. Functions that you return from `useEffect` will be triggered when the component is going to unmount.

Now, let's look at the App component, which renders and removes the Timer component:

```
const ShowHideTimer = ({ show }) => (show ? <Timer /> : null);

function App() {
  const [show, setShow] = React.useState(false);

  return (
    <>
      <button onClick={() => setShow(!show)}>
        {show ? "Hide Timer" : "Show Timer"}
      </button>
      <ShowHideTimer show={show} />
    </>
  );
}
```

The App component renders a button that is used to toggle the show state. This state value determines whether or not the Timer component is rendered, but by using the ShowHideTimer convenience component. If show is true, <Timer /> is rendered; otherwise, Timer is removed, triggering our useEffect cleanup behavior.

Here's what the screen looks like when it first loads:

Show Timer

Figure 3.5: A button used to initiate the state change

The Timer component isn't rendered because the show state of the App component is false. Try clicking on the show timer button. This will change the show state and render the Timer component:

Hide Timer

Timer: 100

Figure 3.6: Displays the timer

You can click on the **Hide Timer** button once more to remove the Timer component. Without the cleanup interval that we added to useEffect, this will create new listeners every time the timer is rendered, which will affect the memory leak.

React allows us to control when we want to run our effects. For example, when we want to all API requests after the first render, or we want to perform effects when a particular state changes. We'll take a look at how to do this next.

Optimizing side-effect actions

By default, React assumes that every effect that is run needs to be cleaned up and it should be run on every render. This typically isn't the case. For example, you might have specific property or state values that require cleanup and run one more time when they change. You can pass an array of values to watch as the second argument to useEffect: for example, if you have a resolved state that requires cleanup when it changes, you would write your effect code like this:

```
const [resolved, setResolved] = useState(false);
useEffect(() => {
  // ...the effect code...
  return () => {
    // ...the cleanup code
  };
}, [resolved]);
```

In this code, the effect will be triggered and only ever run if the resolved state value changes. If the effect runs and the resolved state hasn't changed, then the cleanup code will not run and the original effect code will not run a second time. Another common case is never running the cleanup code, except for when the component is removed. In fact, this is what we want to happen in the example from the section on fetching user data. Right now, the effect runs after every render. This means that we're repeatedly fetching the user API data when all we really want is to fetch it once when the component is first mounted.

Let's make some modifications to the App component from the fetching component data requests example:

```
React.useEffect(() => {
  fetchUser().then((user) => {
    setId(user.id);
```

```
    setName(user.name);
  });
}, []);
```

We've added a second argument to useEffect, an empty array. This tells React that there are no values to watch and that we only want to run the effect once it is rendered and cleanup code when the component is removed. We've also added console.count('fetching user') to the fetchUser function. This makes it easier to look at the browser dev tools console and make sure that our component data is only fetched once. If you remove the [] argument that is passed to useEffect, you'll notice that fetchUser is called several times.

In this section, you learned about side effects in React components. Effects are an important concept, as they are the bridge between your React components and the outside world. One of the most common use cases for effects is to fetch data that the component needs, when it is first created, and then clean up after the component when it is removed.

Now, we're going to look at another way to share data with React components: context.

Sharing data using context Hooks

React applications often have a few pieces of data that are global in nature. This means that several components, possibly every component in an app, share this data: for example, information about the currently logged-in user might be used in several places. This is where the **Context API** comes in handy. The Context API provides a way to create a shared data store that can be accessed by any component in the tree, regardless of its depth.

To utilize the Context API, we need to create a context using the createContext function from the **React** library:

```
import { createContext } from 'react';

const MyContext = createContext();
```

In the example above, we create a context called MyContext using createContext. This creates a context object that contains a Provider and a Consumer.

The Provider component is responsible for providing the shared data to its child components. We wrap the relevant portion of the component tree with the Provider and pass the data using the value prop:

```
<MyContext.Provider value={/* shared data */}>
```

```
  {/* Child components */}
</MyContext.Provider>
```

Any component within the `MyContext.Provider` can access the shared data using the `Consumer` component or the `useContext` hook. Let's take a look at how to read context using a hook:

```
import React, { useContext } from 'react';

const MyComponent = () => {
  const value = useContext(MyContext);

  // Render using the shared data
};
```

By utilizing the Context API, we can avoid the prop-drilling problem where data needs to be passed through multiple levels of components. It simplifies the process of sharing data and allows components to access the shared data directly, making the code more readable and maintainable.

It's worth noting that the Context API is not intended for all scenarios and should be used judiciously. It is most useful for sharing data that is truly global or relevant to a large portion of the component tree. For smaller-scale data sharing, props are still the recommended approach.

Memoization with Hooks

In React, function components are called on every render, which means that expensive computations and function creations can negatively impact performance. To optimize performance and prevent unnecessary recalculations, React provides three Hooks: `useMemo`, `useCallback`, and `useRef`. These Hooks allow us to memoize values, functions, and references, respectively.

useMemo Hook

The `useMemo` hook is used to memoize the result of a computation, ensuring that it is only recomputed when the dependencies have changed. It takes a function and an array of dependencies and returns the memoized value.

Here's an example of using the `useMemo` hook:

```
import { useMemo } from 'react';

const Component = () => {
  const expensiveResult = useMemo(() => {
```

```
    // Expensive computation
    return computeExpensiveValue(dependency);
  }, [dependency]);

  return <div>{expensiveResult}</div>;
};
```

In this example, the expensiveResult value is memoized using useMemo. The computation inside the function is only executed when the dependency value changes. If the dependency remains the same, the previously memoized value is returned instead of recomputing the result.

useCallback hook

We already explored useCallback hook in this chapter, but I want to highlight one important use case. When a function component renders, all of its functions are recreated, including any inline callbacks defined within the component. This can lead to unnecessary re-renders of child components that receive these callbacks as props, as they perceive the callback as a new reference and trigger re-renders. Let's take a look at the example:

```
const MyComponent = () => {
  return <MyButton onClick={() => console.log("click")} />;
};
```

In this example, the inline function we provide to the onClick prop will be created every time MyComponent renders. It means the MyButton component will receive a new function reference each time, and as we already know, it will result in a new render for the MyButton component.

Here's an example that demonstrates the use of the useCallback hook:

```
const MyComponent = () => {
  const clickHandler = React.useCallback(() => {
    console.log("click");
  }, []);

  return <MyButton onClick={clickHandler} />;
};
```

In this example, the clickHandler function is memoized using useCallback. The empty dependency array [] indicates that the function has no dependencies and should remain constant throughout the component's lifecycle.

As a result, the same function instance is provided to MyButton on each render of MyComponent, preventing unnecessary re-renders of the child.

useRef hook

The useRef hook allows us to create a mutable reference that persists across component renders. It is commonly used to store values or references that need to be preserved between renders without triggering re-renders. Additionally, useRef can be used to access the DOM node or a React component instance:

```
const Component = () => {
  const inputRef = useRef();

  const handleButtonClick = () => {
    inputRef.current.focus();
  };

  return (
    <div>
      <input type="text" ref={inputRef} />
      <button onClick={handleButtonClick}>Focus Input</button>
    </div>
  );
};
```

In this example, the inputRef is created using useRef, and it is assigned to the ref attribute of the input element. This allows us to access the DOM node using the inputRef.current property. In the handleButtonClick function, we call the focus method on the inputRef.current to focus the input element when the button is clicked.

By using useRef to access the DOM node, we can interact with the underlying DOM elements directly without triggering re-renders of the component.

By leveraging memoization with the useMemo, useCallback, and useRef Hooks, we can optimize the performance of our React applications by avoiding unnecessary computations, preventing unnecessary re-renders, and preserving values and references across renders. This results in a smoother user experience and more efficient use of resources.

Summary

This chapter introduced you to React components and React Hooks. You learned about component properties or props by implementing code that passed property values from JSX to the component. Next, you found out what state is and how to manipulate it with the useState hook. Then, you learned about useEffect, which enables lifecycle management in functional React components, such as fetching API data when a component is mounted and cleaning up any pending async operations when it is removed. Then, you learned how to use the useContext() hook in order to access global application data. Lastly, you learned about memoization with the useMemo, useCallback, and useMemo Hooks.

In the following chapter, you'll learn about event handling with React components.

4

Event Handling in the React Way

The focus of this chapter is **event handling**. React has a unique approach to handling events: declaring event handlers in JSX. We'll get things started by looking at how event handlers for particular elements are declared in JSX. Then, we'll explore **inline** and **higher-order event handler** functions.

Afterward, you'll learn how React maps event handlers to DOM elements under the hood. Finally, you'll learn about the synthetic events that React passes to event handler functions and how they're pooled for performance purposes. Once you've completed this chapter, you'll be comfortable implementing event handlers in your React components. At that point, your applications come to life for your users because they are then able to interact with them.

The following topics are covered in this chapter:

- Declaring event handlers
- Declaring inline event handlers
- Binding handlers to elements
- Using synthetic event objects
- Understanding event pooling

Technical requirements

The code presented in this chapter can be found at the following link: https://github.com/PacktPublishing/React-and-React-Native-5E/tree/main/Chapter04

Declaring event handlers

The differentiating factor with event handling in React components is that it's declarative. Compare this with something such as **jQuery**, where you have to write imperative code that selects the relevant DOM elements and attaches event handler functions to them.

The advantage of the declarative approach to event handlers in JSX markup is that they're part of the UI structure. Not having to track down code that assigns event handlers is mentally liberating.

In this section, you'll write a basic event handler so that you can get a feel for the declarative event handling syntax found in React applications. Then, you'll learn how to use generic event handler functions.

Declaring handler functions

Let's take a look at a basic component that declares an event handler for the click event of an element:

```
function MyButton(props) {
  const clickHandler = () => {
    console.log("clicked");
  };

  return <button onClick={clickHandler}>{props.children}</button>;
}
```

The event handler `clickHandler` function is passed to the `onClick` property of the `<button>` element. By looking at this markup, you can see exactly which code will run when the button is clicked.

 View the official React documentation for the full list of supported event property names at `https://react.dev/reference/react-dom/components/common`.

Next, let's take a look at how to respond to more than one type of event using different event handlers with the same element.

Multiple event handlers

What I really like about the declarative event handler syntax is that it's easy to read when there's more than one handler assigned to an element. Sometimes, for example, there are two or three handlers for an element. Imperative code is difficult to work with for a single event handler, let alone several of them. When an element needs more handlers, it's just another JSX attribute. This scales well from a code-maintainability perspective, as this example shows:

```
function MyInput() {
  const onChange = () => {
    console.log("changed");
  };

  const onBlur = () => {
    console.log("blured");
  };

  return <input onChange={onChange} onBlur={onBlur} />;
}
```

This `<input>` element could have several more event handlers and the code would be just as readable.

As you keep adding more event handlers to your components, you'll notice that a lot of them do the same thing. Next, you'll learn about inline event handler functions.

Declaring inline event handlers

The typical approach to assigning handler functions to JSX properties is to use a **named** function. However, sometimes, you might want to use an **inline** function, where the function is defined as part of the markup. This is done by assigning an arrow function directly to the event property in the JSX markup:

```
function MyButton(props) {
  return (
    <button onClick={(e) => console.log("clicked", e)}>
      {props.children}
    </button>
  );
}
```

The main use of inlining event handlers like this is when you have a **static parameter** value that you want to pass to another function. In this example, you're calling console.log with the clicked string. You could have set up a special function for this purpose outside of the JSX markup by creating a new function or by using a higher-order function. But then you would have to think of yet another name for yet another function. Inlining is just easier sometimes.

Next, you'll learn about how React binds handler functions to the underlying DOM elements in the browser.

Binding handlers to elements

When you assign an event handler function to an element in JSX, React doesn't actually attach an event listener to the underlying DOM element. Instead, it adds the function to an internal mapping of functions. There's a single event listener on the document for the page. As events bubble up through the DOM tree to the document, the React handler checks to see whether any components have matching handlers. The process is illustrated here:

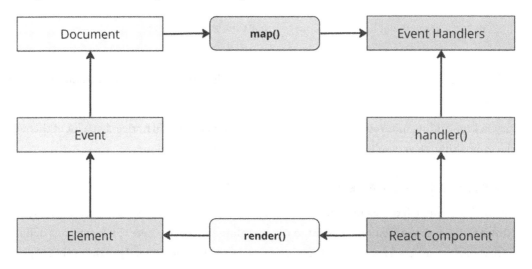

Figure 4.1: The event handler cycle

Why does React go through all of this trouble, you might ask? It's the same principle that I've been covering in the last few chapters: keep the declarative UI structures separated from the DOM as much as possible. The DOM is merely a render target; React's architecture allows it to remain agnostic about the final rendering destination and event system.

For example, when a new component is rendered, its event handler functions are simply added to the internal mapping maintained by React. When an event is triggered and it hits the document object, React maps the event to the handlers. If a match is found, it calls the handler. Finally, when the **React component** is removed, the handler is simply removed from the list of handlers.

None of these DOM operations actually touch the DOM. It's all abstracted by a single event listener. This is good for performance and the overall architecture (in other words, keeping the render target separate from the application code).

In the following section, you'll learn about the synthetic event implementation used by React to ensure good performance and safe asynchronous behavior.

Using synthetic event objects

When you attach an event handler function to a DOM element using the native addEventListener function, the callback will get an event argument passed to it. Event handler functions in React are also passed an event argument but it's not the standard event instance. It's called SyntheticEvent and it's a simple wrapper for native event instances.

Synthetic events serve two purposes in React:

- They provide a consistent event interface, normalizing browser inconsistencies.
- They contain information that's necessary for propagation to work.

Here's a diagram of the synthetic event in the context of a **React component**:

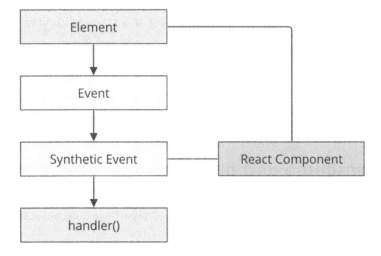

Figure 4.2: How synthetic events are created and processed

When a DOM element that is part of a **React component** dispatches an event, React will handle the event because it sets up its own listeners for them. Then, it will either create a new **synthetic event** or reuse one from the pool, depending on availability. If there are any event handlers declared for the component that match the DOM event that was dispatched, they will run with the synthetic event passed to them.

The event object in React has properties and methods similar to those in native JavaScript events. You can access properties such as event.target to retrieve the DOM element that triggered the event, or event.currentTarget to refer to the element to which the event handler is attached.

Additionally, the event object provides methods like event.preventDefault() to prevent the default behavior associated with the event, such as form submissions or link clicks. You can also use event.stopPropagation() to stop the event from propagating further up the component tree, preventing event bubbling.

Event propagation works differently in React compared to traditional JavaScript event handling. In the traditional approach, events typically bubble up through the DOM tree, triggering handlers on ancestor elements.

In React, event propagation is based on the component hierarchy rather than the DOM hierarchy. When an event occurs in a child component, React captures the event at the root of the component tree and then traverses down to the specific component that triggered the event. This approach, known as event delegation, simplifies event handling by centralizing the event logic at the root of the component tree.

React's event delegation provides several benefits. First, it reduces the number of event listeners attached to individual DOM elements, resulting in improved performance. Second, it allows you to handle events for dynamically created or removed elements without worrying about attaching or detaching event listeners manually.

In the next section, you'll see how these synthetic events are pooled for performance reasons and the implications of this on asynchronous code.

Understanding event pooling

One challenge of wrapping native event instances is that it can cause performance issues. Every synthetic event wrapper that's created will also need to be garbage collected at some point, which can be expensive in terms of CPU time.

When the garbage collector is running, none of your JavaScript code is able to run. This is why it's important to be memory-efficient; frequent garbage collection means less CPU time for code that responds to user interactions.

For example, if your application only handles a few events, this wouldn't matter much. But even by modest standards, applications respond to many events, even if the handlers don't actually do anything with them. This is problematic if React constantly has to allocate new synthetic event instances.

React deals with this problem by allocating a **synthetic instance pool**. Whenever an event is triggered, it takes an instance from the pool and populates its properties. When the event handler has finished running, the **synthetic event** instance is released back into the pool, as shown here:

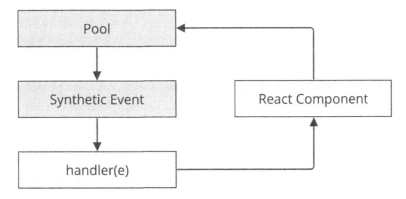

Figure 4.3: Synthetic events are reused to save memory resources

This prevents the garbage collector from running frequently when a lot of events are triggered. The pool keeps a reference to the synthetic event instances, so they're never eligible for garbage collection. React never has to allocate new instances either.

However, there is one gotcha that you need to be aware of. It involves accessing the synthetic event instances from asynchronous code in your event handlers. This is an issue because, as soon as the handler has finished running, the instance goes back into the pool. When it goes back into the pool, all of its properties are cleared.

Here's an example that shows how this can go wrong:

```
function fetchData() {
  return new Promise((resolve) => {
    setTimeout(() => {
```

```
      resolve();
    }, 1000);
  });
}

function MyButton(props) {
  function onClick(e) {
    console.log("clicked", e.currentTarget.style);

    fetchData().then(() => {
      console.log("callback", e.currentTarget.style);
    });
  }

  return <button onClick={onClick}>{props.children}</button>;
}
```

The second call to console.log is attempting to access a synthetic event property from an asynchronous callback that doesn't run until the event handler completes, which causes the event to empty its properties. This results in a warning and an undefined value.

 The aim of this example is to illustrate how things can break when you write asynchronous code that interacts with events. Just don't do it!

In this section, you learned that events are pooled for performance reasons, which means that you should never access event objects in an asynchronous way.

Summary

This chapter introduced you to event handling in React. The key differentiator between React and other approaches to event handling is that handlers are declared in JSX markup. This makes tracking down which elements handle which events much simpler.

You learned that having multiple event handlers on a single element is a matter of adding new JSX properties. Then, you learned about inline event handler functions and their potential use, as well as how React actually binds a single DOM event handler to the document object.

Synthetic events are abstractions that wrap native events; you learned why they're necessary and how they're pooled for efficient memory consumption.

In the next chapter, you'll learn how to create components that are reusable for a variety of purposes. Instead of writing new components for each use case that you encounter, you'll learn the skills necessary to refactor existing components so that they can be used in more than one context.

5

Crafting Reusable Components

The aim of this chapter is to show you how to implement React components that serve more than just one purpose. After reading this chapter, you'll feel confident about how to compose application features.

The chapter starts with a brief look at HTML elements and how they work in terms of helping to implement features versus having a high level of utility. Then, you'll see the implementation of a **monolithic component** and discover the issues that it will cause down the road. The next section is devoted to re-implementing the monolithic component in such a way that the feature is composed of smaller components.

Finally, the chapter ends with a discussion of rendering trees of React components and gives you some tips on how to avoid introducing too much complexity as a result of decomposing components. I'll close the final section by reiterating the concept of high-level feature components versus utility components.

The following topics will be covered in this chapter:

- Reusable HTML elements
- The difficulty with monolithic components
- Refactoring component structures
- Render props
- Rendering component trees

Technical requirements

You can find the code files for this chapter on GitHub at `https://github.com/PacktPublishing/React-and-React-Native-5E/tree/main/Chapter05`.

Reusable HTML elements

Let's think about HTML elements for a moment. Depending on the type of HTML element, it's either feature-centric or utility-centric. Utility-centric HTML elements are more reusable than feature-centric HTML elements. For example, consider the `<section>` element. This is a generic element that can be used just about anywhere but its primary purpose is to compose the structural aspects of a feature: the outer shell of the feature and the inner sections of the feature. This is where the `<section>` element is most useful.

On the other side of the fence, you have elements such as `<p>`, `<span>`, and `<button>`. These elements provide a high level of utility because they're generic by design. You're supposed to use `<button>` elements whenever you have something that's clickable by the user, resulting in an action. This is a level lower than the concept of a feature.

While it's easy to talk about HTML elements that have a high level of utility versus those that are geared toward specific features, the discussion is more detailed when data is involved. HTML is static markup; React components combine static markup with data. The question is, how do you make sure that you're creating the right feature-centric and utility-centric components?

The aim of this chapter is to find out how to go from a monolithic React component that defines a feature to a smaller feature-centric component combined with utility components.

The diffculty with monolithic components

If you could implement just one component for any given feature, it would simplify your job. At the very least, there wouldn't be many components to maintain, and there wouldn't be many communication paths for data to flow through because everything would be internal to the component.

However, this idea doesn't work for a number of reasons. Having monolithic feature components makes it difficult to coordinate any kind of team development effort, such as **version control**, **merge conflicts**, and **parallel development**. The bigger the monolithic components become, the more difficult they are to refactor into something better later on.

There's also the problem of feature overlap and feature communication. Overlap happens because of similarities between features; it's unlikely that an application will have a set of features that are completely unique to one another. That would make the application very difficult to learn and use. Component communication essentially means that the state of something in one feature will impact the state of something in another feature. State is difficult to deal with, and even more so when there is a lot of state packaged up in a monolithic component.

The best way to learn how to avoid monolithic components is to experience one firsthand. You'll spend the remainder of this section implementing a monolithic component. In the following section, you'll see how this component can be refactored into something a little more sustainable.

The JSX markup

The **monolithic component** we're going to implement is a feature that lists articles. It's just for illustrative purposes, so we don't want to go overboard on the size of the component. It'll be simple yet monolithic. The user can add new items to the list, toggle the summary of items in the list, and remove items from the list.

Here is the JSX markup of the component:

```
<section>
    <header>
      <h1>Articles</h1>
      <input placeholder="Title" value={title} onChange={onChangeTitle}
/>
      <input
        placeholder="Summary"
        value={summary}
        onChange={onChangeSummary}
      />
      <button onClick={onClickAdd}>Add</button>
    </header>
    <article>
      <ul>
        {articles.map((i) => (
          <li key={i.id}>
            <a
              href={'#${i.id}'}
              title="Toggle Summary"
```

```
                    onClick={() => onClickToggle(i.id)}
                >
                    {i.title}
                </a>
                 
                <button
                    href={'#${i.id}'}
                    title="Remove"
                    onClick={() => onClickRemove(i.id)}
                >
                    &#10007;
                </button>
                <p style={{ display: i.display }}>{i.summary}</p>
            </li>
        ))}
        </ul>
    </article>
</section>
```

This is definitely more JSX than is necessary in one place. We'll improve on this in the following section, but for now, let's implement the initial state for this component.

Initial state

Now, let's look at the initial state of this component:

```
const [articles, setArticles] = React.useState([
    {
        id: id.next(),
        title: "Article 1",
        summary: "Article 1 Summary",
        display: "none",
    },
    {
        id: id.next(),
        title: "Article 2",
        summary: "Article 2 Summary",
        display: "none",
    },
```

```
  ]);
  const [title, setTitle] = React.useState("");
  const [summary, setSummary] = React.useState("");
```

The state consists of an array of `articles`, a `title` string, and a `summary` string. Each article object in the `articles` array has several string fields to help render the article and an `id` field, which is a number. The number is generated by `id.next()`.

Let's take a look at how this works:

```
const id = (function* () {
  let i = 1;
  while (true) {
    yield i;
    i += 1;
  }
})();
```

The `id` constant is a generator. It is created by defining an inline generator function and calling it right away. This generator will yield numbers infinitely. So, calling `id.next()` the first time returns 1, the next is 2, and so on. This simple utility will come in handy when it's time to add new articles and we need a new unique ID.

Event handler implementation

At this point, you have the initial state and the JSX of the component. Now, it's time to implement the event handlers:

```
const onChangeTitle = useCallback((e) => {
  setTitle(e.target.value);
}, []);

const onChangeSummary = useCallback((e) => {
  setSummary(e.target.value);
}, []);
```

The `onChangeTitle()` and `onChangeSummary()` methods use the hook's `setState()` to update the `title` and `summary` state values, respectively. The new values come from the `target.value` property of the event argument, which is the value that the user types into the text input:

```
const onClickAdd = useCallback(() => {
```

```
      setArticles((state) => [
        ...state,
        {
          id: id.next(),
          title: title,
          summary: summary,
          display: "none",
        },
      ]);
      setTitle("");
      setSummary("");
    }, [summary, title]);
```

The onClickAdd() method adds a new article to the articles state. This state value is an array. We use the spread operator to build a new array from the existing array ([...state]), and the new object gets added to the end of the new array. The reason we're building a new array and passing it to setArticles() is so that there are no surprises. In other words, we're treating state values as immutable so that other code that updates the same state doesn't accidentally cause problems. Next, we'll use a handler to remove the article:

```
    const onClickRemove = useCallback((id) => {
      setArticles((state) =>
        state.filter((article) => article.id !== id)
      );
    }, []);
```

The onClickRemove() method removes the article with the given ID from the articles state. It does this by calling filter() on the array, which returns a new array, so the operation is immutable. The filter removes the object with the given ID:

```
    const onClickToggle = useCallback((id) => {
      setArticles((state) => {
        const articles = [...state];
        const index = articles.findIndex((article) => article.id === id);

        articles[index] = {
          ...articles[index],
          display: articles[index].display ? "" : "none",
        };
```

```
    return articles;
  });
}, []);
```

The onClickToggle() method toggles the visibility of the article with the given ID. We carry out two immutable operations in this method. First, we build a new articles array. Then, based on the index of the given ID, we replace the article object at the index with a new object. We use the object spread operator to fill in the properties ({...articles[index]}), and then the display property value is toggled based on the existing display value.

Here's a screenshot of the output rendered:

Figure 5.1: Rendered articles

At this point, we have a component that does everything that we need our feature to do. However, it's monolithic and difficult to maintain. Imagine if we had other places in our app that use the same pieces of MyFeature. They have to re-invent them because they cannot be shared. In the following section, we'll work on breaking down MyFeature into smaller reusable components.

Refactoring component structures

You have a monolithic feature component: *now what*? Let's make it better.

In this section, you'll learn how to take the feature component that you just implemented in the preceding section and split it into more maintainable components. You'll start with the **JSX**, as this is probably the best refactor starting point. Then, you'll implement new components for the feature.

Next, you'll make these new components functional instead of class-based. Finally, you'll learn how to use **render props** to reduce the number of direct component dependencies in your application, and how to remove classes entirely by using hooks to manage state within functional components.

Starting with the JSX

The **JSX** of any **monolithic component** is the best starting point for figuring out how to refactor it into smaller components. Let's visualize the structure of the component that we're currently refactoring:

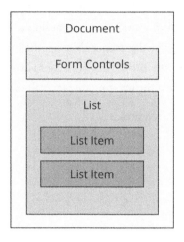

Figure 5.2: Visualization of the JSX that makes up a React component

The top part of the JSX is the form controls, so this could easily become its own component:

```
<header>
  <h1>Articles</h1>
  <input
    placeholder="Title"
    value={title}
    onChange={onChangeTitle} />
  <input
    placeholder="Summary"
    value={summary}
    onChange={onChangeSummary} />
  <button onClick={onClickAdd}>Add</button>
</header>;
```

Next, you have the list of articles:

```
<ul>
  {articles.map((i) => (
    <li key={i.id}>
```

```
    <a
      href={`#${i.id}`}
      title="Toggle Summary"
      onClick={() => onClickToggle(i.id)}
    >
      {i.title}
    </a>
     
    <button
      href={'#${i.id}'}
      title="Remove"
      onClick={() => onClickRemove(i.id)}
    >
      &#10007;
    </button>
    <p style={{ display: i.display }}>{i.summary}</p>
  </li>
))}
</ul>
```

Within this list, there's potential for an article component, which would be everything in the `<li>` tag. Let's try building this next.

Implementing an article list component

Here's what the ArticleList component implementation looks like:

```
function ArticleList({ articles, onClickToggle, onClickRemove }) {
  return (
    <ul>
      {articles.map((i) => (
        <li key={i.id}>
          <a
            href={'#${i.id}'}
            title="Toggle Summary"
            onClick={() => onClickToggle(i.id)}
          >
            {i.title}
```

```
              </a>
               
              <button
                href={'#${i.id}'}
                title="Remove"
                onClick={() => onClickRemove(i.id)}
              >
                &#10007;
              </button>
              <p style={{ display: i.display }}>{i.summary}</p>
            </li>
          ))}
        </ul>
      );
    }
```

We're taking the relevant JSX out of the monolithic component and putting it here. Now, let's see what the feature component of JSX looks like:

```
      <section>
        <header>
          <h1>Articles</h1>
          <input placeholder="Title" value={title} onChange={onChangeTitle}
  />
          <input
            placeholder="Summary"
            value={summary}
            onChange={onChangeSummary}
          />
          <button onClick={onClickAdd}>Add</button>
        </header>
        <ArticleList
          articles={articles}
          onClickRemove={onClickRemove}
          onClickToggle={onClickToggle}
        />
      </section>
```

The list of articles is now rendered by the `ArticleList` component. The list of articles to render is passed to this component as a property along with two of the event handlers.

Why are we passing event handlers to a child component? The reason is so that the `ArticleList` component doesn't have to worry about the state or how the state changes. All it cares about is rendering content and making sure the appropriate event callbacks are hooked up to the appropriate DOM elements. This is a container component concept that I'll expand upon later in this chapter.

Now that we have an `ArticleList` component, let's see whether we can further break it down into smaller reusable components.

Implementing an article item component

After implementing the article list component, you might decide that it's a good idea to break this component.

Another way to look at it is this: if it turns out that we don't actually need the item as its own component, this new component doesn't introduce much indirection or complexity. Without further ado, here's the article item component:

```
function ArticleItem({ article, onClickRemove }) {
  const [isOpened, setIsOpened] = React.useState(article.display !==
"none");

  const onClickToggle = React.useCallback(() => {
    setIsOpened((state) => !state);
  }, []);

  return (
    <li>
      <a href={'#${article.id}'} title="Toggle Summary"
onClick={onClickToggle}>
        {article.title}
      </a>
       
      <button
        href={'#${article.id}'}
        title="Remove"
```

```
        onClick={() => onClickRemove(article.id)}
      >
        &#10007;
      </button>
      <p style={{ display: isOpened ? "block" : "none" }}>{article.
summary}</p>
    </li>
  );
}
```

Essentially, the component remains unchanged except for one enhancement: we have relocated the logic for expanding and collapsing the article to the ArticleItem component, which offers several advantages. Firstly, we reduced the original MyFeature component, since it doesn't need to know when we hide or expand an article at all. Secondly, we have improved the performance of the application due to the fact that when expanding an article, we no longer recreate the array of articles using the spread operator but only change the state locally. As a result, when expanding the article, the list of articles remains the same and React does not re-render the page, but only one component is re-rendered.

Here's the new ArticleItem component being rendered by the ArticleList component:

```
function ArticleList({ articles, onClickRemove }) {
  return (
    <ul>
      {articles.map((article) => (
        <ArticleItem
          key={article.id.value}
          article={article}
          onClickRemove={onClickRemove}
        />
      ))}
    </ul>
  );
}
```

Do you see how this list just maps the list of articles? What if you wanted to implement another article list that does some filtering too? If so, it's beneficial to have a reusable ArticleItem component. Next, we'll move the add article markup into its own component.

Implementing an AddArticle component

Now that we're done with the article list, it's time to think about the form controls used to add a new article. Let's implement a component for this aspect of the feature:

```
function AddArticle({
  name,
  title,
  summary,
  onChangeTitle,
  onChangeSummary,
  onClickAdd,
}) {
  return (
    <section>
      <h1>{name}</h1>
      <input placeholder="Title" value={title} onChange={onChangeTitle} />
      <input placeholder="Summary" value={summary}
onChange={onChangeSummary} />
      <button onClick={onClickAdd}>Add</button>
    </section>
  );
}
```

Now, our feature component only needs to render `<AddArticle>` and `<ArticleList>` components:

```
<section>
  <AddArticle
    name="Articles"
    title={title}
    summary={summary}
    onChangeTitle={onChangeTitle}
    onChangeSummary={onChangeSummary}
    onClickAdd={onClickAdd}
  />
  <ArticleList articles={articles} onClickRemove={onClickRemove} />
</section>
```

The focus of this component is on the feature data, while it defers to other components for rendering UI elements. In the next section, we'll look at how render props make it possible to pass components around as properties instead of directly importing them as dependencies.

Render props

Imagine implementing a feature that is composed of several smaller components, like what you've been working on in this chapter. The MyFeature component depends on ArticleList and AddArticle. Now, imagine using MyFeature in different parts of your application where it makes sense to use a different implementation of ArticleList or AddArticle. The fundamental challenge is substituting one component for another.

Render props are a nice way to address this challenge. The idea is that you pass a property to your component whose value is a function that returns a component to render. This way, instead of having the feature component directly depend on its child components, you can configure them as you like; they pass them in as render prop values. Let's look at an example. Instead of having MyFeature directly depend on AddArticle and ArticleList, you can pass them as render props. Here's what the MyFeature looks like when it's using render props to fill in the holes where add used to be:

```
<section>
  {addArticle({
    title,
    summary,
    onChangeTitle,
    onChangeSummary,
    onClickAdd,
  })}
  {articleList({ articles, onClickRemove })}
</section>
```

The addArticle() and articleList() functions are called with the same property values that would have been passed to <AddArticle> and <ArticleList>, respectively. The difference now is that this module no longer imports AddArticle or ArticleList as dependencies.

Now, let's take a look at the main.js file where <MyFeature> is rendered:

```
const root = ReactDOM.createRoot(document.getElementById("root"));
root.render(
  <MyFeature
```

```
      addArticle={({
        title,
        summary,
        onChangeTitle,
        onChangeSummary,
        onClickAdd,
      }) => (
        <AddArticle
          name="Articles"
          title={title}
          summary={summary}
          onChangeTitle={onChangeTitle}
          onChangeSummary={onChangeSummary}
          onClickAdd={onClickAdd}
        />
      )}
      articleList={({ articles, onClickRemove }) => (
        <ArticleList articles={articles} onClickRemove={onClickRemove} />
      )}
    />
  );
```

There's a lot more going on here now than there was when it was just <MyFeature> being rendered. Let's break down why that is. Here is where you pass the addArticle and articleList render props. These prop values are functions that accept argument values from MyComponent. For example, the onClickRemove() function comes from MyFeature and is used to change the state of that component. You can use the **render prop** function to pass this to the component that will be rendered, along with any other values. The return value of these functions is what is ultimately rendered.

In this section, you learned that by passing render property values: functions that render JSX markup: you can avoid hardcoding dependencies in places where you might want to share functionality. Passing a different property value to a component is usually easier than changing the dependencies used by a given module.

Rendering component trees

Let's take a moment to reflect on what we've accomplished so far in this chapter. The feature component that was once monolithic ended up focusing almost entirely on the state data. It handled the initial state and handled transforming the state and it would handle network requests that fetch state, if there were any. This is a typical container component in a React application, and it's the starting point for data.

The new components that you implemented to better compose the feature were the recipients of this data. The difference between these components and their container is that they only care about the properties that are passed into them at the time they're rendered. In other words, they only care about data snapshots at a particular point in time. From here, these components might pass the property data into their own child components as properties. The generic pattern for composing React components is as follows:

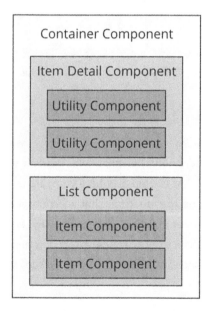

Figure 5.3: A pattern for composing larger React components from smaller components

The **container component** will typically contain one direct **child**. In this diagram, you can see that the container has either an **item detail component** or a **list component**. Of course, there will be variations in these two categories, as every application is different. This generic pattern has three levels of component composition. Data flows in one direction from the **container** all the way down to the **utility** components.

Once you add more than three layers, the application architecture becomes difficult to comprehend. There will be the odd case where you'll need to add four layers of React components but, as a rule of thumb, you should avoid this.

Feature components and utility components

In the **monolithic component** example that we have worked on in this chapter, you started with a single component that was entirely focused on a feature. This means that the component has very little utility elsewhere in the application.

The reason for this is that top-level components deal with the application state. **Stateful components** are difficult to use in any other context. As you refactored the monolithic feature component, you created new components that moved further away from the data. The general rule is that the further your components move from stateful data, the more utility they have because their property values could be passed in from anywhere in the application.

Summary

This chapter was about avoiding a monolithic component design. However, monoliths are often a necessary starting point in the design of any React component.

You began by learning about how the different HTML elements have varying degrees of utility. Next, you learned about the issues with monolithic React components and walked through the implementation of a monolithic component.

Then, you spent several sections learning how to refactor the monolithic component into a more sustainable design. From this exercise, you learned that container components should only have to think in terms of handling state, while smaller components have more utility because their property values can be passed from anywhere. You also learned that you could use render props for better control over component dependencies and substitution.

In the next chapter, you'll learn about the component props validation and type checking.

6

Type-Checking and Validation with TypeScript

In this chapter, we'll explore the importance of **property validation** in React components for creating robust, bug-free applications. We'll introduce **TypeScript**, which is a powerful tool for static type-checking in JavaScript.

We'll guide you through setting up TypeScript in the project and cover its basic and advanced concepts. We'll also provide examples of how to use TypeScript for type-checking in React components.

By the end of this chapter, you'll have a solid foundation in property validation and type-checking, and be ready to create more predictable, reliable components using TypeScript.

The following topics will be covered in this chapter:

- Knowing what to expect
- An introduction to TypeScript
- Using TypeScript in React

Technical requirements

The code files for this chapter can be found on GitHub at https://github.com/PacktPublishing/
React-and-React-Native-5E/tree/main/Chapter05.

Knowing what to expect

In any application, predictability is key. A predictable application behaves in expected ways, reducing bugs, improving user experience, and simplifying maintenance. When we talk about predictability in the context of React, we often refer to how components behave based on the props they receive. Props is short for properties and serves as the inputs to React components, determining their behavior and rendering. This is where the concept of **props validation** comes into play.

The importance of props validation

Props validation is a way to ensure that components receive the right type of data. It's like a contract between components. When a component specifies the types of props it expects to receive, it makes a promise that it will behave in a certain way if it receives props of those types.

Props validation is crucial for a few reasons, as follows:

- It **helps catch errors early in the development process**: If a component receives a prop of an unexpected type, it might not behave as expected, leading to bugs that can be hard to track down. By validating props, we can catch these errors before they cause problems.

- **Props validation improves code readability**: By looking at a component's prop types, you can quickly understand what data the component expects to receive. This makes it easier to use and reuse components throughout your application.

- **Props validation makes components more predictable**: When a component clearly specifies the types of props it expects to receive, it's easier to understand how the component will behave based on its props.

Potential issues without props validation

Without adequate props validation, components can become unpredictable and prone to bugs. Let's take a look at a component:

```
const MyList = ({ list }) => (
  <ul>
    {list.map((user) => (
      <li key={user.name}>
        {user.name} ({user.email})
      </li>
    ))}
  </ul>
);
```

In this example, a component expects to receive a **list prop**, which should be an array of objects with name and email properties. If this component receives a list prop that is a string, a number, or even an array, but without objects, it might try to access user.name or user.email, which would result in an error.

These types of errors can be hard to debug, especially in larger applications with many components. It also might be difficult to understand what exactly we should provide to the component without reading every single line of code of this component. Errors can also lead to crashes or unexpected behavior in your application. But what if we can add a props validation to our components that can help us catch these errors early and ensure that your components behave as expected? Let's explore it.

Options for props validation

There are several tools you can use for props validation in React and React Native. One of these is PropTypes, a library that allows you to specify the types of props a component should receive. Another option is TypeScript, a statically typed superset of JavaScript that provides powerful tools for type-checking.

Now, I would like to show you examples of the MyList component with PropTypes. Take a look at this component:

```
import PropTypes from 'prop-types';

const MyList = ({ list }) => (
  <ul>
    {list.map((user) => (
      <li key={user.name}>
        {user.name} ({user.email})
      </li>
    ))}
  </ul>
);

MyList.propTypes = {
  list: PropTypes.arrayOf(
    PropTypes.shape({
      name: PropTypes.string.isRequired,
      email: PropTypes.string.isRequired,
```

```
    })
  ).isRequired,
};
```

In this example, we're using PropTypes to specify that the list prop should be an array of objects, and each object should have a name and an email property, both of which should be strings.

Next, let's take a look at the TypeScript example:

```
type User = {
  name: string;
  email: string;
};

type MyListProps = {
  list: User[];
};

const MyList = ({ list }: MyListProps) => (
  <ul>
    {list.map((user) => (
      <li key={user.name}>
        {user.name} ({user.email})
      </li>
    ))}
  </ul>
);
```

In this TypeScript example, we're defining a User type and a MyListProps type. The User type is an object with a name and an email property, both of which are strings. The MyListProps type is an object with a list property, which is an array of User objects.

While both PropTypes and TypeScript offer valuable tools for props validation, we'll be focusing on TypeScript for the remainder of this book. TypeScript provides a more comprehensive and powerful approach to type-checking, and it's becoming increasingly popular in the React and React Native communities.

In the following chapters, all examples will use TypeScript. By the end of this book, you'll have a solid understanding of TypeScript and how to use it in your own React and React Native projects. So, let's dive in and start exploring the world of TypeScript!

Introduction to TypeScript

As we embark on this journey to learn about type-checking and validation, let's momentarily step away from React and React Native and turn our attention to TypeScript. You might be wondering, "What exactly is TypeScript?"

TypeScript is a statically typed superset of **JavaScript**, developed and maintained by Microsoft. This means that it adds additional features to JavaScript, one of the most significant being static typing. While JavaScript is dynamically typed, TypeScript introduces a type system that allows you to explicitly define the type of data that variables, function parameters, and function return values can have.

But don't worry, TypeScript is completely compatible with JavaScript. In fact, any valid JavaScript code is also valid TypeScript code. TypeScript uses a transpiler (a type of compiler) to convert TypeScript code, which browsers can't understand directly, into JavaScript code, which can run in any environment where JavaScript runs.

Consider the following JavaScript function:

```javascript
function greet(name) {
  return "Hello, " + name;
}

console.log(greet("Mike")); // "Hello, Mike"
console.log(greet(32)); // "Hello, 32"
```

This function works as expected when you pass a string as an argument. But if you pass a number, it doesn't throw an error, even though it doesn't make much sense to greet a number.

Now, let's see how we could write this function in TypeScript:

```typescript
function greet(name: string) {
  return "Hello, " + name;
}

console.log(greet("Mike")); // "Hello, Mike"
console.log(greet(32)); // Error: Argument of type 'number' is not
assignable to parameter of type 'string'.
```

In the TypeScript version, we've added a type annotation to the name parameter. This tells Type-Script that name should always be a string. If we try to call greet with a number, TypeScript will give us an error. This helps us catch the mistake before we even run the code.

This is a simple example, but it illustrates one of the key benefits of TypeScript: it can help us catch errors early before they lead to bugs in our code. It's like having a helpful co-pilot who points out potential issues before they become problematic.

Why use TypeScript?

Now that we've introduced what TypeScript is, let's delve into why you might want to learn and use it in your projects:

- **Catch errors early**: We've already discussed it, but it's worth putting it in the first place on the list. One of the biggest advantages of TypeScript is its ability to catch errors at compile time, before even running the code. This can help prevent many common errors that might not be caught until runtime in regular JavaScript.

- **Improve code readability**: TypeScript's **type annotations** make it clear what kind of values a function expects as arguments or what type of value a function returns. This can make the code easier to read and understand, especially for other developers who might be working on the same code base.

- **Easier refactoring**: TypeScript's static typing also makes it easier to refactor code. If you change the type of a variable or the signature of a function, TypeScript can help you find all the places in your code where you need to make corresponding changes.

- **Community and tooling support**: TypeScript has gained significant popularity in the JavaScript community and is used by many large companies like Microsoft, Google, and Airbnb. This implies that there's a large community of developers who can provide support and a wealth of resources for learning TypeScript. Additionally, many code editors have excellent support for TypeScript, providing features like **autocompletion, type inference**, and **error highlighting**.

- **Integration with modern frameworks and libraries**: TypeScript integrates well with modern JavaScript frameworks like React and React Native, which have built-in TypeScript definitions, making it easier to build strongly typed applications. Moreover, a vast majority of popular JavaScript libraries have TypeScript definitions available. These definitions, often contributed by the community, provide type information about the library's functions and objects, making it easier and safer to use these libraries in your TypeScript projects.

This widespread adoption of TypeScript in the JavaScript ecosystem ensures that you can leverage the benefits of TypeScript almost anywhere in your code base.

- **Increasing job market demand**: The popularity of TypeScript extends beyond just development practices: it's also increasingly sought after in the job market. Many companies, from start-ups to large corporations, are adopting TypeScript for their projects, and as a result, there's a growing demand for developers who are proficient in TypeScript. This is particularly true for roles involving React and React Native, where TypeScript is often used for its benefits in scaling and maintaining large code bases. By learning TypeScript, you're not only gaining a valuable skill for your projects but also making yourself more marketable as a developer.

In summary, TypeScript offers a range of benefits that can help you write more robust, maintainable code. It's a valuable tool in any JavaScript developer's toolkit, and its growing popularity in the job market makes it a worthwhile investment for your career development.

But understanding the benefits of TypeScript is just the first step. To truly harness its power, you need to know how to use it in your projects. In the next section, we'll guide you through the process of setting up TypeScript in a React project. We'll cover everything from installing TypeScript to configuring your project to use it. So, let's dive in and start exploring the practical side of TypeScript!

Setting up TypeScript in a project

In the first chapter, we walked through the process of creating a new React project using **Vite**. Now, let's see how we can create a TypeScript project.

Vite provides a template for creating a new React and TypeScript project. You can create a new project with the following command:

```
npm create vite@latest my-react-app -- --template react-ts
```

This command creates a new Vite project with the `react-ts` template, which includes TypeScript. The project based on this template will include the `tsconfig.json` file in the root of your project. This file is used to configure TypeScript for your project.

Here's what the `tsconfig.json` file might look like:

```
{
  "compilerOptions": {
    "target": "esnext",
```

```
    "module": "esnext",
    "jsx": "react-jsx",
    "strict": true,
    "moduleResolution": "node",
    "esModuleInterop": true
  }
}
```

These settings tell TypeScript to compile your code to the latest version of JavaScript ("target":
"esnext"), to use the latest module system ("module": "esnext"), and to use the new JSX transform introduced in *React 17* ("jsx": "react-jsx"). The "strict": true option enables a wide
range of type-checking behavior to catch more issues.

With TypeScript set up, let's write some code. However, TypeScript uses different file extensions
than JavaScript: *.ts for files without JSX, and *.tsx for files with JSX. So, let's create our first
React component using TypeScript:

```
type AppProps = {
  message: string;
};


function App({ message }: AppProps) {
  return <div>{message}</div>;
}
```

In this example, we're defining an AppProps type for the props of the App component. This tells
TypeScript that the message prop should be a string.

Now, let's take a look at the figure of how main.tsx looks like right now:

```
ReactDOM.createRoot(document.getElementById("root")!).render(
  <React.StrictMode>
    <App />    Property 'message' is missing in type '{}' but required in type 'AppProps'.
  </React.StrictMode>
);
```

Figure 6.1: App component in the main.tsx file with the error from TypeScript

This is how TypeScript checks and validates props usage in components. Here, we should pass
the message prop:

```
ReactDOM.createRoot(document.getElementById("root")!).render(
  <React.StrictMode>
    <App message="Hello TypeScript" />
  </React.StrictMode>
```

Figure 6.2: App component in the main.tsx file without errors

Finally, you can run your project with the following command:

```
npm run dev
```

This command starts the **Vite development server**. If there are any **type errors** in your code, TypeScript will show them in the console as well.

Basic types in TypeScript

One of the key features of TypeScript is its rich type system. TypeScript introduces several basic types that you can use to describe the shape of your data. To specify the type of a variable, you use a colon after the variable name, followed by the type.

Let's explore these basic types:

- **Boolean**: The most basic datatype is the simple `true`/`false` value, which JavaScript and TypeScript call a Boolean:

  ```
  let isDone: boolean = false;
  ```

- **Number**: As in JavaScript, all numbers in TypeScript are floating point values. These floating point numbers get the type number:

  ```
  let age: number = 32;
  ```

- **String**: Another fundamental part of creating programs in JavaScript for web pages and servers alike is working with **textual data**. As in other languages, we use the type string to refer to these textual datatypes:

  ```
  let color: string = "blue";
  ```

- **Array**: TypeScript, like JavaScript, allows you to work with arrays of values. Array types can be written in one of two ways. In the first, you use the type of the elements followed by [ ] to denote an array of that element type:

  ```
  let list: number[] = [1, 2, 3];
  ```

The second way uses a generic array type, `Array<elemType>`:

```
let list: Array<number> = [1, 2, 3];
```

- **Tuple**: Tuple types allow you to express an array where the type of a fixed number of elements is known but does not need to be the same. For example, you may want to represent a value as a pair of a `string` and a `number`:

```
let x: [string, number];
x = ["hello", 10]; // OK
```

- **Enum**: A helpful addition to the standard set of datatypes from JavaScript is the enum. As in languages like C#, an enum is a way of giving more friendly names to sets of numeric values:

```
enum Color {
  Red,
  Green,
  Blue,
}
let c: Color = Color.Green;
```

- **Any**: We may need to describe the type of variables that we do not know when we are writing an application. These values may come from dynamic content, for example, from the user or a third-party library. In these cases, we want to opt out of type-checking and let the values pass through compile-time checks. To do so, we label these with the any type:

```
let notSure: any = 4;
notSure = "maybe a string instead";
notSure = false; // okay, definitely a Boolean
```

- **Unknown**: The unknown type is a type-safe counterpart of any. Anything is assignable to unknown, but unknown isn't assignable to anything but itself and any without a type assertion or a control flow-based narrowing. Likewise, no operations are permitted on an unknown without first asserting or narrowing to a more specific type:

```
let notSure: unknown = 4;
notSure = "maybe a string instead";

// OK, because of structural typing
notSure = false;
```

```
let surelyNotAString: string = notSure; // Error, 'unknown' is not
assignable to 'string'
```

In this example, we can't assign notSure to surelyNotAString without a type-check, because notSure is of the unknown type. This helps prevent errors because we can't inadvertently perform operations on variables of the unknown type without first checking their types.

A common use case for unknown is in a catch clause, where the type of the error object is not known:

```
try {
  // some operation that might throw
} catch (error: unknown) {
  if (error instanceof Error) {
    console.log(error.message);
  }
}
```

In this example, we don't know what the error type might be, so we give it the unknown type. This forces us to check its type before we can interact with it.

- **Void**: void is a little like the opposite of any: the absence of having any type at all. You may commonly see this as the return type of functions that do not return a value:

```
function warnUser(): void {
  console.log("This is my warning message");
}
```

- **Null and undefined**: In TypeScript, both undefined and null actually have their own types named undefined and null respectively. Much like void, they're not extremely useful on their own:

```
let u: undefined = undefined;
let n: null = null;
```

However, undefined plays a crucial role in optional types. In TypeScript, you can make a type optional by adding ? after the type name. This means the value can be of the specified type or undefined. For example:

```
function greet(name?: string) {
```

```
    return 'Hello ${name}';
}

greet("Mike");
greet(undefined); // OK
greet(); // Also OK
```

- **Never:** The never type in TypeScript represents a type of value that never occurs. It's used in situations where a function never returns a value or reaches the end of its execution path. For example, a function that throws an error or one that has an infinite loop can be annotated with the never type:

```
function throwError(errorMsg: string): never {
    throw new Error(errorMsg);
}

function infiniteLoop(): never {
    while (true) {
    }
}
```

Understanding these basic types is a crucial first step in working with TypeScript. As you start to use TypeScript in your projects, you'll find that these types are powerful tools for writing robust, maintainable code.

In the next section, we'll delve deeper into TypeScript's type system and explore interfaces and type aliases, which provide a way to define complex types.

Interfaces and type aliases

While the basic types are useful for simple data types, when dealing with more complex data structures, we need more powerful tools. This is where interfaces and type aliases come in. They allow us to define complex types and give them a name.

Interfaces

An interface in TypeScript is a way of defining a contract for complex types. It describes the shape an object should have. Here's an example:

```
interface User {
  name: string;
```

```
    email: string;
  }
```

In this example, we've defined a User interface with two properties: name and email, both of which are strings. We can use this interface to type-check objects:

```
const user: User = {
  name: "Alice",
  email: "alice@example.com",
};
```

If we try to assign an object that doesn't match the User interface to the user variable, TypeScript will give us an error.

Type aliases

Type aliases are very similar to interfaces, but can be used for other types as well, not just objects. Here's an example of a type alias:

```
type Point = {
  x: number;
  y: number;
};

type ID = number | string;
```

In this example, we've defined a Point type that represents a point in a two-dimensional space and ID that can be a string or number. We can use these type aliases in the same way we use interfaces:

```
const point: Point = {
  x: 10,
  y: 20,
};

const id: ID = 100;
```

Interfaces vs type aliases

So, when should you use an interface, and when should you use a type alias? In many cases, the two are interchangeable, and it's mostly a matter of personal preference.

However, there are some differences. Interfaces are more extensible because they can be declared multiple times, and they will be merged together. Type aliases can't be re-opened to add new properties. On the other hand, type aliases can represent other types like union types, intersection types, tuples, and any other types that aren't currently available in an interface.

In general, if you're defining the shape of an object, either an interface or a type alias would work. If you're defining a type that could be something other than an object, you'll need to use a type alias.

In this section, we've taken our first steps into the world of TypeScript. We've learned about its setup in a **Vite** project, its basic types, and how to define complex types using interfaces and type aliases.

Now let's explore how we can use TypeScript with React components, state, event handlers.

Using TypeScript in React

Alright, we've made it this far! We've learned about the basics of TypeScript and talked about its benefits. Now, it's time to roll up our sleeves and get our hands dirty with some practical TypeScript in React.

In this section, we're going to explore how to use TypeScript to type-check all the different parts of a React application. We'll look at components, props, state, event handlers, context, and even refs. Don't worry: I'll walk you through plenty of examples to help illustrate these concepts.

Type-checking props in React components

In a React application, one of the primary areas where we can leverage TypeScript is in our components, specifically with props. Let's see the example:

```
type GreetingProps = {
  name: string;
};

const Greeting = ({ name }: GreetingProps) => {
  return <h1>Hello, {name}!</h1>;
};
```

In this example, we're defining a GreetingProps type that specifies the shape of the props that Greeting should receive. We're then using this type to type-check the name prop in the Greeting component.

This is a simple example with just one prop, but the same approach can be used for components with more complex props. For example, if a component receives an object or an array as a prop, we can define a type that describes the shape of that object or array. Here's an example:

```
type UserProps = {
  user: {
    name: string;
    email: string;
  };
};

const UserCard = ({ user }: UserProps) => {
  return (
    <div>
      <h1>{user.name}</h1>
      <p>{user.email}</p>
    </div>
  );
};
```

In this example, the UserCard component receives a user prop that is an object with name and email properties. We define a UserProps type that describes the shape of this object and use it to type-check the user prop.

Let's consider another common scenario in React: **optional props**. Sometimes, a component has props that aren't always required. In these cases, we can provide a default value for the prop, and mark it as optional in our type definition. Here's an example:

```
type ButtonProps = {
  children: React.ReactNode;
  disabled?: boolean;
};
```

```
const Button = ({ children, disabled = false }: ButtonProps) => {
  return <button disabled={disabled}>{children}</button>;
};
```

In the `ButtonProps` type, we're using `React.ReactNode` for the children prop. This is a special type provided by React that can accept any kind of renderable content. This includes strings, numbers, JSX elements, arrays of these types, or even functions that return these types. By using `React.ReactNode`, we're saying that the `children` prop can be any kind of content that React can render. Also, we're using the `disabled` prop, which is optional. We indicate that `disabled` is optional by adding a ? after the prop name in the `ButtonProps` type. We also provide a default value of false for disabled in the component function parameters.

This way, we can use the `Button` component with or without the `disabled` prop, and TypeScript will still type-check it correctly:

```
<Button>Click me!</Button> // OK
<Button disabled>Don't click me!</Button> // OK
```

Typing state

Just as we type-checked our props, we can also use TypeScript to type-check the state in our components. This ensures that we're always using the correct types of state values, providing another layer of safety to our code.

Let's look at an example of how we can apply TypeScript to state in a functional component:

```
const Counter = () => {
  const [count, setCount] = React.useState<number>(0);

  return (
    <div>
      <p>Count: {count}</p>
      <button
        onClick={() => {
          setCount(count + 1);
        }}
      >
        Increment
      </button>
```

```
      </div>
    );
  };
```

In this `Counter` component, we're using `React.useState<number>(0)` to declare a state variable `count` with an initial value of `0`. By providing `<number>` as a type argument to `useState`, we're telling TypeScript that `count` should always be a number. By the way: we can omit passing `<number>` because TypeScript is smart enough to infer that `count` should be a number based on the initial value type.

This also means that the `setCount` function will only accept numbers. If we try to call `setCount` with a non-number argument, TypeScript will give us an error.

Typing event handlers

Another area where TypeScript can be very useful in a React application is in **event handlers**. By type-checking our event handlers, we can ensure that we're using the correct event types and accessing the right properties on the event objects.

Let's look at an example of a functional component with an input field and a typed event handler:

```
  const InputField = () => {
    const [value, setValue] = React.useState("");

    const handleChange = (event: React.ChangeEvent<HTMLInputElement>) => {
      setValue(event.target.value);
    };

    return <input value={value} onChange={handleChange} />;
  };
```

In this `InputField` component, we're defining a `handleChange` function that will be called whenever the input field's value changes. We're using the `React.ChangeEvent<HTMLInputElement>` type for the event parameter to specify that this function should receive a change event from an input field.

This type includes all the properties we would expect from a change event on an input field, such as `event.target.value`. If we try to access a property that doesn't exist on this type of event, TypeScript will give us an error.

Typing context

When using TypeScript with React, we can also type-check our context to ensure that we're always using the correct types of values. Let's look at an example:

```
type ThemeContextType = {
  theme: string;
  setTheme: (theme: string) => void;
};


const ThemeContext = React.createContext<ThemeContextType | null>(null);



const ThemeProvider = ({ children }: { children: React.ReactNode }) => {
  const [theme, setTheme] = React.useState('light');

  return (
    <ThemeContext.Provider value={{ theme, setTheme }}>
      {children}
    </ThemeContext.Provider>
  );
};

const useTheme = () => {
  const context = React.useContext(ThemeContext);
  if (context === null) {
    throw new Error('useTheme must be used within a ThemeProvider');
  }
  return context;
};
```

In this example, we're creating a ThemeContext with React.createContext. We're providing a ThemeContextType as a type argument to createContext to specify the shape of the context value. This type includes a theme string and a setTheme function.

We're then creating a ThemeProvider component that provides the theme and setTheme values to the context. Inside the useTheme hook, we're using React.useContext to consume the ThemeContext. If the context is null, we throw an error.

This is a common pattern to ensure that the context is used within a provider.

With this example, I want to highlight an important TypeScript feature. In the `useTheme` hook, we don't specify the type. It returns the context value, which TypeScript knows is of the `ThemeContextType` type and not `null`, thanks to the error check. This means that when we use `useTheme`, TypeScript will automatically provide the correct, non-null context type.

Typing refs

Now, let's turn our attention to another powerful feature in React: refs. As you already know from *Chapter 3*, *Understanding React Components and Hooks*, refs give us a way to access **DOM nodes** or **React elements** directly within our components. But how do we ensure we're using refs correctly? TypeScript coming to the rescue.

Consider this example where we apply TypeScript to refs:

```
const InputWithRef = () => {
  const inputRef = React.useRef<HTMLInputElement>(null);

  const focusInput = () => {
    if (inputRef.current) {
      inputRef.current.focus();
    }
  };

  return (
    <div>
      <input ref={inputRef} type="text" />
      <button onClick={focusInput}>Focus the input</button>
    </div>
  );
};
```

In this `InputField` component, we're creating a ref with `React.useRef`. We're providing `HTMLInputElement` as a type argument to `useRef` to specify the type of the ref. `HTMLInputElement` is a type provided by TypeScript's built-in DOM typings, and it represents an input element in the DOM. This type corresponds to the type of the DOM element that the ref is attached to.

This means that `inputRef.current` will be of the `HTMLInputElement | null` type, and TypeScript will know that it has a `focus` method.

Summary

In this chapter, we delved into the world of type-checking and validation in React. We started with the importance of props validation, then introduced TypeScript and its benefits for robust type-checking.

We then applied TypeScript to React, demonstrating its use in type-checking various aspects of React components, from props and state to event handlers, context, and refs. All of it allows you to create applications that are not only more dependable but also easier to maintain, allowing for early detection of errors and significantly improving both the quality of your code and your efficiency as a developer.

As we move to the next chapter, *Handling Navigation with Routes*, we'll shift our focus to navigation in React applications. We'll learn how to set up and use routes to navigate between different parts of our application.

7

Handling Navigation with Routes

Almost every web application requires routing, which is the process of responding to a URL based on a set of route handler declarations. In other words, this is a mapping from the URL to rendered content. However, this task is more involved than it seems at first, due to the complexities of managing different URL patterns and mapping them to appropriate content rendering. This includes handling nested routes and dynamic parameters and ensuring proper navigation flow. The complexities of these tasks are why you're going to leverage the `react-router` package in this chapter, the de facto routing tool for React.

First, you'll learn the basics of declaring routes using JSX syntax. Then, you'll learn about the dynamic aspects of routing, such as dynamic path segments and query parameters. Next, you'll implement links using components from `react-router`.

Here are the high-level topics that we'll cover in this chapter:

- Declaring routes
- Handling route parameters
- Using link components

Technical requirements

You can find the code files for this chapter on GitHub at https://github.com/PacktPublishing/React-and-React-Native-5E/tree/main/Chapter07.

Declaring routes

With react-router, you can collocate routes with the content that they render. By defining routes using JSX syntax alongside the components they are associated with, react-router empowers developers to create a clear and logical structure for their React applications. This collocation makes it easier to understand how different parts of the application are connected and navigated, leading to improved readability and maintainability of the code base.

Throughout this chapter, we'll explore the fundamentals of routing in React applications using react-router. We'll start by creating a basic example route to familiarize ourselves with the syntax and structure of route declarations. Then, we'll dive deeper into organizing routes by feature, rather than relying on a monolithic routing module. Finally, we'll implement a common parent-child routing pattern to demonstrate how to handle more complex routing scenarios.

Hello route

Before we start writing code, let's set up the react-router project. Run the following command to add react-router-dom to the dependencies:

```
npm install react-router-dom
```

Let's create a simple route that renders a simple component:

1. First, we have a small React component that we want to render when the route is activated:

    ```
    function MyComponent() {
      return <p>Hello Route!</p>;
    }
    ```

2. Next, let's look at the route definition:

    ```
    import React from "react";
    import ReactDOM from "react-dom/client";
    import { createBrowserRouter, RouterProvider } from "react-router-
    dom";
    import MyComponent from "./MyComponent";

    const router = createBrowserRouter([
      {
        path: "/",
        element: <MyComponent />,
      },
    ```

```
  ]);

  ReactDOM.createRoot(document.getElementById("root")!).render(
    <React.StrictMode>
      <RouterProvider router={router} />
    </React.StrictMode>
  );
```

The `RouterProvider` component is the top-level component of the application. Let's break it down to find out what's happening within the router.

You have the actual routes declared in the `createBrowserRouter` function. There are two key properties of any route: `path` and `element`. When the `path` property is matched against the active URL, the component is rendered. But where is it rendered, exactly? The router doesn't actually render anything itself; it's responsible for managing how other components are connected based on the current URL. In other words, the router checks the current URL and returns the corresponding component from the `createBrowserRouter` declaration. Sure enough, when you look at this example in a browser, `<MyComponent>` is rendered as expected:

Hello Route!

Figure 7.1: The rendered output of our component

When the `path` property matches the current URL, the route component is replaced by the `element` property value. In this example, the route returns `<MyComponent>`. If a given route doesn't match, nothing is rendered.

This example shows the fundamentals of routing in React. It's really simple and intuitive to declare routes. To further solidify your understanding of `react-router`, I encourage you to experiment with the concepts we've covered. Try creating more routes on your own, and observe how they impact the behavior of your application. After that, you can try more advanced techniques like lazy loading components using React.lazy and Suspense (you'll learn more about these in the next chapter), and implement route-based code splitting to optimize your application's performance. By diving deeper into these topics and applying them to your own projects, you'll gain a greater appreciation for the capabilities of `react-router` and its role in building modern, efficient, and user-friendly React applications.

Decoupling route declarations

The difficulty with routing happens when your application has dozens of routes declared within a single module since it's more difficult to mentally map routes to features.

To help with this, each top-level feature of the application can define its own routes. This way, it's clear which routes belong to which feature. So, let's start with the App component:

```
const router = createBrowserRouter([
  {
    path: "/",
    element: <Layout />,
    children: [
      {
        index: true,
        element: <h1>Nesting Routes</h1>,
      },
      routeOne,
      routeTwo,
    ],
  },
]);


export const App = () => <RouterProvider router={router} />;
```

In this example, the application has two routes: one and two. These are imported as route objects and placed inside `createBrowserRouter`. The first `element` in this router is the `<Layout />` component, which renders a page template with data that never changes and serves as a place for our route data. Let's take a look at the `<Layout />` component:

```
function Layout() {
  return (
    <main>
      <nav>
        <Link to="/">Main</Link>
        <span> | </span>
        <Link to="/one">One</Link>
        <span> | </span>
        <Link to="/two">Two</Link>
```

```
        </nav>
        <Outlet />
      </main>
   );
 }
```

This component contains a small navigation toolbar with links and the `<Outlet />` component. It's a built-in `react-router` component that will be replaced with matched route elements.

The router only gets as big as the number of application features, instead of the number of routes, which could be substantially larger. Let's take a look at one of the feature routes:

```
const routes: RouteObject = {
  path: "/one",
  element: <Outlet />,
  children: [
    {
      index: true,
      element: <Redirect path="/one/1" />,
    },
    {
      path: "1",
      element: <First />,
    },
    {
      path: "2",
      element: <Second />,
    },
  ],
};
```

This module, one/index.js, exports a configuration object with three routes:

- When the /one path is matched, redirect to /one/1.
- When the /one/1 path is matched, render the First component.
- When the /one/2 path is matched, render the Second component.

This means that when the app loads the URL, /one, the `<Redirect>` component, will send the user to /one/1. Like the RouterProvider, the Redirect component lacks UI elements inside; it solely manages logic.

This aligns with React's practice of embedding components in layouts to handle specific functionalities. This approach allows for a clean separation of concerns, with components focused solely on rendering UI elements and others, like Redirect, dedicated to handling routing logic. The Redirect component in react-router is responsible for programmatically navigating the user to a different route. It's commonly used to redirect users from one URL to another based on certain conditions, such as authentication status or route parameters. By abstracting away the navigation logic into a separate component, it promotes code reusability and maintainability within the application.

You're using Redirect here because we don't have content on the root route. Often, your application doesn't actually have content to render at the root of a feature, or at the root of the application itself. This pattern allows you to send the user to the appropriate route and the appropriate content. Here's what you'll see when you open the app and click on the **One** link:

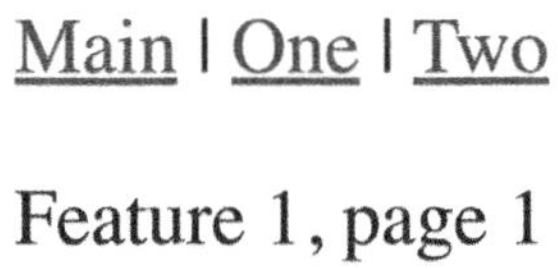

Main | One | Two

Feature 1, page 1

Figure 7.2: The contents of page 1

The second feature follows the exact same pattern as the first. Here's what the First component looks like:

```
export default function First() {
  return <p>Feature 1, page 1</p>;
}
```

Each feature, in this example, uses the same minimal rendered content. These components are ultimately what the user needs to see when they navigate to a given route. By organizing routes this way, you've made your features self-contained with regard to routing.

In the following section, you'll learn how to further organize your routes into parent-child relationships.

Handling route parameters

The URLs that you've seen so far in this chapter have all been static. Most applications will use both **static** and **dynamic** routes. In this section, you'll learn how to pass dynamic URL segments to your components, how to make these segments optional, and how to get query string parameters.

Resource IDs in routes

One common use case is to make the ID of a resource part of the URL. This makes it easy for your code to get the ID and then make an **API** call that fetches the relevant resource data. Let's implement a route that renders a user detail page. This will require a route that includes the user ID, which then needs to somehow be passed to the component so that it can fetch the user.

Let's start with the App component that declares the routes:

```
const router = createBrowserRouter([
  {
    path: "/",
    element: <UsersContainer />,
    errorElement: <p>Route not found</p>,
  },
  {
    path: "/users/:id",
    element: <UserContainer />,
    errorElement: <p>User not found</p>,
    loader: async ({ params }) => {
      const user = await fetchUser(Number(params.id));
      return { user };
    },
  },
]);

function App() {
  return <RouterProvider router={router} />;
}
```

The : syntax marks the beginning of a URL variable. The id variable will be passed to the UserContainer component. Before displaying the component, the loader function is triggered, asynchronously fetching data for the specified user ID. In the case of data loading errors, the errorElement prop provides a fallback to handle such situations effectively. Here's how UserContainer is implemented:

```
function UserContainer() {
  const params = useParams();
  const { user } = useLoaderData() as { user: User };
```

```
  return (
    <div>
      User ID: {params.id}
      <UserData user={user} />
    </div>
  );
}
```

The useParams() hook is used to get any dynamic parts of the URL. In this case, you're interested in the id parameter. Then, we get user from the loader function using the useLoaderData hook. If the URL is missing the segment completely, then this code won't run at all; the router will revert us to the errorElement component.

Now, let's take a look at the API functions that were used in this example:

```
export type User = {
  first: string;
  last: string;
  age: number;
};



const users: User[] = [
  { first: "John", last: "Snow", age: 40 },
  { first: "Peter", last: "Parker", age: 30 },
];



export function fetchUsers(): Promise<User[]> {
  return new Promise((resolve) => {
    resolve(users);
  });
}



export function fetchUser(id: number): Promise<User> {
  return new Promise((resolve, reject) => {
```

```
    const user = users[id];

    if (user === undefined) {
      reject('User ${id} not found');
    } else {
      resolve(user);
    }
  });
}
```

The `fetchUsers()` function is used by the `UsersContainer` component to populate the list of user links. The `fetchUser()` function will find and resolve a value from the `users` array of the mock data.

Here is the `User` component, which is responsible for rendering the user details:

```
type UserDataProps = {
  user: User;
};

function UserData({ user }: UserDataProps) {
  return (
    <section>
      <p>{user.first}</p>
      <p>{user.last}</p>
      <p>{user.age}</p>
    </section>
  );
}
```

When you run this app and navigate to /, you should see a list of users that looks like this:

- <u>John</u>
- <u>Peter</u>

Figure 7.3: The contents of the app home page

Clicking on the first link should take you to /users/0, which looks like this:

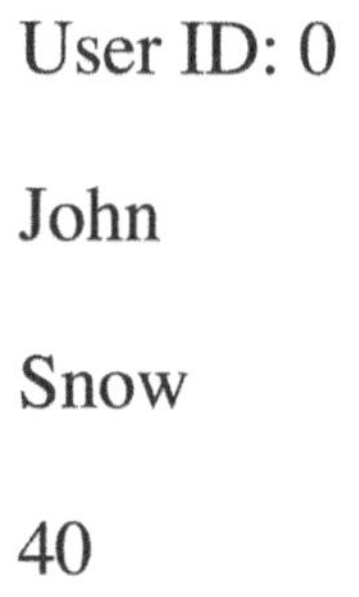

User ID: 0

John

Snow

40

Figure 7.4: The contents of the user page

If you navigate to a user that doesn't exist, for example, /users/2, here's what you'll see:

User not found

Figure 7.5: When a user isn't found

The reason that you get this error message instead of a 500 error is that the API endpoint knows how to deal with missing resources:

```
if (user === undefined) {
  reject('User ${id} not found');
}
```

This rejection will be handled by react-router with the provided errorElement component.

In the next section, we'll look at defining optional route parameters.

Query parameters

Sometimes, we need optional URL path values or query parameters. URLs work best for simple options, and query parameters work best if there are many values that the component can use.

Let's implement a user list component that renders a list of users. Optionally, you want to be able to sort the list in descending order. Let's make this with the route that can accept a query string:

```
const router = createBrowserRouter([
  {
    path: "/",
    element: <UsersContainer />,
  },
```

```
]);

ReactDOM.createRoot(document.getElementById("root")!).render(
  <React.StrictMode>
    <RouterProvider router={router} />
  </React.StrictMode>
);
```

There is no special setup in the router for handling query parameters. It's up to the component to handle any query strings provided to it. So, while the route declaration doesn't provide a mechanism to define accepted query strings, the router will still pass the query parameters to the component. Let's take a look at the user list container component:

```
export type SortOrder = "asc" | "desc";

function UsersContainer() {
  const [users, setUsers] = useState<string[]>([]);
  const [search] = useSearchParams();

  useEffect(() => {
    const order = search.get("order") as SortOrder;

    fetchUsers(order).then((users) => {
      setUsers(users);
    });
  }, [search]);

  return <Users users={users} />;
}
```

This component looks for either of the order query strings. It uses this as an argument to the fetchUsers() API to determine the sort order.

Here's what the Users component looks like:

```
type UsersProps = {
  users: string[];
};

function Users({ users }: UsersProps) {
```

```
  return (
    <ul>
      {users.map((user) => (
        <li key={user}>{user}</li>
      ))}
    </ul>
  );
}
```

Here is what's rendered when you navigate to /:

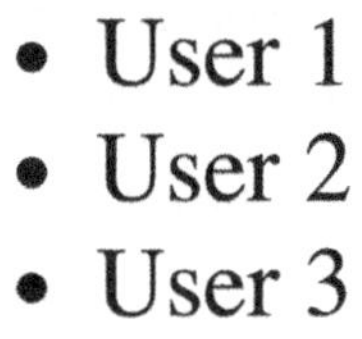

- User 1
- User 2
- User 3

Figure 7.6: Rendering the user list in default order

If you include the order query parameter by navigating to /?order=desc, here's what you get:

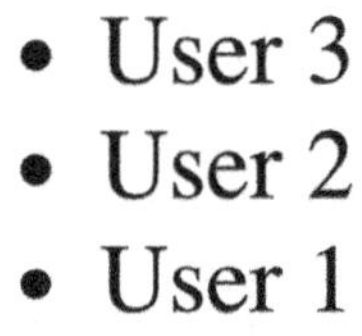

- User 3
- User 2
- User 1

Figure 7.7: Rendering the user list in descending order

In this section, you learned about parameters in routes. Perhaps the most common pattern is to have the ID of a resource in your app as part of the URL, which means that components need to be able to parse out this information in order to interact with the API. You also learned about query parameters in routes, which are useful for dynamic content, filtering, or passing temporary data between components. Next, you'll learn about link components.

Using link components

In this section, you'll learn how to create links. You might be tempted to use the standard <a> elements to link to pages controlled by react-router. The problem with this approach is that these links, in simple terms, will try to locate the page on the backend by sending a GET request. This isn't what you want because the route configuration is already in the app and we can handle routes locally.

First, you'll see an example that illustrates how <Link> components behave somewhat like <a> elements, except that they work locally. Then, you'll see how to build links that use URL parameters and query parameters.

Basic linking

The idea of links in React apps is that they point to routes that point to components, which render new content. The Link component also takes care of the browser history API and looks up route-component mappings. Here's an application component that renders two links:

```
function Layout() {
  return (
    <>
      <nav>
        <p>
          <Link to="first">First</Link>
        </p>
        <p>
          <Link to="second">Second</Link>
        </p>
      </nav>
      <main>
        <Outlet />
      </main>
    </>
  );
}

const router = createBrowserRouter([
  {
    path: "/",
    element: <Layout />,
    children: [
      {
        path: "/first",
        element: <First />,
      },
      {
```

```
        path: "/second",
        element: <Second />,
      },
    ],
  },
]);

function App() {
  return <RouterProvider router={router} />;
}
```

The to property specifies the route to activate when clicked. In this case, the application has two routes: /first and /second. Here is what the rendered links look like:

<u>First</u>

<u>Second</u>

Figure 7.8: Links to the first and second pages of the app

When you click the **First** link, the page content changes to look like this:

<u>First</u>

<u>Second</u>

First

Figure 7.9: The first page when the app is rendered

Now that you can use Link components to render links to basic paths, it's time to learn about building dynamic links with parameters.

URL and query parameters

Constructing the dynamic segments of a path that is passed to <Link> involves string manipulation. Everything that's part of the path goes to the to property. This means that you have to write more code to construct the string, but it also means less behind-the-scenes magic happening in the router.

Let's create a simple component that will echo back whatever is passed to the echo URL segment or the echo query parameter:

```
function Echo() {
  const params = useParams();
  const [searchParams] = useSearchParams();

  return <h1>{params.msg || searchParams.get("msg")}</h1>;
}
```

In order to get search parameters that were passed to a route, you can use the useSearchParams() hook, which gives you a URLSearchParams object. In this case, we can call searchParams. get("msg") to get the parameter we need.

Now, let's take a look at the App component that renders two links. The first will build a string that uses a dynamic value as a URL parameter. The second will use URLSearchParams to build the query string portion of the URL:

```
const param = "From Param";
const query = new URLSearchParams({ msg: "From Query" });

export default function App() {
  return (
    <section>
      <p>
        <Link to={'echo/${param}'}>Echo param</Link>
      </p>
      <p>
        <Link to={'echo?${query.toString()}'}>Echo query</Link>
      </p>
    </section>
  );
}
```

Here's what the two links look like when they're rendered:

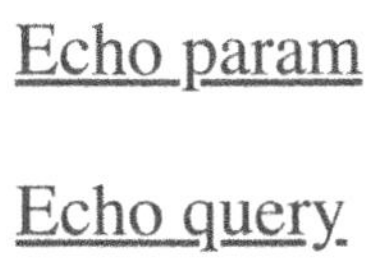

Echo param

Echo query

Figure 7.10: Different types of link parameters

The **Param** link takes you to /echo/From%20Param, which looks like this:

From Param

Figure 7.11: The param version of the page

The **Query** link takes you to /echo?msg=From+Query, which looks like this:

From Query

Figure 7.12: The query version of the page

In learning about the Link component and dynamic link construction, you've unlocked a more interactive and navigable web experience, empowering users to move through your application with URL and query parameters that enrich their journey.

Summary

In this chapter, you learned about routing in React applications. The job of a router is to render content that corresponds to a URL. The react-router package is the standard tool for this job. You learned how routes are JSX elements, just like the components they render. Sometimes, you need to split routes into feature-based modules. A common pattern for structuring page content is to have a parent component that renders the dynamic parts as the URL changes. Then, you learned how to handle the dynamic parts of URL segments and query strings. You also learned how to build links throughout your application using the <Link> element.

Understanding routing in React applications lays the groundwork for building complex applications with efficient navigation, preparing you for the subsequent chapters that delve into performance optimization, state management, and integrating external APIs, ensuring a seamless user experience.

In the next chapter, you'll learn how to split your code into smaller chunks using lazy components.

8

Code Splitting Using Lazy Components and Suspense

Code splitting has been a significant part of React applications for many years, even before official support was included in the **React API**. The evolution of React has brought about APIs that are specifically designed to assist in code-splitting scenarios. Code splitting becomes crucial when dealing with large applications containing a vast amount of JavaScript code that needs to be delivered to a browser.

In the past, **monolithic JavaScript bundles** containing an entire application could cause usability issues due to long initial page load times. Thanks to code splitting, we now have much more granular control over how code is transferred from the server to the browser. This gives us ample opportunities to optimize load-time **User Experience (UX)**.

In this chapter, we will revisit how to implement this in your React applications by using the lazy() API and the Suspense components. These features are very powerful tools in the React toolbox. By gaining a thorough understanding of how these components function, you'll be fully equipped to seamlessly integrate code splitting into your applications.

We'll cover the following topics in this chapter:

- Using the lazy() API
- Using the Suspense component
- Avoiding **lazy components**
- Exploring **lazy pages** and **routes**

Technical requirements

You can find the code files of this chapter on GitHub at `https://github.com/PacktPublishing/` `React-and-React-Native-5E/tree/main/Chapter08`.

Using the lazy API

There are two pieces involved with using the `lazy()` API in React. First, there's bundling components into their own separate files so that they can be downloaded by the browser separately from other parts of the application. Second, once you have created the bundles, you can build React components that are lazy: they don't download anything until they are needed. Let's look at both of these.

Dynamic imports and bundles

The code examples in this book use the **Vite** tooling for creating bundles. The nice thing about this approach is that you don't have to maintain any bundle configuration. Instead, bundles are created for you automatically, based on how you import your modules. If you're using the plain `import` statement (not to be confused with the `import` method) everywhere, your app will be downloaded all at once in one bundle. When your app gets bigger, there will likely be features that some users never use or don't use as frequently as others. You can use the `import()` function to import modules on demand. By using this function, you're telling Vite to create a separate bundle for the code that you're importing dynamically.

Let's look at a simple component that we might want to bundle separately from the rest of the application:

```
export default function MyComponent() {
  return <p>My Component</p>;
}
```

Now, let's take a look at how we would import this module dynamically using the `import()` function, resulting in a separate bundle:

```
function App() {
  const [MyComponent, setMyComponent] = React.useState<() => React.
ReactNode>(
    () => () => null
  );
```

```
  React.useEffect(() => {
    import("./MyComponent").then((module) => {
      setMyComponent(() => module.default);
    });
  }, []);

  return <MyComponent />;
}
```

When you run this example, you'll see the <p> text rendered right away. If you open the browser dev tools and look at the network requests, you'll notice that a separate call is made to fetch the bundle containing the MyComponent code. This happens because of the call to import("./MyComponent"). The import() function returns a promise that resolves with the module object. Since we need the default export to access MyComponent, we reference module.default when we call setMyComponent().

The reason why we're setting a component as the MyComponent state is that when the App component renders for the first time, we don't have the MyComponent code loaded yet. Once it loads, MyComponent will reference the proper value, which results in the correct text being rendered.

Now that you have an idea of how bundles get created and are fetched by the app, it's time to see how the lazy() API greatly simplifies this process for us.

Making components lazy

Instead of manually handling the promise returned by import() by returning the default export and setting state, you can lean on the lazy() API. This function takes a function that returns an import() promise. The return value is a lazy component that you can just render. Let's modify the App component to use this API:

```
import * as React from "react";

const MyComponent = React.lazy(() => import("./MyComponent"));

function App() {
  return <MyComponent />;
}
```

The MyComponent value is created by calling lazy(), passing in the dynamic module import as an argument. Now, you have a separate bundle for your component and a lazy component that loads the bundle when it's first rendered.

In this section, you learned how code splitting works. You learned that the import() function handles bundle creation for you. You also learned that the lazy() API makes your components lazy and handles all of the gritty work of importing components for you. But there's one last thing we need, the Suspense component, to help display placeholders while components are loading.

Using the Suspense component

In this section, we'll explore some of the more common usage scenarios of the Suspense component. We'll look at where to place Suspense components in your component tree, how to simulate latency when fetching bundles, and some of the options available to us to use as the fallback content.

Top-level Suspense components

Lazy components need to be rendered inside of a Suspense component. However, they do not have to be direct children of Suspense though, which is important because this means that you can have one Suspense component handle every lazy component in your app. Let's illustrate this concept with an example. Here's a component that we would like to bundle separately and use lazily:

```
export default function MyFeature() {
  return <p>My Feature</p>;
}
```

Next, let's make the MyFeature component lazy and render it inside of a MyPage component:

```
const MyFeature = React.lazy(() => import("./MyFeature"));

function MyPage() {
  return (
    <>
      <h1>My Page</h1>
      <MyFeature />
    </>
  );
}
```

Here, we're using the `lazy()` API to make the `MyFeature` component lazy. This means that when the `MyPage` component is rendered, the code bundle that contains `MyFeature` will be downloaded because `MyFeature` was also rendered. What's important to note with the `MyPage` component is that it is rendering a lazy component (`MyFeature`) but isn't rendering a `Suspense` component. This is because our hypothetical app has many page components, each with its own lazy components. Having each of these components render its own `Suspense` component would be redundant. Instead, we can render one `Suspense` component inside of our App component, like so:

```
function App() {
  return (
    <React.Suspense fallback={"loading..."}>
      <MyPage />
    </React.Suspense>
  );
}
```

While the `MyFeature` code bundle is being downloaded, `<MyPage>` is replaced with the fallback text passed to `Suspense`. So, even though `MyPage` isn't lazy itself, it renders a lazy component that `Suspense` knows about and will replace its children with the fallback content while this happens.

So far, we haven't really been able to see the fallback content that displays while our lazy components load their code bundles. This is because when developing locally, these bundles load almost instantly. To be able to see fallback component and loading process, you can enable throttling in **Network** tab of the dev tools:

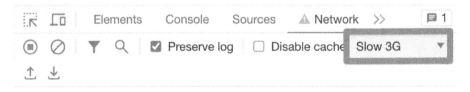

Figure 8.1: Enabling throttling in the browser

This setting emulates a slow internet connection. Instead of loading instantly, the page will be rendering for a few seconds and you will see a **loading ...** fallback.

In the next section, we'll look at an approach to use loading spinners as a fallback component.

Working with spinner fallbacks

The simplest fallback that you can use with the Suspense component is some text that indicates to the user that something is happening. The fallback property can be any valid React element, which means that we can enhance the fallback to be something more visually appealing. For example, the react-spinners package has a selection of spinner components, all of which can be used as a fallback with Suspense.

Let's modify the App component from the last section to include a spinner from the react-spinners package as the Suspense fallback:

```
import * as React from "react";
import { FadeLoader } from "react-spinners";
import MyPage from "./MyPage";

function App() {
  return (
    <React.Suspense fallback={<FadeLoader color="lightblue" />}>
      <MyPage />
    </React.Suspense>
  );
}
```

The FadeLoader component will render a spinner that we've configured with a color value of lightblue. The rendered element of the FadeLoader component is passed to the fallback property. With the Slow 3G throttling, you should be able to see the spinner when you first load the app:

Figure 8.2: The image rendered by the loader component

Now, instead of text, we're showing an animated spinner. This likely provides a user experience that your users are more accustomed to. The react-spinners package has several spinners for you to choose from, each of which has several configuration options. There are other spinner libraries that you can use or implement on your own.

In this section, you learned that you can use a single Suspense component that will display its fallback content for any lazy components that are lower in the tree. You learned how to simulate latency during local development so that you can experience what your users will experience with your Suspense fallback content. Finally, you learned how to use components from other libraries as the fallback content to provide something that looks better than plain text.

In the next section, you'll learn about why it doesn't make sense to make every component in your app a lazy component.

Avoiding lazy components

It might be tempting to make most of your React components lazy components that live in their own bundle. After all, there isn't much extra work that needs to happen to set up separate bundles and make lazy components. However, there are some downsides to this. If you have too many lazy components, your app will end up making several HTTP requests to fetch them: at the same time. There's no benefit to having separate bundles for components used on the same part of the app. You're better off trying to bundle components together in a way that one HTTP request is made to load what is needed on the current page.

A helpful way to think of this is to associate **pages** with **bundles**. If you have lazy page components, everything on that page will also be lazy yet bundled together with other components on the page. Let's build an example that demonstrates how to organize our lazy components. Let's say that your app has a couple of pages and a few features on each page. We don't necessarily want to make these features lazy if they're all going to be needed when the page loads. Here's the App component that shows the user a selector to pick which page to load:

```
const First = React.lazy(() => import("./First"));
const Second = React.lazy(() => import("./Second"));


function ShowComponent({ name }: { name: string }) {
  switch (name) {
    case "first":
      return <First />;

    case "second":
      return <Second />;

    default:
```

```
        return null;
    }
}
```

The First and Second components are the pages that make up our app, so we want them to be lazy components that load their bundles on demand. The ShowComponent component renders the appropriate page when the user changes the selector:

```
function App() {
  const [component, setComponent] = React.useState("");

  return (
    <>
      <label>
        Load Component:{" "}
        <select
          value={component}
          onChange={(e) => setComponent(e.target.value)}
        >
          <option value="">None</option>
          <option value="first">First</option>
          <option value="second">Second</option>
        </select>
      </label>
      <React.Suspense fallback={<p>loading...</p>}>
        <ShowComponent name={component} />
      </React.Suspense>
    </>
  );
}
```

Next, let's look at the first page and see how it's composed, starting with the First component:

```
import One from "./One";
import Two from "./Two";
import Three from "./Three";

export default function First() {
  return (
```

```
      <>
        <One />
        <Two />
        <Three />
      </>
    );
  }
```

The First component pulls in three components and renders them: One, Two, and Three. These three components will be part of the same bundle. While we could make them lazy, there would be no point, as all we would be doing is making three HTTP requests for bundles at the same time instead of one.

Now that you have a better understanding of how to map the page structures of your application to bundles, let's look at another use case where we use a router component to navigate around our app.

Exploring lazy pages and routes

In the *Avoiding lazy components* section, you saw where to avoid making components lazy when there is no benefit in doing so. The same pattern can be applied when you're using react-router as the mechanism to navigate around your application. Let's take a look at an example. Here are the imports we'll need:

```
const First = React.lazy(() => import("./First"));
const Second = React.lazy(() => import("./Second"));

function Layout() {
  return (
    <section>
      <nav>
        <span>
          <Link to="first">First</Link>
        </span>
        <span> | </span>
        <span>
          <Link to="second">Second</Link>
        </span>
      </nav>
```

```
        <section>
          <React.Suspense fallback={<FadeLoader color="lightblue" />}>
            <Outlet />
          </React.Suspense>
        </section>
      </section>
    );
  }




export default function App() {
  return (
    <Router>
      <Routes>
        <Route path="/" element={<Layout />}>
          <Route path="/first" element={<First />} />
          <Route path="/second" element={<Second />} />
        </Route>
      </Routes>
    </Router>
  );
}
```

In the preceding code, we have two lazy page components that will be bundled separately from the rest of the app. The fallback content in this example uses the same FadeLoader spinner component that was introduced in the *Working with spinner fallbacks* section.

Note that the Suspense component is placed beneath the navigation links. This means that the fallback content will be rendered in the spot where the page content will eventually show when it loads. The children of the Suspense component are the Route components that will render our lazy page components: for example, when the /first route is activated, the First component is rendered for the first time, triggering the bundle download.

That brings us to the end of this chapter.

Summary

This chapter was all about code splitting and bundling, which are important concepts for large React applications. We started by looking at how code is split into bundles in your React applications by using the import() function. Then, we looked at the lazy() React API and how it helps to simplify loading bundles when components are rendered for the first time. Next, we looked more deeply at the Suspense component, which is used to manage content while component bundles are being fetched. The fallback property is how we specify the content to be shown while bundles are being loaded. You typically don't need more than one Suspense component in your app, as long as you follow a consistent pattern for bundling pages of your app.

In the next chapter, you'll learn how to use the **Next.js** framework to handle rendering React components on the server. The Next.js framework allows you to create pages that act as React components and can be rendered on the server and in the browser. This is an important capability for applications that need good initial page load performance: that is, all applications.

User Interface Framework Components

When you are developing a React application, it's typical to rely on an existing **UI library** rather than building one from scratch. There are lots of React UI component libraries available to choose from, and there's no wrong choice, as long as the components make your life simpler.

In this chapter, we delve into the **Material UI** React library, a popular choice for React development. Material UI stands out due to its comprehensive suite of customizable components, adherence to Google's Material Design principles, and extensive documentation, making it an optimal choice for developers seeking efficiency and aesthetic coherence in their UI design. Here are the specific topics that we'll cover:

- Layout and UI organization
- Using **navigation components**
- Collecting user input
- Working with **styles** and **themes**

Technical requirements

You can find the code files present in this chapter on GitHub at https://github.com/ PacktPublishing/React-and-React-Native-5E/tree/main/Chapter09.

You can also find more information about Material UI components and its API at https://mui. com/material-ui/.

Layout and organization

Material UI excels in simplifying the complex process of designing application layouts. By offering a robust set of components, specifically **containers** and **grids**, it empowers developers to efficiently structure and organize UI elements. **Containers** serve as the foundation, providing a flexible way to encapsulate and align content within the overall layout. **Grids**, on the other hand, allow more granular control, enabling precise placement and alignment of components across different screen sizes, ensuring responsiveness and consistency.

This section aims to unpack the functionality of containers and grids within Material UI. We'll explore how these tools can be leveraged to create intuitive and aesthetically pleasing layouts, which are crucial for enhancing user experience.

Using containers

Aligning components horizontally on a page often presents a significant challenge due to the intricate balance required between spacing, alignment, and responsiveness. This complexity arises from the need to maintain a visually appealing and functional layout across various screen sizes, ensuring that elements are evenly distributed and maintain their intended appearance without unintended overlaps or gaps. The `Container` component from Material UI is a simple but powerful layout tool. It controls the horizontal width of its children. Let's look at an example to see what's possible:

```
import Typography from "@mui/material/Typography";
import Container from "@mui/material/Container";

export default function MyApp() {
  const textStyle = {
    backgroundColor: "#cfe8fc",
    margin: 1,
    textAlign: "center",
  };

  return (
    <>
      <Container maxWidth="sm">
        <Typography sx={textStyle}>sm</Typography>
```

```
      </Container>
      <Container maxWidth="md">
        <Typography sx={textStyle}>md</Typography>
      </Container>
      <Container maxWidth="lg">
        <Typography sx={textStyle}>lg</Typography>
      </Container>
    </>
  );
}
```

This example has three Container components, each of which wraps a Typography component. The Typography component is used to render text in Material UI applications. Each Container component used in this example takes a maxWidth property. It accepts a breakpoint string value. These breakpoints represent common screen sizes. This example uses small (sm), medium (md), and large (lg). When the screen reaches these breakpoint sizes, the container width will stop growing. Here's what the page looks like when the width is smaller than the sm breakpoint:

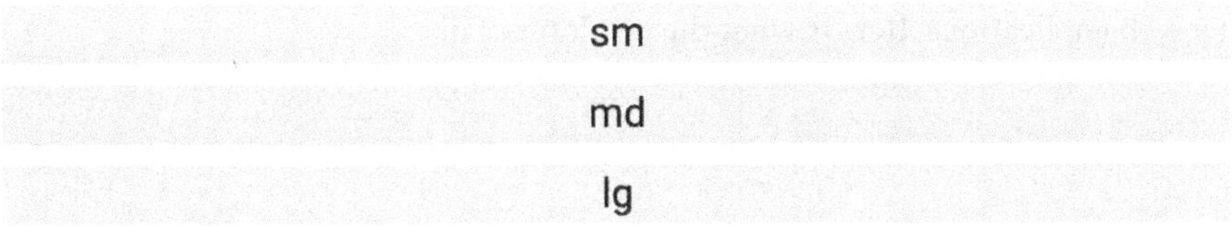

Figure 9.1: The sm breakpoint

Now, if we were to resize the screen so that it was larger than the md breakpoint, but smaller than the lg breakpoint, here is what it would look like:

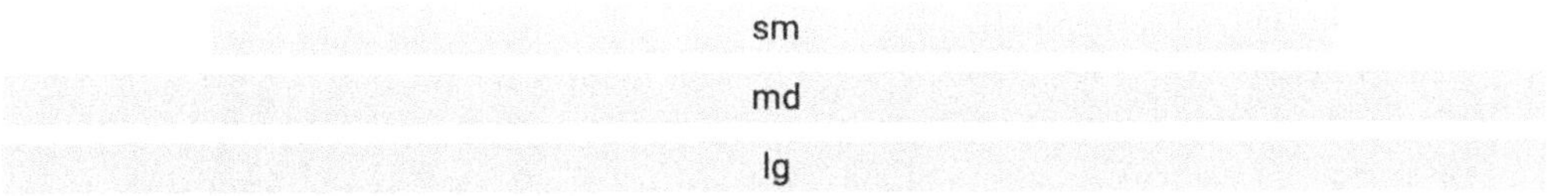

Figure 9.2: The lg breakpoint

Notice how the first container stays at a fixed width now that we've exceeded its maxWidth breakpoint. The md and lg containers just keep growing along with the screen until their breakpoints have been passed.

Let's see what these Container components look like when the screen width surpasses all breakpoints:

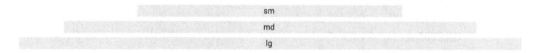

Figure 9.3: All breakpoints

The Container component gives you control over how your page elements grow horizontally. They're also responsive, so your layouts will be updated as the screen dimensions change.

In the next section, we'll look at using Material UI components to build more complex and responsive layouts.

Building responsive grid layouts

Material UI has a Grid component that we can use to compose responsive complex layouts. At a high level, a Grid component can be either a container or an item within a container. By combining these two roles, we can achieve any type of layout for our app. To get familiar with Material UI grid layouts, let's put together an example that uses a common layout pattern that we'll find in many web applications. Here is what the result looks like:

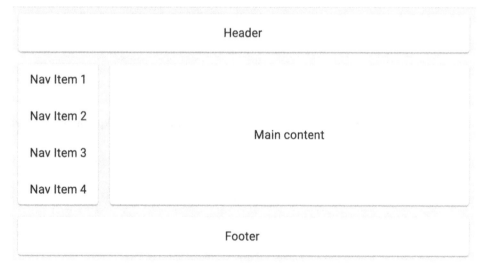

Figure 9.4: A sample responsive grid layout

As you can see, this layout has familiar sections that are typical in many web applications. This is just an example layout; you can use the `Grid` component to build any type of layout you can imagine. Let's look at the code that created this layout:

```
const headerFooterStyle = {
  textAlign: "center",
  height: 50,
};
const mainStyle = {
  textAlign: "center",
  padding: "8px 16px",
};
const Item = styled(Paper)(() => ({
  height: "100%",
  display: "flex",
  alignItems: "center",
  justifyContent: "center",
}));

export default function App() {
  return (
    <Grid container spacing={2} sx={{ backgroundColor: "#F3F6F9" }}>
      <Grid xs={12}>
        <Item sx={headerFooterStyle}>
          <Typography sx={mainStyle}>Header</Typography>
        </Item>
      </Grid>
      <Grid xs="auto">
        <Item>
          <Stack spacing={1}>
            <Typography sx={mainStyle}>Nav Item 1</Typography>
            <Typography sx={mainStyle}>Nav Item 2</Typography>
            <Typography sx={mainStyle}>Nav Item 3</Typography>
            <Typography sx={mainStyle}>Nav Item 4</Typography>
          </Stack>
        </Item>
      </Grid>
```

```
      <Grid xs>
        <Item>
          <Typography sx={mainStyle}>Main content</Typography>
        </Item>
      </Grid>
      <Grid xs={12}>
        <Item sx={headerFooterStyle}>
          <Typography sx={mainStyle}>Footer</Typography>
        </Item>
      </Grid>
    </Grid>
  );
}
```

Let's break down how the sections in this layout are created. We'll start with the header section:

```
<Grid xs={12}>
  <Item sx={headerFooterStyle}>
    <Typography sx={mainStyle}>Header</Typography>
  </Item>
</Grid>
```

The xs breakpoint property value of 12 means that the header will always span the entire width of the screen since 12 is the highest value you can use here. Next, let's look at the navigation items:

```
<Grid xs="auto">
  <Item>
    <Stack spacing={1}>
      <Typography sx={mainStyle}>Nav Item 1</Typography>
      <Typography sx={mainStyle}>Nav Item 2</Typography>
      <Typography sx={mainStyle}>Nav Item 3</Typography>
      <Typography sx={mainStyle}>Nav Item 4</Typography>
    </Stack>
  </Item>
</Grid>
```

In the navigation section, we have a grid with the xs="auto" prop. It matches the column's size with the width of its content. Also, you can see that we use a Stack component to place components in a vertical direction with spacing.

Next, we'll look at the main content section:

```
<Grid xs>
  <Item>
    <Typography sx={mainStyle}>Main content</Typography>
  </Item>
</Grid>
```

The xs breakpoint is a true value used to fill all free space after the navigation section in the grid.

In this section, you were introduced to what Material UI has to offer in the way of layouts. You can use the Container component to control the width of sections and how they change in response to screen dimension changes. You then learned that the Grid component is used to put together more complex grid layouts.

In the following section, we'll look at some of the navigational components found in Material UI.

Using navigation components

Once we have an idea of how the layout of our application is going to look and work, we can start to think about the navigation. This is an important piece of our UI because it's how the user gets around the application, and it will be used frequently. In this section, we'll learn about two of the navigational components offered by Material UI.

Navigating with drawers

The Drawer component, just like a physical drawer, slides open to reveal content that is easily accessed. When we're finished, the drawer closes again. This works well for navigation because it stays out of the way, allowing more space on the screen for the active task that the user is engaged with. Let's look at an example, starting with the App component:

```
<BrowserRouter>
  <Button onClick={toggleDrawer}>Open Nav</Button>
  <section>
    <Routes>
      <Route path="/first" element={<First />} />
      <Route path="/second" element={<Second />} />
      <Route path="/third" element={<Third />} />
    </Routes>
  </section>
  <Drawer open={open} onClose={toggleDrawer}>
```

```
    <div
      style={{ width: 250 }}
      role="presentation"
      onClick={toggleDrawer}
      onKeyDown={toggleDrawer}
    >
      <List component="nav">
        {links.map((link) => (
          <NavLink
            key={link.url}
            to={link.url}
            style={{ color: "black", textDecoration: "none" }}
          >
            {(({ isActive }) => (
              <ListItemButton selected={isActive}>
                <ListItemText primary={link.name} />
              </ListItemButton>
            )}
          </NavLink>
        ))}
      </List>
    </div>
  </Drawer>
</BrowserRouter>
```

Let's look at what's happening here. Everything that this component renders is within the BrowserRouter component because the items in the drawer are links to routes:

```
<Button onClick={toggleDrawer}>Open Nav</Button>
<section>
  <Routes>
    <Route path="/first" element={<First />} />
    <Route path="/second" element={<Second />} />
    <Route path="/third" element={<Third />} />
  </Routes>
</section>
```

The First, Second, and Third components are used to render the main application content when the user clicks on a link in the drawer. The drawer itself is opened when the Open Nav button is clicked. Let's take a closer look at the state that's used to control this:

```
const [open, setOpen] = useState(false);

const toggleDrawer = ({ type, key }: { type?: string; key?: string }) => {
  if (type === "keydown" && (key === "Tab" || key === "Shift")) {
    return;
  }

  setOpen(!open);
};
```

The open state controls the visibility of the drawer. The onClose property of the Drawer component calls this function, too, meaning that the drawer closes when any of the links within it are activated. Next, let's look at how the links within the drawer are generated:

```
<List component="nav">
  {links.map((link) => (
    <NavLink
      key={link.url}
      to={link.url}
      style={{ color: "black", textDecoration: "none" }}
    >
      {({ isActive }) => (
        <ListItemButton selected={isActive}>
          <ListItemText primary={link.name} />
        </ListItemButton>
      )}
    </NavLink>
  ))}
</List>
```

The items that are displayed in a Drawer component are actually list items, as you can see here. The links property has all the link objects with the url and name properties. Each item in the items array is mapped to the NavLink, which is used to handle navigation and highlight the active route. Within NavLink, we have the ListItemButton component, which generates the list item with text by rendering a ListItemText component.

Finally, let's look at the default value for the `links` property:

```
const links = [
  { url: "/first", name: "First Page" },
  { url: "/second", name: "Second Page" },
  { url: "/third", name: "Third Page" },
];
```

Here's what the drawer looks like when it's opened after the screen first loads:

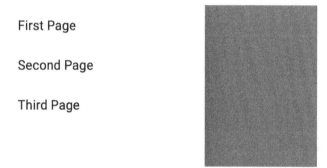

First Page

Second Page

Third Page

Figure 9.5: A drawer showing links to our pages

Try clicking on the `First Page` link. The drawer closes and renders the content of the `/first` route. Then, when you open the drawer again, you'll notice that the `First Page` link is rendered as the active link:

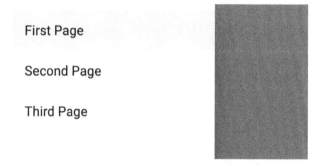

First Page

Second Page

Third Page

Figure 9.6: The First Page link is styled as the active link in the drawer

In this section, you learned how to use the `Drawer` component as the main navigation for your application. In the following section, we'll look at the `Tabs` component.

Navigating with tabs

Tabs are another common navigation pattern found in modern web apps. The Material UI Tabs component lets us use tabs as links and hook them up to a router. Let's look at an example of how to do this. Here is the App component:

```
export default function App() {
  return <RouterProvider router={router} />;
}
const router = createBrowserRouter([
  {
    path: "/",
    element: <RouteLayout />,
    children: [
      {
        path: "/page1",
        element: <Typography>Item One</Typography>,
      }, // same routes for /page2 and /page3
    ],
  },
]);

function RouteLayout() {
  const routeMatch = useRouteMatch(["/", "/page1", "/page2", "/page3"]);
  const currentTab = routeMatch?.pattern?.path;
  return (
    <Box>
      <Tabs value={currentTab}>
        <Tab label="Item One" component={Link} to="/page1" value="/page1"
/>
        <Tab label="Item Two" component={Link} to="/page2" value="/page2"
/>
        <Tab label="Item Three" component={Link} to="/page3" value="/
page3" />
      </Tabs>
      <Outlet />
    </Box>
  );
}
```

In the interest of space, I've left out the route configuration for /page2 and /page3; it follows the same pattern as /page1. The Tabs and Tab components from Material UI don't actually render any content underneath the selected tab. It's up to us to provide the content as the Tabs component only looks after showing the tabs and marking one of them as selected. This example aims to have the Tab components use Link components that link to content rendered by routes.

Let's now take a closer look at the RouteLayout component. Each Tab component uses the Link component so that, when it is clicked, the router is activated with the route specified in the to property. The Outlet component is then used as a child of our route content. To match the active tab, we use a simple approach to handle the current route using useRouteMatch:

```
function useRouteMatch(patterns: readonly string[]) {
  const { pathname } = useLocation();
  for (let i = 0; i < patterns.length; i += 1) {
    const pattern = patterns[i];
    const possibleMatch = matchPath(pattern, pathname);
    if (possibleMatch !== null) {
      return possibleMatch;
    }
  }

  return null;
}
```

The useRouteMatch hook uses useLocation to get the current pathname and then check whether it matches our patterns.

Here's what the page looks like when it first loads:

Figure 9.7: Tabs with the first item active

If you click on the **ITEM TWO** tab, the URL will update, the active tab will change, and the page content below the tabs will change:

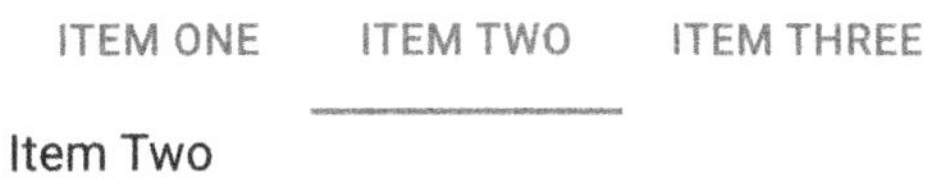

ITEM ONE   ITEM TWO   ITEM THREE

Item Two

Figure 9.8: Tabs with the second item active

By now, you have learned about two of the navigation approaches that you can use in your Material UI application. The first is to use a Drawer that is only displayed when the user needs to access navigational links. The second is to use Tabs that are always visible. In the following section, you'll learn about collecting input from users.

Collecting user input

Collecting input from users can be difficult. There are many nuanced things about every field that we need to consider if we plan on getting the user experience right. Thankfully, the Form components available in Material UI take care of a lot of usability concerns for us. In this section, you'll get a brief sampling of the input controls that you can use.

Checkboxes and radio buttons

Checkboxes are useful for collecting true/false answers from users, while radio buttons are useful for getting the user to select an option from a short number of choices. Let's take a look at an example of these components in Material UI:

```
export default function Checkboxes() {
  const [checkbox, setCheckbox] = React.useState(false);
  const [radio, setRadio] = React.useState("First");

  return (
    <div>
      <FormControlLabel
        label={'Checkbox ${checkbox ? "(checked)" : ""}'}
        control={
          <Checkbox
            checked={checkbox}
            onChange={() => setCheckbox(!checkbox)}
          />
        }
      />
```

```
      <FormControl component="fieldset">
        <FormLabel component="legend">{radio}</FormLabel>
        <RadioGroup value={radio} onChange={(e) => setRadio(e.target.
value)}>
          <FormControlLabel value="First" label="First" control={<Radio
/>} />
          <FormControlLabel value="Second" label="Second" control={<Radio
/>} />
          <FormControlLabel value="Third" label="Third" control={<Radio
/>} />
        </RadioGroup>
      </FormControl>
    </div>
  );
}
```

This example has two pieces of state information. The checkbox state controls the value of the Checkbox component, while the radio value controls the state of the RadioGroup component. The checkbox state is passed to the checked property of the Checkbox component, while the radio state is passed to the value property of the RadioGroup component. Both components have onChange handlers that call their respective state setter functions: setCheckbox() and setRadio(). You'll notice that many other Material UI components are involved in the display of these controls. For example, the label for the checkbox is displayed using the FormControlLabel component, while the radio control uses a FormControl component and a FormLabel component.

Here is what the two input controls look like:

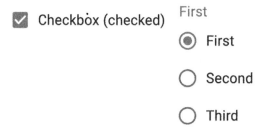

Figure 9.9: A checkbox and a radio group

The labels for both of these controls are updated to reflect the state of the components as they change. The checkbox labels show whether the checkbox is checked, and the radio labels show the currently selected value. In the next section, we'll look at text inputs and select components.

Text inputs and select inputs

Text fields allow our users to enter text, while Select allows them to choose from several options. The difference between selects and radio buttons is that selects require less space on the screen since the options are only displayed when the user opens the options menu.

Let's look at a Select component now:

```
import { useState } from "react";
import InputLabel from "@mui/material/InputLabel";
import MenuItem from "@mui/material/MenuItem";
import FormControl from "@mui/material/FormControl";
import Select from "@mui/material/Select";


export default function MySelect() {
  const [value, setValue] = useState<string | undefined>();

  return (
    <FormControl>
      <InputLabel id="select-label">My Select</InputLabel>
      <Select
        labelId="select-label"
        id="select"
        label="My Select"
        value={value}
        onChange={(e) => setValue(e.target.value)}
        inputProps={{ id: "my-select" }}
      >
        <MenuItem value="first">First</MenuItem>
        <MenuItem value="second">Second</MenuItem>
        <MenuItem value="third">Third</MenuItem>
      </Select>
    </FormControl>
  );
}
```

The value state used in this example controls the selected value in the Select component. When the user changes their selection, the setValue() function changes the value.

The MenuItem component is used to specify the available options in the select field; the value property is set as the value state when a given item is selected. Here's what the select field looks like when the menu is displayed:

Figure 9.10: A menu with the first item active

Next, let's look at a TextField component example:

```
export default function MyTextInput() {
  const [value, setValue] = useState("");

  return (
    <TextField
      label="Name"
      value={value}
      onChange={(e) => setValue(e.target.value)}
      margin="normal"
    />
  );
}
```

The value state controls the value of the text input and changes as the user types. Here's what the text field looks like:

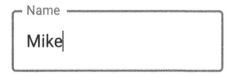

Figure 9.11: A text field with user-provided text

Unlike other `FormControl` components, the `TextField` component doesn't require several other supporting components. Everything that we need can be specified via properties. In the next section, we'll look at the `Button` component.

Working with buttons

Material UI buttons are very similar to HTML button elements. The difference is that they're React components that work well with other aspects of Material UI, such as theming and layout. Let's look at an example that renders different styles of buttons:

```
type ButtonColor = "primary" | "secondary";


export default function App() {
  const [color, setColor] = useState<ButtonColor>("secondary");

  const updateColor = () => {
    setColor(color === "secondary" ? "primary" : "secondary");
  };

  return (
    <Stack direction="row" spacing={2}>
      <Button variant="contained" color={color} onClick={updateColor}>
        Contained
      </Button>

      <Button color={color} onClick={updateColor}>
        Text
      </Button>

      <Button variant="outlined" color={color} onClick={updateColor}>
        Outlined
      </Button>

      <IconButton color={color} onClick={updateColor}>
        <AndroidIcon />
      </IconButton>
```

```
     </Stack>
   );
}
```

This example renders four different button styles. We're using the `Stack` component to render the row of buttons. When the buttons are clicked on, the state toggles to primary and vice versa.

Here's what the buttons look like when they're first rendered:

Figure 9.12: Four styles of Material UI buttons

Here's what the buttons look like when they've each been clicked on:

Figure 9.13: What the buttons look like after they've been clicked on

In this section, you learned about some of the user input controls available in Material UI. `Checkboxes` and `radio` buttons are useful when the user needs to turn something on or off or choose an option. Text inputs are necessary when the user needs to type in some text, while `select` fields are useful when you have a list of options to choose from but limited space to display those options. Finally, you learned that Material UI has several styles of buttons that can be used when the user needs to initiate an action. In the following section, we'll look at how styles and themes work in Material UI.

Working with styles and themes

Included with Material UI are systems for extending the styles of UI components and extending **theme styles** that are applied to all components. In this section, you'll learn about using both of these systems.

Making styles

Material UI comes with a `styled()` function that can be used to create styled components based on JavaScript objects. The return value of this function is a new component with the new styles applied.

Let's take a closer look at this approach:

```
const StyledButton = styled(Button)(({ theme }) => ({
  "&.MuiButton-root": { margin: theme.spacing(1) },
  "&.MuiButton-contained": { borderRadius: 50 },
  "&.MuiButton-sizeSmall": { fontWeight: theme.typography.fontWeightLight
},
}));

export default function App() {
  return (
    <>
      <StyledButton>First</StyledButton>
      <StyledButton variant="contained">Second</StyledButton>
      <StyledButton size="small" variant="outlined">
        Third
      </StyledButton>
    </>
  );
}
```

The names used in this style (`MuiButton-root`, `MuiButton-contained`, and `MuiButton-sizeSmall`) aren't something that we came up with. These are part of the **Button CSS API**. The root style is applied to all buttons, so, in this example, all three buttons will have the margin value that we've applied here. The `contained` style is applied to buttons that use the contained variant. The `sizeSmall` style is applied to buttons that have a small value for the size property.

Here's what the custom button styles look like:

Figure 9.14: Buttons using customized styles

Now that you know how to change the look and feel of individual components, it's time to think about customizing the look and feel of the application as a whole.

Customizing themes

Material UI comes with a default theme. We can use this as the starting point to create our own theme. There are two main steps to creating a new theme in Material UI:

1. Use the `createTheme()` function to customize the default theme settings and return a new theme object.

2. Use the `ThemeProvider` component to wrap our application so that the appropriate theme is applied.

Let's look at how this process works in practice:

```
import Menu from "@mui/material/Menu";
import MenuItem from "@mui/material/MenuItem";
import { ThemeProvider, createTheme } from "@mui/material/styles";


const theme = createTheme({
  typography: {
    fontSize: 11,
  },
  components: {
    MuiMenuItem: {
      styleOverrides: {
        root: {
          marginLeft: 15,
          marginRight: 15,
        },
      },
    },
  },
});

export default function App() {
  return (
    <ThemeProvider theme={theme}>
      <Menu anchorEl={document.body} open={true}>
        <MenuItem>First Item</MenuItem>
        <MenuItem>Second Item</MenuItem>
```

```
            <MenuItem>Third Item</MenuItem>
        </Menu>
     </ThemeProvider>
   );
 }
```

The custom theme that we've created here does two things:

- It changes the default font size for all components to 11.
- It updates the left and right margin values for the MenuItem components.

Many values can be set in a Material UI theme; refer to the customization documentation for more. The components section is used for component-specific customizations. This is useful when you need to style every instance of a component in your application.

Summary

This chapter was a very brief introduction to Material UI, the most popular React UI framework. We started by looking at the components used to assist with the layout of our pages. We then looked at components that can help the user navigate around your application. Next, you learned how to collect user input using Material UI form components. Finally, you learned how to style your Material UI using styles and modifying themes.

The insights gained from this chapter allow you to build complex interfaces without the overhead of developing UI components from scratch, accelerating your development process. Furthermore, React application development inherently relies on the synergistic use of various auxiliary libraries. A deep understanding of the React ecosystem and its key libraries empowers developers to rapidly prototype and iterate on their applications, making development effective.

In the next chapter, we'll look at ways to improve the efficiency of your component state updates using the latest functionality available in the latest version of React.

10

High-Performance State Updates

State represents the dynamic aspect of your React application. When the state changes, your components react to those changes. Without state, you would have nothing more than a fancy HTML template language. Usually, the time required to perform a state update and have the changes rendered on the screen is barely, if at all, noticeable. However, there are times that complex state changes can lead to noticeable lag for your users. The goal of this chapter is to address these cases and find out how we can avoid those lags.

In this chapter, you'll learn how to do the following:

- Batch your state changes together for minimal re-rendering
- Prioritize state updates to render content that's critical for your user experience first
- Develop strategies for performing asynchronous actions while **batching** and prioritizing **state updates**

Technical requirements

For this chapter, you'll need your code editor (**Visual Studio Code**). The code we'll be following can be found here: https://github.com/PacktPublishing/React-and-React-Native-5E/tree/main/Chapter10.

You can open the terminal within Visual Studio Code and run `npm install` to make sure you're able to follow along with the examples as you read through the chapter.

Batching state updates

In this section, you'll learn about how React can **batch state** updates together to prevent unnecessary rendering when multiple state changes happen simultaneously. In particular, we'll look at the changes introduced in **React 18** that make **automatic batching** of state updates commonplace.

When your React component issues a state change, this causes the React internals to re-render the parts of your component that have changed visually as a result of this state update. For example, imagine you have a component with a name state that's rendered inside of a `<span>` element, and you change the name state from Adam to Ashley. That's a straightforward change that results in a re-render that's too fast for the user to even notice. Unfortunately, state updates in web applications are rarely this straightforward. Instead, there might be dozens of state changes in 10 milliseconds. For example, the name state might follow changes like this:

1. Adam
2. Ashley
3. Andrew
4. Ashley
5. Aaron
6. Adam

Here, we have six changes that took place with the name state in a short amount of time. This means that React would have re-rendered the **DOM** six times, once for each value that was set as the name state. What's interesting to note about this scenario is the final state update: we're back where we started with Adam. This means that we just re-rendered the DOM five times for no reason. Now, imagine these wasted re-renders on a web application scale and how these types of state updates might cause problems for performance. For example, when the app uses complex animations, user interactions like drag and drops, timeouts, and intervals can all lead to unnecessary re-renders, negatively impacting performance.

The answer to this problem is **batching**. This is how React takes several state updates that were made in our component code and treats them as a single state update. Rather than process every state update individually, while re-rendering the DOM between each update, the state changes are all merged, which results in one DOM re-render. In the aggregate, this reduces the amount of work that our web applications need to do by a lot.

In **React 17**, automatic batching of state updates only happened inside of event handler functions. For example, let's say you have a button with an onClick() handler that performs five state updates. React will batch all of these state updates together so that only one re-render is necessary. The problem arises when your event handlers make asynchronous calls, usually to fetch some data, and then make state updates when the asynchronous call finishes. These state changes are no longer automatically batched because they're not running directly inside of the event handler function. Instead, they're running in the callback code of the asynchronous operation and React 17 will not batch these updates. This is a challenge because it's common for our React components to fetch data asynchronously and perform state updates in response to events!

Now we know how we can handle the most common problem with unnecessary re-renders, which is multiple changes to a state in a short time. Now, let's understand it by example.

React 18 batching

Let's turn our attention to some code now to see how **React 18** addresses the batching problem that we've just outlined. For this example, we'll render a button that, when clicked, will perform 100 state updates. We'll use setTimeout() so that the updates are performed asynchronously, outside of the event handler function. The idea is to show the difference between how this code is handled by two different React versions. To do this, we can open the **React profiler** in the browser dev tools and hit record before we press the button to execute our state changes. Here's what the code looks like:

```
import * as React from "react";

export default function BatchingUpdates() {
  let [value, setValue] = React.useState("loading...");

  function onStart() {
    setTimeout(() => {
      for (let i = 0; i < 100; i++) {
        setValue('value ${i + 1}');
      }
    }, 1);
  }

  return (
    <div>
```

```
      <p>
        Value: <em>{value}</em>
      </p>
      <button onClick={onStart}>Start</button>
    </div>
  );
}
```

By clicking the button that this component renders, we call the onStart() event handler function defined by our component. Then, our handler calls setValue() 100 times inside a loop. Ideally, we do not want to perform 100 re-renders because this will hurt the performance of our application, and it doesn't need to. Only the final call to setValue() matters here.

Let's first take a look at the profile captured for this component using React 17:

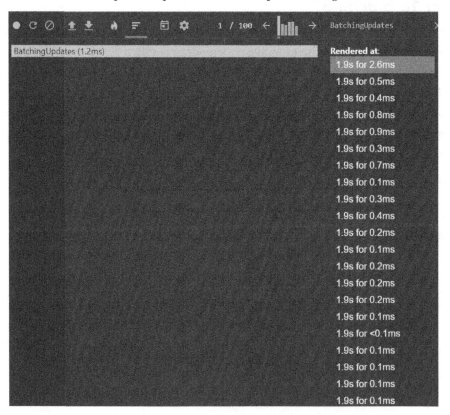

Figure 10.1: Using React dev tools to view re-renders every time state updates are made

By pressing the button with our event handler attached to it, we're making 100 state update calls. Since this is done outside of the event handler function in setTimeout(), automatic batching doesn't happen. We can see this in the profile output of the BactchingUpdates component, where there's a long list of renders. Most of these aren't necessary and contribute to the amount of work React needs to do in response to user interactions, hurting the overall performance of our application.

Let's capture a profile of the same component being rendered using React 18:

Figure 10.2: React dev tools showing only one render with automatic batching enabled

Automatic batching is applied everywhere that state updates are made, even in common asynchronous scenarios such as this one. As the profile shows, there's only one re-render when we click the button instead of 100. We didn't have to make any adjustments to our component code to make this happen either. However, there is one change that's required in order to make state updates batch automatically. Let's say you used ReactDOM.render() to render your root component, like so:

```
ReactDOM.render(
  <React.StrictMode>
    <App />
  </React.StrictMode>,
  document.getElementById("root")
);
```

Instead, you can use ReactDOM.createRoot() and render that:

```
ReactDOM.createRoot(document.getElementById("root")!).render(
  <React.StrictMode>
    <App />
  </React.StrictMode>
);
```

By creating and rendering your root node this way, you can ensure that with **React 18**, you'll get batched state updates throughout your application. You no longer need to worry about manually optimizing state updates so that they take place immediately: React does this for you now. However, sometimes, you'll have state updates that are of higher priority than others. In cases like these, we need a way to tell React to prioritize certain state updates over others, instead of batching everything together.

Prioritizing state updates

When something happens in our React application, we usually make several state updates so that the UI can reflect these changes. Typically, you can make these state changes without much thought about how the rendering performance is impacted. For example, let's say you have a long list of items that need to be rendered. This will probably have some impact on the UI: while the list is being rendered, the user probably won't be able to interact with certain page elements because the JavaScript engine is 100% utilized for a brief moment.

However, this can become an issue when expensive rendering disrupts the normal browser behavior that users expect. For example, if the user types in a text box, they expect the character they just typed to show up immediately. But if your component is busy rendering a large item list, the text box state cannot be updated right away. This is where the new React state update prioritization API comes in handy.

The `startTransition()` API is used to mark certain state updates as transitional, meaning that the updates are treated as a lower priority. If you think about a list of items either being rendered for the first time or being changed to another list of items, this is a transition that doesn't have to be immediate. On the other hand, state updates such as changing the value in a text box should be as close to immediate as possible. By using `startTransition()`, you tell React that any state updates within can wait if there are more important updates.

A good rule of thumb for `startTransition()` is to use it for the following:

- Anything that has the potential to perform a lot of rendering work
- Anything that doesn't require immediate feedback from the user in response to their interactions

Let's walk through an example that renders a large list of items in response to a user typing in a text box to filter a list.

This component will render a text box that the user can type in to filter a list of 25,000 items. I've chosen this number based on the performance of the laptop I'm using to write this code: you might want to tweak it up if there's no delay or down if it takes too long to render anything. When the page first loads, you should see a filter text box that looks like this:

Figure 10.3: The filter box before the user types anything

When you start typing in the filter text box, the filtered items will render underneath it. It might take a second or two, since there are so many items to render:

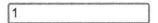

- Item 1
- Item 10
- Item 11
- Item 12
- Item 13
- Item 14
- Item 15

Figure 10.4: Filtered items underneath the filter input when the user starts typing

Now, let's walk through the code, starting with a large array of items:

```
let unfilteredItems = new Array(25000)
  .fill(null)
  .map((_, i) => ({ id: i, name: 'Item ${i}' }));
```

The size of the array is specified in the array constructor, and then it's filled with numbered string values that we can filter by.

Next, let's look at the state used by this component:

```
let [filter, setFilter] = React.useState("");
let [items, setItems] = React.useState([]);
```

The filter state represents the value of the filter text box and defaults to an empty string. The items state represents the filtered items from our unfilteredItems array. This array is populated when the user types in the filter text box.

Next, let's look at the markup rendered by this component:

```
<div>
  <div>
    <input
      type="text"
      placeholder="Filter"
      value={filter}
      onChange={onChange}
    />
  </div>
  <div>
    <ul>
      {items.map((item) => (
        <li key={item.id}>{item.name}</li>
      ))}
    </ul>
  </div>
</div>
```

The filter text box is rendered by an `<input>` element, while the filtered results are rendered as a list by iterating over the `items` array.

Finally, let's look at the event handler function that's fired when the user types in the filter text box:

```
const onChange = (e) => {
  setFilter(e.target.value);
  setItems(
    e.target.value === ""
      ? []
      : unfilteredItems.filter((item) => item.name.includes(e.target.
value))
  );
};
```

The `onChange()` function is called when the user types in the filter text box and sets two state values. First, it uses `setFilter()` to set the value of the filter text box. Then, it calls `setItems()` to set the filtered items to render unless the filter text is empty, in which case, we render nothing.

When interacting with this example, you might notice a problem with the responsiveness of the text box when typing in it. This is because, in this function, we're setting not only the text box value but also the filtered items. This means that before the text value can be rendered, we have to wait for thousands of items to be rendered.

Even though these are two separate state updates (setFilter() and setItems()), they're batched and treated as a single state update. Likewise, when the rendering starts, React makes all the changes at once, which means that the CPU won't let the user interact with the text box because it's fully utilized, rendering the long list of filter results. Ideally, we want to prioritize the text box state update while letting the items render afterward. To put it another way, we want to deprioritize the item rendering, since it's expensive and the user doesn't interact with it directly.

This is where the startTransition() API comes in. Any state updates that take place within the function that's passed to startTransition() will be treated with lower priority than any state updates that happen outside of it. In our filtering example, we can fix the text box responsiveness issue by moving the setItems() state change inside of startTransition().

Here's what our new onChange() event handler looks like:

```
const onChange = (e) => {
  setFilter(e.target.value);
  React.startTransition(() => {
    setItems(
      e.target.value === ""
        ? []
        : unfilteredItems.filter((item) => item.name.includes(e.target.
value))
    );
  });
};
```

Note that we didn't have to make any changes to how the item's state is updated: the same code is moved to a function that's passed to startTransition(). This tells React to only execute this state change after any other state changes are complete. In our case, this allows the text box to update and render before the setItems() state change runs. If you run the example now, you'll see that the responsiveness of the text box is no longer affected by how long it takes to render a long list of items.

Before this new API was introduced, you could achieve state update prioritizations via work-arounds with `setTimeout()`. The main disadvantage of this approach is that the internal React scheduler knows nothing about your state updates and their priorities. For example, by using `startTransitiion()`, React can cancel the update entirely if the state changes again before completion or if the component is unmounted.

In real applications, it isn't simply a matter of prioritizing which state updates should run first. Rather, it's a combination of fetching data asynchronously while making sure that priorities are taken into account. In the final section of this chapter, we'll tie all of this together.

Handling asynchronous state updates

In this final section of the chapter, we'll look at the common scenario of fetching data asynchronously and setting render priorities. The key scenario that we want to address is making sure that users aren't interrupted when typing or doing any other interaction that requires immediate feedback. This requires both proper prioritization and handling asynchronous responses from the server. Let's start by looking at the React APIs that can potentially help with this scenario.

The `startTransition()` API can be used as a **Hook**. When we do this, we also get a Boolean value that we can check to see whether the transition is still pending. This is useful for showing the user that things are loading. Let's modify the example from the previous section to use an asynchronous data-fetching function for our items. We'll also use the `useTransition()` Hook and add loading behavior to the output of our component:

```
let unfilteredItems = new Array(25000)
  .fill(null)
  .map((_, i) => ({ id: i, name: 'Item ${i}' }));


function filterItems(filter: string) {
  return new Promise((resolve) => {
    setTimeout(() => {
      resolve(unfilteredItems.filter((item) => item.name.
includes(filter)));
    }, 1000);
  });
}


export default function AsyncUpdates() {
  const [isPending, startTransition] = React.useTransition();
```

```
  const [isLoading, setIsLoading] = React.useState(false);
  const [filter, setFilter] = React.useState("");
  const [items, setItems] = React.useState<{ id: number; name: string }
[]>([]);

  const onChange: React.ChangeEventHandler<HTMLInputElement> = async (e)
=> {
    setFilter(e.target.value);

    startTransition(() => {
      if (e.target.value === "") {
        setItems([]);
      } else {
        filterItems(e.target.value).then((result) => {
          setItems(result);
        });
      }
    });
  };


  return (...);
}
```

What this example shows is that once you start typing in the filter text box, it will trigger the onChange() handler, which will call the filterItems() function. We also have an isLoading value that we can use to show the user that something is happening in the background:

```
<div>
  <div>
    <input
      type="text"
      placeholder="Filter"
      value={filter}
      onChange={onChange}
    />
  </div>
  <div>
    {isPending && <em>loading...</em>}
```

```
    <ul>
      {items.map((item) => (
        <li key={item.id}>{item.name}</li>
      ))}
    </ul>
  </div>
</div>
```

Here's what the user will see when isLoading is true:

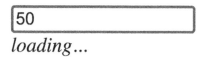

Figure 10.5: A loading indicator while a state transition is pending

However, there's a slight problem with our approach. You might have noticed the loading message flash briefly when typing into the text box. But then, you probably had a longer period when the items still weren't visible, and the loading message disappeared. What's happening here? Well, the isPending value that comes from the useTransition() Hook can be misleading. We've designed our component in such a way that isPending will be true in the following situations:

- If the filterItems() function is still fetching our data
- If the setItems() state update is still performing an expensive render with lots of items

Unfortunately, this isn't how isPending works. The only time this value is true is before the function we pass to startTransition() is run. This is why you'll see the loading indicator flash briefly instead of being displayed throughout the data-fetching operation and the rendering operation. Remember, React schedules state updates internally, and by using startTransition(), we've scheduled setItems() to run after other state updates.

Another way to think about isPending is that it's true while high-priority updates are still running. We can call it highPriorityUpdatesPending to avoid confusion. That said, the uses of this value are narrow, but they do happen from time to time. For our more common case of fetching data and performing an expensive render, we need to think of another solution. Let's walk through our code and refactor it in such a way that the loading indicator is displayed while the fetch and the higher-priority updates happen. First, let's introduce a new isLoading state that defaults to false:

```
const [isLoading, setIsLoading] = React.useState(false);
const [filter, setFilter] = React.useState("");
```

```
const [items, setItems] = React.useState([]);
```

Now, inside of our onChange() handler, we can set the state to true. Inside of the transition that runs after the data fetch completes, we set it back to false:

```
const onChange: React.ChangeEventHandler<HTMLInputElement> = async (e) =>
{
  setFilter(e.target.value);
  setIsLoading(true);

  React.startTransition(() => {
    if (e.target.value === "") {
      setItems([]);
      setIsLoading(false);
    } else {
      filterItems(e.target.value).then((result) => {
        setItems(result);
        setIsLoading(false);
      });
    }
  });
};
```

Now that we're keeping track of the isLoading state, we know exactly when all the heavy lifting is done and can hide the loading indicator. The final change is to base the indicator display on isLoading instead of isPending:

```
<div>
  {isLoading && <em>loading...</em>}
  <ul>
    {items.map((item) => (
      <li key={item.id}>{item.name}</li>
    ))}
  </ul>
</div>
```

When you run the example with these changes, the results should be a lot more predictable. The setLoading() and setFilter() state updates are high-priority and execute immediately. The call to fetch data using filterItems() isn't made until the high-priority state updates are completed.

Only after we have the data do we hide the loading indicator.

Summary

This chapter introduced you to the new APIs available in React 18 that help you achieve high-performance state updates. We started with a look at the changes to automatic state update batching in React 18 and how to best take advantage of them. We then explored the new startTransition() API and how it can be used to mark certain state updates as having a lower priority than those that require immediate feedback for user interactions. Finally, we looked at how state update prioritization can be combined with asynchronous data fetching.

In the next chapter, we'll go over fetching data from the server.

11

Fetching Data from a Server

The evolution of web technologies has made the interaction of browsers with servers and the processing of server data an integral part of web development. Today, it's challenging to draw a clear line between traditional web pages and full-fledged web applications. At the heart of this evolution is the ability of JavaScript in the browser to make requests to the server, efficiently process the received data, and dynamically display it on the page. This process has become the foundation for creating the interactive and responsive web applications we see today. In this chapter, we will explore various approaches and methods used to fetch data from the server, discuss their impact on the architecture of web applications, and acquaint ourselves with modern practices in this area.

So, in this chapter, we will cover the following topics:

- Working with remote data
- Using the **Fetch API**
- Using **Axios**
- Using **TanStack Query**
- Using **GraphQL**

Technical requirements

You can find the code files for this chapter on GitHub at https://github.com/PacktPublishing/React-and-React-Native-5E/tree/main/Chapter11.

Working with remote data

In the realm of web development, the journey of fetching data from servers has seen remarkable transformations. In the early 90s, the web's infancy with **HTTP 1.0** marked the beginning of server communication. Web pages were static, and HTTP requests were basic, fetching whole pages or static assets. Every request meant establishing a new connection, and interactivity was minimal, mostly limited to HTML forms. Security was also basic, reflecting the nascent state of the web.

The turn of the millennium witnessed a significant shift with the rise of **Asynchronous JavaScript and XML (AJAX)**. This brought an era of enhanced interactivity, allowing web applications to communicate with the server in the background without reloading the whole page. It was powered by the XMLHttpRequest object. Here's a simple example of using XMLHttpRequest to fetch data:

```
var xhr = new XMLHttpRequest();
xhr.onreadystatechange = function() {
  if (xhr.readyState == XMLHttpRequest.DONE) {
    if (xhr.status === 200) {
      console.log(xhr.responseText);
    } else {
      console.error('Error fetching data');
    }
  }
};
xhr.open('GET', 'http://example.com', true);
xhr.send();
```

This example illustrates a typical **XHR request**. Success and error responses are managed with callback functions. This reflects the time when asynchronous code relied heavily on callbacks.

As we progressed, HTTP evolved to version **1.1**, enhancing efficiency with persistent connections and standardizing **RESTful APIs**. These APIs used standard HTTP methods and were designed around identifiable resources, greatly improving scalability and developer productivity.

The advent of the **Fetch API** provided a modern, promise-based mechanism to make network requests. Fetch is more powerful and flexible compared to XMLHttpRequest. Here's an example of using Fetch:

```
fetch('http://example.com/data')
  .then(response => response.json())
```

```
    .then(data => console.log(data))
    .catch(error => console.error('Error:', error));
```

Moreover, there are a lot of tools based on top of the Fetch API and XHR, developed by the community. For example, Axios, GraphQL, and React Query have further simplified server communication and data fetching, enhancing developer experiences.

Axios, a modern HTTP client library, further simplified fetching data with its promise-based API and a host of useful features, such as intercepting requests and responses. Here's how you can use Axios to make a **GET** request:

```
  axios.get('http://example.com/data')
    .then(response => console.log(response.data))
    .catch(error => console.error('Error:', error));
```

The example might look identical to the **Fetch** API, but in real projects where you set up interceptors, it becomes a game-changer that saves a lot of time with less code. **Interceptors** allow you to intercept and modify requests before they are sent and responses before they are handled. A common use case is to refresh access tokens when they expire. Interceptors can add the new token to all subsequent requests. By using a library like Axios, a lot of the low-level networking code is abstracted away, allowing you to focus on making requests and handling responses. Interceptors, error handling, and other features help address cross-cutting concerns in a reusable way, leading to cleaner code.

Next is **GraphQL**, which revolutionized data fetching by allowing clients to request exactly the data they need, eliminating over-fetching and under-fetching issues. It offers a flexible and efficient way to retrieve data from servers. Instead of predefined endpoints, clients specify their data requirements, and servers respond with precisely the requested data. This reduces network load and enhances application performance.

```
  import { GraphQLClient, gql } from 'graphql-request';

  const endpoint = 'http://example.com/graphql';
  const client = new GraphQLClient(endpoint);

  const query = gql'
    query {
      user(id: 123) {
        name
```

```
      email
    }
  }
';

client.request(query)
  .then(data => console.log(data))
  .catch(error => console.error('Error:', error));
```

Here, we request the user by ID, specifying only two fields: name and email. Regardless of the user object's size, the GraphQL server efficiently handles it, sending only the requested data to the client.

One more tool I would like to explore is **React Query**. The library is designed to simplify data fetching and state management in React applications. It abstracts away the complexities of fetching and caching data, handles background updates, and provides Hooks for easy integration with components. React Query enhances the development process by making it straightforward to work with server data in a highly efficient and maintainable manner.

```
import { useQuery } from 'react-query';

function UserProfile({ userId }) {
  const { data, error, isLoading } = useQuery(userId, fetchUser);

  if (isLoading) return <div>Loading...</div>;
  if (error) return <div>Error: {error.message}</div>;

  return (
    <div>
      <h1>{data.name}</h1>
      <p>Email: {data.email}</p>
    </div>
  );
}
```

As you can see, we don't even need to handle errors or set up and update the loading state manually. Everything is provided by one Hook.

Another remarkable development in server communication is **WebSockets,** enabling real-time, bidirectional communication. This is a game-changer for applications requiring live data updates, like chat apps or trading platforms. Below is a basic example of using WebSockets:

```
const socket = new WebSocket('ws://example.com');

socket.onopen = function(event) {
  console.log('Connection established');
};

socket.onmessage = function(event) {
  console.log('Message from server ', event.data);
};

socket.onerror = function(error) {
  console.error('WebSocket Error ', error);
};
```

Here, we are still using the callback approach due to the mental model of bidirectional communication.

In conclusion, the evolution of server communication in web development has been pivotal in enhancing user experiences and developer productivity. From the rudimentary stages of **HTTP 1.0** to the sophisticated tools of today, we have witnessed a significant transformation. The introduction of technologies like Ajax, the Fetch API, Axios, GraphQL, and React Query not only streamlined server interactions but also standardized asynchronous behavior in applications. These advancements have been critical in efficiently managing states like loading, errors, and offline scenarios. The integration of these tools in modern web applications signifies a leap forward in building more responsive, robust, and user-friendly interfaces. It's a testament to the ever-evolving nature of technology and its profound impact on both the creation and consumption of web content.

In the next section, we will explore real examples of how to fetch data from a server using the Fetch API.

Using the Fetch API

Let's explore how we can retrieve data from a server in practice. We'll start with the **Fetch API,** the most common and fundamental approach provided by web browsers.

Before we begin, let's create a small application that fetches user data from GitHub and displays their avatar and basic information on the screen. To do this, we'll need an empty **Vite** project with React. You can create it with the following command:

```
npm create vite@latest
```

Since we're using **TypeScript** in our examples, let's start by defining the `GitHubUser` interface and all the necessary parameters.

To find out what data the server returns, we often need to refer to the documentation, usually provided by backend developers. In our case, since we're using the GitHub REST API, we can find user information in the official GitHub documentation at this link: `https://docs.github.com/en/rest/users/users?apiVersion=2022-11-28`.

Let's create the `GitHubUser` interface as follows:

```typescript
export interface GitHubUser {
  login: string;
  id: number;
  avatar_url: string;
  html_url: string;
  gists_url: string;
  repos_url: string;
  name: string;
  company: string | null;
  location: string | null;
  bio: string | null;
  public_repos: number;
  public_gists: number;
  followers: number;
  following: number;
}
```

These are the essential fields we will use in our application. In reality, there are more fields in the user object, but I've included the ones we'll use.

Now that we know the fields the user will have, let's create a component that will display the user data on the screen:

```typescript
const UserInfo = ({ user }: GitHubUserProps) => {
  return (
```

```
      <div>
        <img src={user.avatar_url} alt={user.login} width="100" height="100"
  />
        <h2>{user.name || user.login}</h2>
        <p>{user.bio}</p>
        <p>Location: {user.location || "Not specified"}</p>
        <p>Company: {user.company || "Not specified"}</p>
        <p>Followers: {user.followers}</p>
        <p>Following: {user.following}</p>
        <p>Public Repos: {user.public_repos}</p>
        <p>Public Gists: {user.public_gists}</p>
        <p>
          GitHub Profile:{" "}
          <a href={user.html_url} target="_blank" rel="noopener noreferrer">
            {user.login}
          </a>
        </p>
      </div>
    );
  };
```

Here, we render their avatar and some useful information about the user together with a link to open their GitHub profile page.

Let's now take a look at the App component, where we handle the server data retrieval logic:

```
function App() {
  const [user, setUser] = useState<GitHubUser>();
  const [loading, setLoading] = useState(true);

  useEffect(() => {
    setLoading(true);

    fetch("https://api.github.com/users/sakhnyuk")
      .then((response) => response.json())
      .then((data) => setUser(data))
      .catch((error) => console.log(error))
      .finally(() => setLoading(false));
  }, []);
```

We use the useState hook to store user data and loading state. In the useEffect, we make a Fetch API request to fetch data from the GitHub API. As you can see, the fetch function takes a URL as an argument. We process the response, save it in the state, handle errors with the catch block, and finally, turn off the loading process with the finally block.

To complete the application, we display the retrieved user data:

```
return (
  <div>
    {loading && <p>Loading...</p>}
    {!loading && !user && <p>No user found.</p>}
    {user && <UserInfo user={user} />}
  </div>
);
}
```

You can run your application using the following command:

```
npm run dev
```

Open the link that will appear in the terminal and you'll see:

Michael Sakhniuk

Software Engineer at KappaPay (kappapay.com)

Location: Barcelona, Spain

Company: @kappapay

Followers: 67

Following: 22

Public Repos: 15

Public Gists: 2

GitHub Profile: sakhnyuk

Figure 11.1: GitHub user requested by the Fetch API

Now you know how to fetch data using the Fetch API. Let's explore the implementation of a similar application where we request data using other tools.

Using Axios

In this section, we will explore one of the most popular libraries for working with the server, called **Axios**. This library is similar to the Fetch API but also provides additional features that make it a powerful tool for handling requests.

Let's take our previous project and make some changes to it. First, let's install Axios as a dependency:

```
npm install axios
```

One of Axios's features is the ability to create instances with specific configurations, such as headers, base URLs, interceptors, and more. This allows us to have a preconfigured instance tailored to our needs, reducing code repetition and making it more scalable.

Let's create an API class that encapsulates all the necessary logic for working with the server:

```
class API {
  private apiInstance: AxiosInstance;

  constructor() {
    this.apiInstance = axios.create({
      baseURL: "https://api.github.com",
    });

    this.apiInstance.interceptors.request.use((config) => {
      console.log("Request:", '${config.method?.toUpperCase()} ${config.
url}');
      return config;
    });

    this.apiInstance.interceptors.response.use(
      (response) => {
        console.log("Response:", response.data);
        return response;
      },
      (error) => {
```

```
        console.log("Error:", error);
        return Promise.reject(error);
      }
    );
  }

  getProfile(username: string) {
    return this.apiInstance.get<GitHubUser>('/users/${username}');
  }
}


export default new API();
```

In the constructor of this class, we create and store an Axios instance and set the base URL, eliminating the need to repeat this domain in future requests. Next, we configure interceptors for each request and response. This is done for demonstration purposes, so when we run the application, we can see all the requests and responses in the console logs:

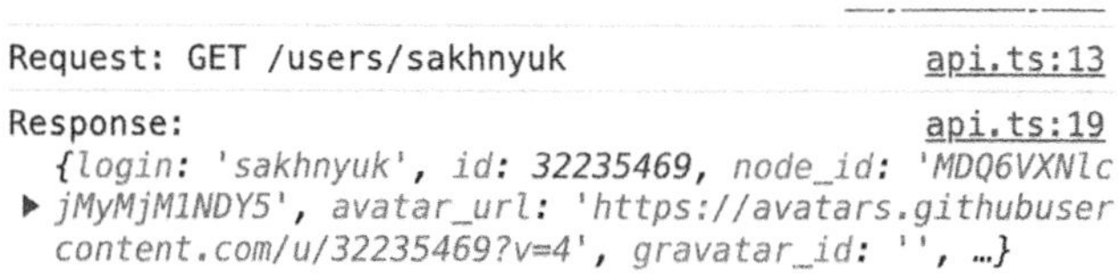

```
Request: GET /users/sakhnyuk                                api.ts:13
Response:                                                    api.ts:19
  {login: 'sakhnyuk', id: 32235469, node_id: 'MDQ6VXNlc
▶ jMyMjM1NDY5', avatar_url: 'https://avatars.githubuser
  content.com/u/32235469?v=4', gravatar_id: '', …}
```

Figure 11.2: Axios interceptor logs

Now, let's see how the App component, which uses our new API class, will look:

```
function App() {
  const [user, setUser] = useState<GitHubUser>();
  const [loading, setLoading] = useState(true);

  useEffect(() => {
    setLoading(true);

    api
      .getProfile("sakhnyuk")
      .then((res) => setUser(res.data))
      .finally(() => setLoading(false));
  }, []);
```

```
  return (
    <div>
      {loading && <p>Loading...</p>}
      {!loading && !user && <p>No user found.</p>}
      {user && <UserInfo user={user} />}
    </div>
  );
}
```

As mentioned earlier, Axios is not significantly different from the Fetch API, but it offers more powerful functionality, making it easy to create more complex solutions for working with server data.

In the next section, we will explore the same application implemented using TanStack Query.

Using TanStack Query

TanStack Query, more commonly known as **React Query**, is a library that has taken server interaction to a new level. This library allows us to request data and cache it. As a result, we can call the same useQuery hook a lot of times during one rendering, but only one request will be sent to the server. The library also includes built-in loading and error states, simplifying the handling of request states.

To get started, let's install the library as a dependency for our project:

```
npm install @tanstack/react-query
```

Next, we need to configure the library by adding the QueryClientProvider:

```
const queryClient = new QueryClient();

ReactDOM.createRoot(document.getElementById("root")!).render(
  <QueryClientProvider client={queryClient}>
    <App />
  </QueryClientProvider>
);
```

After this setup, we can start working on the app. One of the unique features of this library is that it is agnostic to the tool you use for data fetching. You just need to provide a promise function that returns the data. Let's create such a function using the Fetch API:

```
const userFetcher = (username: string) =>
```

```
fetch("https://api.github.com/users/sakhnyuk")
  .then((response) => response.json());
```

Now, let's take a look at how simple our App component has become:

```
function App() {
  const {
    data: user,
    isPending,
    isError,
  } = useQuery({
    queryKey: ["githubUser"],
    queryFn: () => userFetcher("sakhnyuk"),
  });

  return (
    <div>
      {isPending && <p>Loading...</p>}
      {isError && <p>Error fetching data</p>}
      {user && <UserInfo user={user} />}
    </div>
  );
}
```

Now, all the logic for making the request and handling loading and error states is contained within a single useQuery hook.

In the next section, we will explore an even more powerful tool for data fetching using GraphQL.

Using GraphQL

Earlier in this chapter, we discussed what **GraphQL** is and how it allows us to specify the exact data we want from the server, reducing the amount of transferred data and speeding up data fetching.

In this example, we will explore GraphQL in conjunction with the @apollo/client library, which provides similar functionality to React Query but works with GraphQL queries.

To begin, let's install the necessary dependencies using the following command:

```
npm install @apollo/client graphql
```

Next, we need to add a provider to our application:

```
const client = new ApolloClient({
  uri: "https://api.github.com/graphql",
  cache: new InMemoryCache(),
  headers: {
    Authorization: 'Bearer YOUR_PAT', // Put your GitHub personal access
token here
  },
});

ReactDOM.createRoot(document.getElementById("root")!).render(
  <ApolloProvider client={client}>
    <App />
  </ApolloProvider>
);
```

At this stage, during the client setup, we specify the server URL we want to work with, caching settings, and authentication. In earlier examples, we used the public GitHub API, but GitHub also supports GraphQL. For this, we need to provide a **GitHub personal access token**, which you can obtain in your GitHub profile settings.

For our example, to demonstrate how we can select only the necessary fields we need, let's trim down the user data. Here's how our GraphQL query in the component will look:

```
const GET_GITHUB_USER = gql'
  query GetGithubUser($username: String!) {
    user(login: $username) {
      login
      id
      avatarUrl
      bio
      name
      company
      location
    }
  }
';
```

Now that everything is set up, let's see what the App component will look like:

```
function App() {
  const { data, loading, error } = useQuery(GET_GITHUB_USER, {
    variables: { username: "sakhnyuk" },
  });

  if (loading) return <p>Loading...</p>;
  if (error) return <p>Error fetching data</p>;

  const user = data.user;

  return (
    <div>
      <UserInfo user={user} />
    </div>
  );
}
```

Similar to React Query, we have access to the loading state, errors, and the actual data. When we open the application, we will see the result:

Michael Sakhniuk

Software Engineer at KappaPay (kappapay.com)

Location: Barcelona, Spain

Company: @kappapay

Figure 11.3: GiHub user requested by GraphQL

To ensure that the server returns exactly the data we requested, we can open Chrome Dev Tools, go to the **Network** tab, and inspect our request:

```
Name                        X    Headers    Payload    Preview    Response    Initiator    Timing

{} graphql                  ▼ {data: {user: {login: "sakhnyuk", id: "MDQ6VXNlcjMyMjM1NDY5",…}}}
                              ▼ data: {user: {login: "sakhnyuk", id: "MDQ6VXNlcjMyMjM1NDY5",…}}
                                ▼ user: {login: "sakhnyuk", id: "MDQ6VXNlcjMyMjM1NDY5",…}
                                    avatarUrl: "https://avatars.githubusercontent.com/u/32235469?u=…
                                    bio: "Software Engineer at KappaPay (kappapay.com)"
                                    company: "@kappapay"
                                    id: "MDQ6VXNlcjMyMjM1NDY5"
                                    location: "Barcelona, Spain"
                                    login: "sakhnyuk"
                                    name: "Michael Sakhniuk"
                                    __typename: "User"
```

Figure 11.4: GraphQL request

As shown in *Figure 11.4*, the server sent us precisely the data we specified in the query. You can experiment with query parameters to see the difference.

Summary

In this chapter, we explored how to fetch data from the server. We began by briefly reviewing the history of client-server communication and highlighting the primary methods of interacting with servers. Next, we built an application to retrieve GitHub user data using the Fetch API, Axios, TanStack Query, and Apollo GraphQL.

The techniques you learned in this chapter will enable you to significantly expand the capabilities of your own web applications. By efficiently fetching data from the server, you can create dynamic, data-driven experiences for your users. Whether you are building a social media app that displays real-time feeds, an e-commerce site with up-to-date product information, or a dashboard that visualizes live data, the skills you gained will prove invaluable.

In the next chapter, we will delve into managing the application state using state management libraries.

12

State Management in React

In the previous chapters, we explored the concept of state in React and mastered the basics of working with it using the useState hook. Now it's time to delve deeper into the **global state management** of applications. In this chapter, we will focus on the global state: we'll define what it is, its key advantages, and the strategies for its effective management.

This chapter will cover the following topics:

- What is global state?
- React Context API and useReducer
- Redux
- Mobx

What is global state?

In developing React applications, one of the key aspects that requires special attention is **state management**. We are already familiar with the useState hook, which allows us to create and manage state within a component. This type of state is often referred to as **local**, and it is very effective within a single component and very simple and easy to use.

For a clearer illustration, consider an example with a small form component, where we have two **input** elements and have created two states for each **input**:

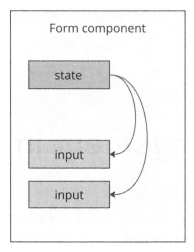

Figure 12.1: Form component with local state

In this example, everything is simple: the user enters something into the input, which triggers an onChange event, where we usually change our state, causing a full re-render of the form, and then we see the result of the input on the screen.

However, as the complexity and size of your application increase, there will inevitably be a need for a more scalable and flexible approach to state management. Let's further consider our example and imagine that after entering information into the form, we need to make a request to the server for user authorization and obtain a **session key**. Then, with this key, we need to request user data: name, surname, and avatar.

Here, we immediately encounter difficulties: where do we store the session key and user data? Perhaps we can retrieve the data right inside the form and then pass it up to the parent component, as it is more global and responsible. Alright, let's illustrate this and take a look:

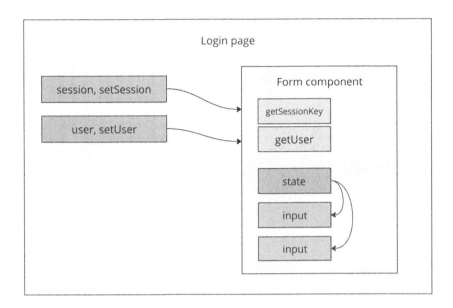

Figure 12.2: Login page with form component

So, now we have a login page, where we have local states for **session** and **user** objects. Using props, we can pass functions like onSessionChange and onUserChange to the form component, which ultimately allows us to transfer data from the form to the login page. Also, in the form, we now have the functions getSessionKey and getUser. These methods interact with the server, and upon successful response, they don't store data locally but call the aforementioned onSessionChange and onUserChange.

One might think that the data storage problem is solved, but likely after user authorization and obtaining their data, we need to redirect the user to some homepage of our application. We could repeat our trick of lifting the data higher once again, but before doing that, let's think ahead and imagine that obtaining user data is probably not just the job of the authorization form, and such a function might be needed on other pages.

Ultimately, we come to understand that in addition to the data itself, we also need to keep the logic for working with the data higher up in the component tree:

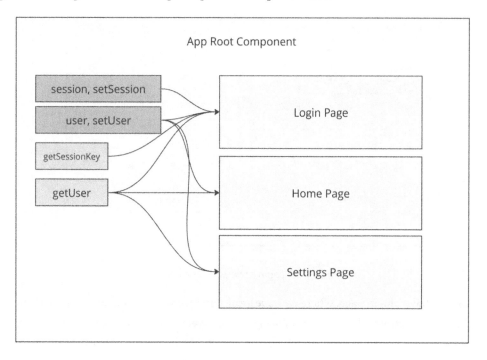

Figure 12.3: App root component

This image clearly demonstrates how the application becomes more complicated when we need to pass down all the necessary data and methods from the topmost component of the application to all its pages and components.

In addition to the complexity of implementing and maintaining such an approach to organizing the application's state, there is also a significant performance problem. For example, having a state in the root component created through useState, every time we update it, the entire application will be re-rendered because the app root component will be redrawn.

So, we have identified the main problems with organizing local state in the components of a large application:

- Overcomplicated component tree, where all important data must be passed down from top to bottom using props. This tightly couples the components, complicating the code and its maintenance.

- Performance issue, where the application may re-render unnecessarily when it's not required.

Looking at the last image, one can think of whether it is possible to break the connection of our components and extract all the data and logic somewhere outside of the components. This is where the concept of global state comes into play.

Global state is a data management approach that allows state to be accessible and modifiable across different levels and components of your application. This solution overcomes the limitations of local state, facilitating data exchange between components and improving state manageability in large-scale projects.

To clearly understand how global state would look in our example, take a look at the image below:

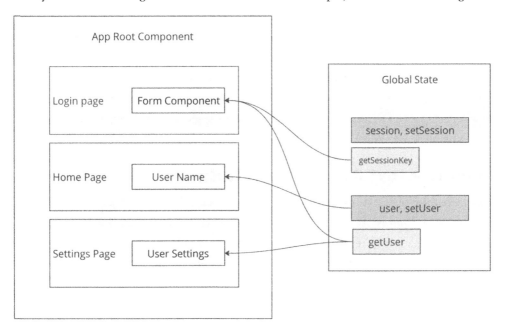

Figure 12.4: App root component and global state

In this example, we have a global state that is located outside of the components and the entire tree. Only the components that actually need any data from the state can directly access it and subscribe to its changes.

By implementing global state, we can solve both problems at once:

- Simplifies the component tree and dependencies, thereby scaling and supporting the application.
- Increases application performance because now, only those components that were subscribed to data from the global state are re-rendered when the state changes.

However, it's important to understand that the local state remains a very powerful tool and should not be abandoned in favor of the global state. We only gain advantages when the state needs to be used across different levels of application components. Otherwise, if we start transferring all variables and states to the global state, we will only complicate the application without gaining any benefits.

Now that we know that the global state is merely a way of organizing data, how do we manage the global state? A **state manager** is a tool that helps organize and manage state in an application, especially when it comes to complex interactions and extensive data. It provides a **centralized repository** for all your application's state and manages its updates in an orderly and predictable manner. In practice, state managers are often represented as npm packages installed as project dependencies. However, it is also possible to manage the global state independently without any libraries using React's API. We will explore one such approach later on.

React Context API and useReducer

To organize the global state on your own, you can use tools that already exist in the React ecosystem, namely the **Context API** and useReducer. They represent a powerful duo for managing state, especially in situations where using third-party state managers seems excessive. These tools are ideal for creating and managing global states in more compact applications.

The **React Context API** is designed to pass data through the component tree without the need to pass props at every level. This simplifies access to data in deeply nested components and reduces **prop drilling** (passing props through many levels), as illustrated in *Figure 12.4*. The React Context API is particularly useful for data such as theme settings, language preferences, or user information.

Here's an example of how to store theme settings using context:

```
const ThemeContext = createContext();

const ThemeProvider = ({ children }) => {
  const theme = 'dark';
  return (
```

```
      <ThemeContext.Provider value={theme}>
        {children}
      </ThemeContext.Provider>
    );
};


  const useTheme = () => useContext(ThemeContext);


  export { ThemeProvider, useTheme };
```

In this example, we created `ThemeContext` using the `createContext` function. Then, we made a `ThemeProvider` component, which should wrap the root component of the application. This will later allow access at any level of nested components using the `useTheme` hook, which was created with the `useContext` hook:

```
  const MyComponent = () => {
    const theme = useTheme();

    return (
      <div>
        <p>Current theme: {theme}</p>
      </div>
    );
};
```

On any level of the component tree, we can access the current theme using the `useTheme` hook.

Next let's take a look at the next one of the duo, the special hook that will help us to build the global state. `useReducer` is a hook that allows you to manage complex states with reducers: functions that take the current state and an action, and then return a new state. `useReducer` is ideal for managing states that require complex logic or multiple sub-states. Let's consider a small example of a counter using `useReducer`:

```
  import React, { useReducer } from 'react';


  const initialState = { count: 0 };


  function reducer(state, action) {
    switch (action.type) {
```

```
      case 'increment':
        return { count: state.count + 1 };
      case 'decrement':
        return { count: state.count - 1 };
      default:
        throw new Error();
    }
  }


  function Counter() {
    const [state, dispatch] = useReducer(reducer, initialState);

    return (
      <>
        Count: {state.count}
        <button onClick={() => dispatch({ type: 'increment' })}>+</button>
        <button onClick={() => dispatch({ type: 'decrement' })}>-</button>
      </>
    );
  }
```

In this example, a reducer is implemented that has two actions: increasing and decreasing the counter.

The combination of the Context API and useReducer provides a powerful mechanism for creating and managing the global state of an application. This approach is convenient for small applications, where ready-made and larger state management solutions might be redundant. However, it's also worth noting that this solution doesn't completely solve the performance issue, as any change in the theme in the useTheme example or the counter in the counter example will cause the provider, and thus the entire component tree, to re-render. This can be avoided, but it requires additional logic and coding.

Therefore, more complex applications require a more powerful tool. For this, there are several ready-made and popular solutions for working with state, each with its unique features and suitable for different use cases.

Redux

The first of such tools is, of course, **Redux**. It is one of the most popular tools for managing state in complex JavaScript applications, especially when used with React. Redux provides predictable state management by maintaining the application's state in a single global object, simplifying the tracking of changes and data management.

Redux is based on three core principles: a single source of truth (one global state), the state is read-only (immutable), and changes are made using pure functions (reducers). These principles ensure an orderly and controlled data flow.

```
function counterReducer(state = { count: 0 }, action) {
  switch (action.type) {
    case 'INCREMENT':
      return { count: state.count + 1 };
    case 'DECREMENT':
      return { count: state.count - 1 };
    default:
      return state;
  }
}

const store = createStore(counterReducer);

store.subscribe(() => console.log(store.getState()));

store.dispatch({ type: 'INCREMENT' });
store.dispatch({ type: 'DECREMENT' });
```

In this example, the state of the application has been implemented from the counter example. We have a counterReducer, which is a regular function that takes the current state and the action to be performed on it. The reducer always returns a new state.

Implementing asynchronous operations in the Redux world is a complex issue, as out of the box it offers nothing but middleware, which is used by third-party solutions. One such solution is redux-thunk.

redux-thunk is a middleware that allows you to call action creator functions that return a function instead of an action object. This provides the ability to delay the dispatch of an action or dispatch multiple actions by making asynchronous requests.

```
function fetchUserData() {
  return (dispatch) => {
    dispatch({ type: 'LOADING_USER_DATA' });
    fetch('/api/user')
      .then((response) => response.json())
      .then((data) => dispatch({ type: 'FETCH_USER_DATA_SUCCESS', payload:
data }))
      .catch((error) => dispatch({ type: 'FETCH_USER_DATA_ERROR', error
}));
  };
}


const store = createStore(reducer, applyMiddleware(thunk));
store.dispatch(fetchUserData());
```

As you can see in the example, we create a function, fetchUserData, that doesn't immediately change the state. Instead, it returns another function with a dispatch argument. This dispatch can be used as many times as needed to change the state.

There are also other more powerful but more complex solutions for asynchronous operations. We will not discuss these here.

Redux is well suited for managing complex global state in applications. It offers powerful debugging tools, such as time travel. Redux also facilitates the testing of state and logic due to the clear separation between data and its processing.

To integrate Redux with React, the React-Redux library is used. It provides Provider components, and the useSelector and useDispatch hooks, which allow easy connection of the Redux store to your React application.

```
function Counter() {
  const count = useSelector((state) => state.count);
  const dispatch = useDispatch();

  return (
    <div>
```

```
        <div>Count: {count}</div>
        <button onClick={() => dispatch({ type: 'INCREMENT' })}>+</button>
        <button onClick={() => dispatch({ type: 'DECREMENT' })}>-</button>
      </div>
   );
}
```

In the example above, the Counter component works with the Redux state by subscribing to changes through useSelector. This subscription is more granular, and changing the counter does not lead to the re-rendering of the entire application, but only of the specific component that invokes this hook.

However, it's important to note the drawbacks of Redux. Although it is the most popular solution, it has significant issues that affect my personal choice against this solution:

- Redux is verbose. Implementing a large global state requires writing a lot of boilerplate code in the form of reducers, actions, selectors, etc.

- With the growth of the project, the complexity of maintaining and scaling the Redux state increases disproportionately.

As the project and global state grow, application performance significantly decreases. This happens due to the need for a large number of computations, even if you simply change the state of one value from false to true.

Implementation of asynchronous operations is not supported out of the box by Redux and requires additional solutions, further complicating the understanding and maintenance of the project.

Dividing state and business logic into chunks for lazy loading requires a lot of effort. As a result, the application's size and therefore its initial loading speed are affected.

Despite these drawbacks, many companies and developers still use this solution, as it suits most business tasks, so I believe it is important to know this tool and be able to work with it.

MobX

The next popular solution for managing the global state is the **MobX** library. This library differs significantly from Redux, with a concept that is in some ways even the opposite.

MobX is a state management library that provides reactive and flexible interaction with data. Its main idea is to make the application state as simple and transparent as possible, working through small objects and classes that can be created as many times as desired and nested within each other.

Technically, the library allows for creating not just one global state but many small objects directly linked to some functionality of the application, which gives a significant advantage when working with large applications. To get the difference between one global state and MobX states, you can look at the following diagram:

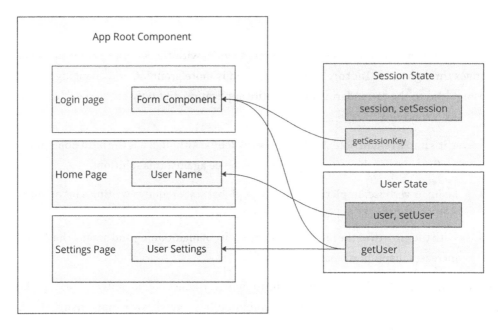

Figure 12.5: MobX state

In MobX, the state of the application is managed using observable method, which automatically track changes and inform related computed values and reactions. This allows the application to automatically update in response to state changes, simplifying the data flow and increasing flexibility.

```
class Store {
  @observable accessor count = 0;

  @computed get doubleCount() {
    return this.count * 2;
  }

  @action increment() {
    this.count += 1;
  }
}
```

```
    @action decrement() {
      this.count -= 1;
    }
  }

  const myStore = new Store();
```

In the example, the same counter is implemented using MobX. In one class, both the actual data and computed data are present, along with actions to change the state.

Speaking about asynchronous operations, MobX doesn't have any issues with that, as you can work in a regular class and add a new method that returns a promise.

```
  class Store {
    @observable count = 0;

    @computed get doubleCount() {
      return this.count * 2;
    }

    @action increment() {
      this.count += 1;
    }

    @action decrement() {
      this.count -= 1;
    }

    @action async fetchCountFromServer() {
      const response = await fetch('/count');
      const data = await response.json();
      this.count = data.count;
    }
  }

  const myStore = new Store();
```

MobX is well suited for applications that require high performance and simplicity in managing complex data dependencies. It offers an elegant and intuitive way to handle complex state, allowing developers to focus on business logic rather than state management.

One drawback of this library is the considerable freedom it provides in organizing state, which can lead to difficulties and scalability issues in inexperienced hands. For example, MobX allows direct manipulation of object data, which can trigger component updates, but this can also lead to unexpected state changes in large projects and debugging challenges. Similarly, this freedom often results in small, clean MobX classes becoming tightly coupled, making testing and project development more challenging.

To integrate MobX with React, the `mobx-react` library is used, which provides the `observer` function. This allows React components to automatically react to changes in observed data.

```
import React from 'react';
import { observer } from 'mobx-react';
import myStore from './myStore';

const Counter = observer(() => {
  return (
    <div>
      <div>Count: {myStore.count}</div>
      <div>Double: {myStore.doubleCount}</div>
      <button onClick={() => myStore.increment()}>-</button>
      <button onClick={() => myStore.decrement()}>+</button>
    </div>
  );
});
```

In the example, the same counter is implemented using MobX. As you can see, we don't use hooks to access the state or providers to store it in the application context. We simply import the variable from the file and use it. The `myStore` created from the `Store` class is the state itself. It's easy to use the observed value of an object in a component because the component immediately subscribes to all changes of that value and will re-render every time it changes.

Just from the examples, you can already see how simple and convenient MobX is for managing state. Since it's just an object, there are no complexities in lazily loading it when needed and clearing the cache and memory of the application when the data is no longer needed. I consider it a powerful tool for state management and highly recommend trying it in a real project.

Summary

In this chapter, we've learned about global state and how to manage it. Using the example of limited local state, we've discussed why it's important to have global state in cases where shared data is needed across different components at different levels of the application.

We've explored an example using the React Context API and identified when to use it and when to prefer more powerful state management solutions. Next, we looked at two such solutions in the form of Redux and MobX.

In the next chapter, we will discuss server-side rendering and the benefits it can bring to our applications.

13

Server-Side Rendering

As we discussed in *Chapter 1*, *Why React?*, the React library is remarkably flexible in terms of how our components can be transformed into various target formats. One such target format, as you might have guessed, is standard HTML markup, presented as a string and generated on the server. In this chapter, we will delve into how **server-side rendering** (**SSR**) works in React and the advantages it offers both users and developers. You will learn why this approach can be valuable for your application and how it enhances the overall user experience and performance.

The following topics are covered in this chapter:

- Working on the server
- Using Next.js
- React Server Components

Technical requirements

You can find the code files of this chapter on GitHub at https://github.com/PacktPublishing/React-and-React-Native-5E/tree/main/Chapter13.

Working on the server

Web technologies have come a long way or, more precisely, have come full circle. It all started with static web pages prepared by a server. Servers were the foundation of all website and application logic, as they were entirely responsible for their functioning. Then, we tried to move away from **SSR** in favor of rendering pages in the browser, which led to a significant leap in the development of web pages as fully fledged applications, now comparable to desktop ones. As a result, browsers became the core of application logic, while servers merely provided data for applications.

Currently, the development cycle has brought us back to SSR and server components, but now we have a unified logic and code for both the server and the client. Why this happened and what conclusions and experiences we have gained with the evolution of technologies are what we will try to understand in this section, and we will simultaneously learn about the types of work our applications do on the server.

Server-side rendering

In a traditional **single-page application (SPA)** approach, we rely solely on local browser rendering. We write all the code, styles, and markup specifically for a browser, and during the application build, we get static HTML, CSS, and JavaScript files, which are then loaded into the browser.

In most cases, the initial HTML file remains empty, without any content. The only important thing to have in this file is the connected JavaScript file, which will render everything we need.

Below is a schematic illustration of how an SPA application is loaded and rendered:

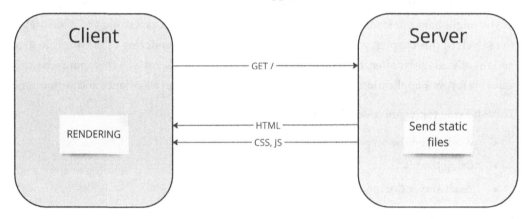

Figure 13.1: SPA application

This approach brought interactivity, making applications feel and function like real desktop applications. There's no longer a need to reload a page every time to update the content and receive notifications, new emails, or messages, as the entire application logic is directly in the browser. Over time, browser applications have almost entirely replaced desktop ones. Now, we can write emails, work with documents, watch movies, and do much more, all within a single browser. Many companies, instead of developing desktop applications, started creating their projects as web applications. The browser's ability to operate across any architecture and operating system significantly reduced development costs.

At the same time, servers also underwent changes, moving away from page templating, caching, etc. Backend developers no longer need to focus on page layout and can devote more time to more complex logic and architecture.

However, SPA applications do have drawbacks, including the long initial load time due to the need to download and process the script. During this process, the user sees a white screen or a loading spinner. Additionally, the empty initial HTML file is not suitable for search engine optimization, as search engines perceive it as a blank page.

In the context of creating, for example, an online store, a regular React SPA might not be suitable because it's important for users and search engines to immediately see the page content. Before the advent of SPAs, such tasks were solved by tools that worked only on the server side, which always prepared the content. In React, solving this problem is more complex because, as we know, React works on the browser side.

The first step in the solution will obviously be the idea of rendering the page content on the server by React. And this won't be a problem. Since its release, React has had the renderToString function for this purpose, which can be called in a **Node.js server** environment. This function returns an HTML string that, when sent to the browser, allows the content to be rendered on the user's screen.

Let's see how SSR with the renderToString function would work:

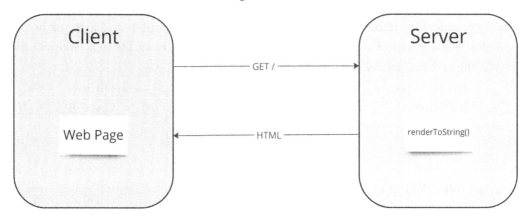

Figure 13.2: Server rendering using renderToString

In this example, when a page is requested in the browser, the server, by calling the function renderToString and passing it to the React component tree, outputs HTML. By sending this HTML string in response to the browser's request, the browser renders the result.

However, in such an example, the HTML generated on the server and rendered in the browser lacks interactivity and the capabilities of a client application. For functionalities like buttons, navigation, and everything we are accustomed to in SPAs, JavaScript is required. Therefore, the next step in implementing an interactive site or application rendered on the server is to transmit not only HTML but also JavaScript, which will provide all the interactivity we need.

To solve this problem, the approach of **isomorphic JavaScript** was introduced. Code written in this style can be executed first on the server and then on the client. This allows you to prepare the initial render on the server and send the ready HTML along with the JavaScript bundle to the client, allowing the browser to then provide interactivity. This approach speeds up the initial load of the application, while maintaining its functionality and allowing search engines to index the page in search results.

When a user opens a page, they immediately see the rendering result performed on the server even before the JavaScript is loaded. This quick initial response significantly improves the user experience. After the page and JS bundle are loaded, it's crucial for the browser to **hydrate** the page, as we know from the renderToString example that all our elements lack interactivity. For this, the script needs to attach all necessary event listeners to the elements. This process is called **hydration** and is a lighter and faster process compared to a full-page render from scratch.

Another important feature of interactivity is the ability to navigate through an application instantly or smoothly without reloading a browser page. With isomorphic JavaScript, this became possible, as it is enough to load the JavaScript code of the next page, and the application can then render the next page locally.

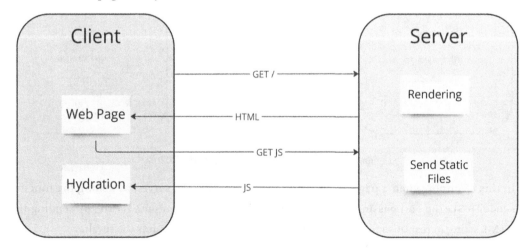

Figure 13.3: SSR

The figure above schematically represents the SSR approach, where the application is fully inter-active. Initially, when a page is requested, the server renders the content and returns HTML with an attached JavaScript bundle. Then, the browser loads the JS file and hydrates all the content previously displayed on the page. This approach is what has come to be known as SSR. It has become widely used among React developers and has found its place in the arsenal of modern web technologies. SSR combines the fast loading of page content and the high performance of server rendering with the flexibility and interactivity of a client application.

Static site and incremental static generation

Although SSR represents a significant improvement, it is not a universal solution and has its drawbacks, including the need to generate a page from scratch for each request. For example, pages that do not have dynamic content must be generated on a server each time, which can cause display delays for the user. Additionally, even for the simplest applications or sites, SSR requires a Node.js server for rendering, unlike SPAs where it was sufficient to use a **content delivery network (CDN)** to position application files closer to the user, thereby speeding up loading.

The solution to these problems was found in the **static site generation (SSG)** approach. The logic of SSG is to render all static pages on a server during the project build process. As a result, we get many HTML pages ready for immediate delivery upon request. As with SSR, in SSG, the JavaScript bundle hydrates the page after it has loaded, making it interactive. In the end, we get the same experience as with SPAs but not with an empty HTML file: rather, one full of content for quick rendering. SSG projects can be hosted on fast web servers or CDNs, which also allows for additional caching and speeding up the loading time of such applications.

SSG became an ideal solution for websites, blogs, and simple online stores, ensuring fast page load times without blocking requests, SEO support, and the same interactivity as SPAs. Moreover, it became possible to combine SSR for dynamic data and SSG for static pages. This hybrid approach opens up new possibilities to implement more complex projects, combining the advantages of both methods. It allows developers to optimize performance and user experience by choosing the best rendering method, depending on the specific requirements of each page of the site or application.

Another issue faced by developers and companies is updating statically generated pages. For example, traditionally, adding a new blog post or updating an online store's inventory required a complete rebuild of a project, which can be time-consuming and inconvenient, especially in large projects. Imagine a blog with 1,000 posts having to be completely rebuilt and re-rendered just because a new post being added.

This problem is solved by an approach known as **incremental static generation (ISR)**. ISR combines the principles of SSG and SSR with caching functionality. To understand this approach, imagine all our generated HTML and JS files at the build stage simply as a **cache**, representing the current result of the project build. As with any cache, we now need to introduce a logic for its revalidation. As long as our cache is valid, all page requests work as before using the SSG approach. But when the revalidation time expires, the next request to the page initiates its re-rendering on the server in SSR mode. The resulting output is sent to the client and simultaneously replaces the old HTML file with a new one, i.e., updates the cache. The application then continues to operate in SSG mode.

Thanks to ISR, it became possible to implement large-scale projects with millions of pages, which do not need to be constantly rebuilt for minor updates. It also became possible to altogether skip the generation of pages at the build stage, as the required pages would be rendered and saved upon request. For huge projects, this provided a significant increase in project build speeds.

Currently, SSG with ISR, combined with traditional SSR, is one of the most popular approaches for implementing both simple websites and blogs, as well as complex applications. However, traditional SPAs remain a very popular solution. But if we know how to create and assemble SPAs, what about everything else we just discussed? In response to this question, it's important to note that you don't need to develop all these approaches manually. There are several frameworks based on React that provide all the functionalities described above:

- **Next.js**: This framework is known for its flexibility and powerful features. Next.js started with SSR but now supports both SSR and SSG, including ISR support. Recently, Next.js has been working extensively on a new concept for implementing applications using server components, which we will discuss at the end of the chapter.

- **Gatsby**: Gatsby's main distinction is its strong focus on generating static sites using data from various sources (such as **CMS** or **Markdown**). While there are not as many differences from Next.js as there used to be, it remains a fairly popular solution.

- **Remix**: This is a relatively new framework that focuses on closer integration with web standards and improving the user experience. Remix offers unique approaches to data handling and routing, where we can work not page by page but by sections of a page, implementing nested navigation by changing and caching only the part of the page that requires dynamics.

All these frameworks collectively provide a similar experience and implementation of the approaches we've discussed. Next, we'll explore how to implement SSR and static generation using Next.js.

Using Next.js

After familiarizing ourselves with the theory of SSR, let's see how we can implement all this in practice using the **Next.js** framework.

Next.js is a popular React-based framework specifically designed to simplify the process of SSR and static site generation. It offers powerful and flexible capabilities for creating high-performance web applications.

The features of Next.js:

- **An easy-to-use API that automates SSR and static generation**: You just need to write code using the provided methods and functions, and the framework will automatically determine which pages should be rendered server-side and which can be rendered during the project build process.
- **File-based routing**: Next.js uses a simple and intuitive routing system based on the folder and file structure in the project. This greatly simplifies the creation and management of routes in the application.
- The ability to create comprehensive full-stack applications, thanks to API routes that allow you to implement server-side REST API endpoints.
- The optimization of images, fonts, and scripts, enhancing the performance of projects.

Another important feature of the framework is its close collaboration with the React Core team on implementing new React features. As a result, Next.js currently supports two types of application implementations, known as the **Pages Router** and the **App Router**. The former implements the main functionality we discussed earlier, while the latter is a newer approach designed for working with React Server Components. We will examine the new approach later in this chapter, but for now, let's start with the Pages Router.

To start working with Next.js, you only need to execute a single command that will set everything up for you:

```
npx create-next-app@latest
```

This CLI command will ask you a few questions:

```
✓ What is your project named? … using-nextjs
✓ Would you like to use TypeScript? … No / Yes
✓ Would you like to use ESLint? … No / Yes
✓ Would you like to use Tailwind CSS? … No / Yes
✓ Would you like to use `src/` directory? … No / Yes
✓ Would you like to use App Router? (recommended) … No / Yes
✓ Would you like to customize the default import alias (@/*)? … No / Yes
✓ What import alias would you like configured? … @/* No / Yes
```

For our current example, you should answer Yes to all questions except for the one about using the App Router. Also, you can access the ready-made example that we'll discuss further at the provided link: https://github.com/PacktPublishing/React-and-React-Native-5E/tree/main/Chapter13/using-nextjs.

In the example, we will create a small website with multiple pages, each using different server rendering approaches. In Next.js, each page of the website should be placed in separate files with names that correspond to the URL path. In our project example:

- The main page of the website, accessible at the root path domain.com/, will be located in the index.tsx file in the pages folder. For the understanding of the following examples, the path to this file, in the case of the main page, will be pages/index.tsx.

- The /about page will be located in the pages/about.tsx file.

- Next, we will create a /posts page at the path pages/posts/index.tsx.

- Each individual post page will be located in a file using the path pages/posts/[post].tsx. Files with names in square brackets indicate to Next.js that this will be a dynamic page, with the post variable as a parameter. This means that pages like /posts/1 and /posts/2 will use this file as the page component.

- This is how the file routing works. The main directory of the project is the pages folder, where we can nest files that will be used to generate website pages based on the structure and names of files and folders.

In the pages folder, there are also two service files that are not actual pages but are used by the framework to prepare pages:

- The _document.tsx file is necessary for preparing the HTML markup. In this file, we have access to the <html> and <body> tags. This file is always rendered on the server.

- The _app.tsx file is used to initialize the page. You can use this component to connect scripts or for the root layout of pages that will be reused between routes.

Let's add a header to our website in the App component. Here's how the _app.tsx file looks:

```
const inter = Inter({ subsets: ["latin"] });

export default function App({ Component, pageProps }: AppProps) {
  return (
    <div className={inter.className}>
      <header className="p-4 flex items-center gap-4">
        <Link href="/">Home</Link>
        <Link href="/posts">Posts</Link>
        <Link href="/about">About</Link>
      </header>

      <div className="p-4">
        <Component {...pageProps} />
      </div>
    </div>
  );
}
```

The App component returns markup that will be used on every page of our project, which means we will see this header on any of our pages. Additionally, we can use the component control where the rest of the dynamic part of the project will be located.

Now, let's take a look at how the main page of our project will look:

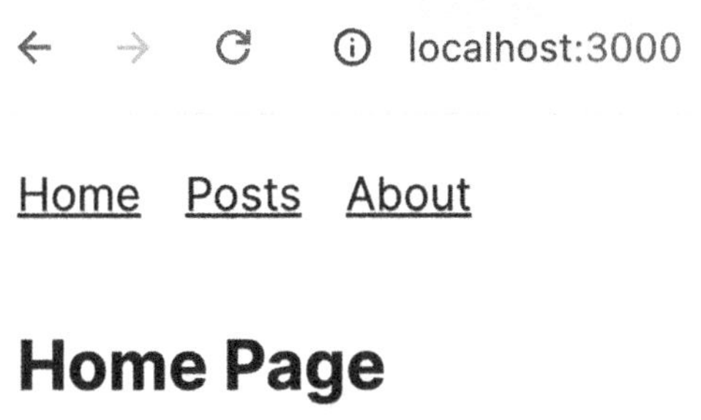

← → C ⓘ localhost:3000

Home **Posts** **About**

Home Page

Figure 13.4: Home Page

On this page, we can see the website header with links and the title, which was taken from the pages/index.tsx file:

```
export default function Home() {
  return (
    <main>
      <h1>Home Page</h1>
    </main>
  );
}
```

The pages/index.tsx file exports only one component with a title inside. It's important to note that this page doesn't have any additional functions or parameters and will be automatically rendered during the project build process. This means that when we visit this page, we get ready-made HTML that the browser can render immediately.

We can confirm that by visiting localhost:3000/, we receive the prepared markup. To do this, we just need to open the browser's developer tools and inspect what is returned for this request.

```
Name                          X   Headers   Preview   Response   Initiator   Timing
localhost                     —        <body>
                              —          <div id="__next">
                              —            <div class="__className_e66fe9">
                              —              <header class="p-4 flex items-center gap-4">
                              —                <a href="/">Home</a>
                              —                <a href="/posts">Posts</a>
                              —                <a href="/about">About</a>
                              —              </header>
                              —              <div class="p-4">
                              —                <main>
                              —                  <h1>Home Page</h1>
                              —                </main>
                              —              </div>
                              —            </div>
                              —          </div>
```

Figure 13.5: Home page response in Chrome DevTools

We can see how Next.js has taken content from the App and Home components and assembled HTML from it. All of this was done on the server side, not in the browser.

Next, let's take a look at the /about page. On this page, we will implement SSR, which means that instead of generating HTML during the build, the page will be rendered on every request. For this purpose, Next.js provides the getServerSideProps function, which runs at the time of the page request and returns props used by the component for rendering.

For our example, I've taken some logic from *Chapter 11, Fetching Data from a Server*, where we fetched user data from GitHub. Let's see what the about.tsx file will look like:

```
export const getServerSideProps = (async () => {
  const res = await fetch("https://api.github.com/users/sakhnyuk");
  const user: GitHubUser = await res.json();

  return { props: { user } };
}) satisfies GetServerSideProps<{ user: GitHubUser }>;
```

In the getServerSideProps function, we request user data using the **Fetch API**. The data we receive is stored in the user variable, which is then returned in the props object.

It's important to understand that this function is part of the Node.js environment, where we can use server-side APIs. This means we can read files, access databases, and more. This provides significant capabilities for implementing complex full-stack projects.

Next, in the same about.tsx file, we have the About component:

```
export default function About({
  user,
}: InferGetServerSidePropsType<typeof getServerSideProps>) {
  return (
    <main>
      <Image src={user.avatar_url} alt={user.login} width="100"
height="100" />
      <h2>{user.name || user.login}</h2>
      <p>{user.bio}</p>
      <p>Location: {user.location || "Not specified"}</p>
      <p>Company: {user.company || "Not specified"}</p>
      <p>Followers: {user.followers}</p>
      <p>Following: {user.following}</p>
      <p>Public Repos: {user.public_repos}</p>
    </main>
  );
}
```

In the About component, we use the user variable that we returned from the getServerSideProps function to create the page's markup. With just this one function, we've implemented SSR.

Next, let's create the /posts and /posts/[post] pages where we will implement SSG and ISR. For this, Next.js provides two functions: getStaticProps and getStaticPaths:

- getStaticProps: This function serves a similar purpose as getServerSideProps but is called during the project build process.
- getStaticPaths: This is used on dynamic pages where the path contains parameters (such as [post].tsx). This function determines which paths should be pre-generated during the build.

Let's take a look at how the Posts page component is implemented:

```
export async function getStaticProps() {
  const posts = ["1", "2", "3"];

  return {
    props: {
      posts,
    },
  };
}


export default function Posts({ posts }: { posts: string[] }) {
  return (
    <main>
      <h1>Posts</h1>

      <ul>
        {posts.map((post) => (
          <li key={post}>
            <Link href={`/posts/${post}`}>Post {post}</Link>
          </li>
        ))}
      </ul>
    </main>
  );
}
```

The getStaticProps function in this example doesn't request any data but simply returns three pages. However, just like in getServerSideProps, you can use getStaticProps to fetch data or work with the filesystem. The Posts component then receives posts as props and uses them to display a list of links to posts.

Here's what the **Posts** page will look like:

Figure 13.6: Posts page

When opening any post, the component from the [post].tsx file will be loaded. Here's how it looks:

```
export const getStaticPaths = (async () => {
  return {
    paths: [
      {
        params: {
          post: "1",
        },
      },
      {
        params: {
          post: "2",
        },
      },
      {
        params: {
          post: "3",
        },
```

```
      },
    ],
    fallback: true,
  };
}) satisfies GetStaticPaths;
```

This function informs the builder that only three pages need to be rendered during the build process. In this function, we can also make network requests. The "fallback" parameter we returned indicates that, theoretically, there may be more post pages than the ones we returned. For example, if we access the /posts/4 page, it will be rendered in SSR mode and saved as the build result:

```
Export const getStaticProps = (async (context) => {
  const content = `This is a dynamic route example. The value of the post
parameter is ${context.params?.post}.`;

  return { props: { content }, revalidate: 3600 };
}) satisfies GetStaticProps<{
  content: string;
}>;
```

In the getStaticProps function, we can now read the page parameter from the context argument. The value of revalidate that we returned from the function enables ISR and tells the server to rebuild this page on the next request, after 3600 from the previous build. Here's how the Post page will look:

```
export default function Post({
  content,
}: InferGetStaticPropsType<typeof getStaticProps>) {
  const router = useRouter();

  return (
    <main>
      <h1>Post - {router.query.post}</h1>

      <p>{content}</p>
    </main>
  );
}
```

When we open any post using the link, we will see the following:

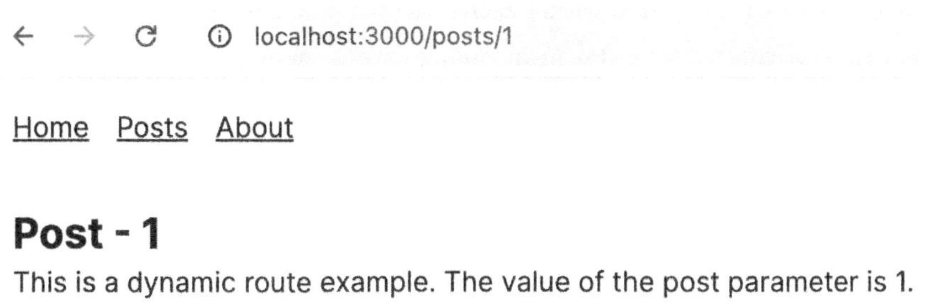

← → C   ⓘ localhost:3000/posts/1

Home Posts About

Post - 1

This is a dynamic route example. The value of the post parameter is 1.

Figure 13.7: Post page

In this example, we've created a website where pages use different server rendering approaches, which is useful and convenient for building large and complex projects. However, Next.js has more capabilities beyond this. Next, we will explore a new approach to building websites using the App Router.

React Server Components

React Server Components represent a new paradigm for working with components in Next.js that eliminates isomorphic JavaScript. The code of such components runs only on a server and can be cached as a result. In this concept, you can directly read the server's filesystem or access the database from the components.

In Next.js, React Server Components allow you to categorize components into two types: **server-side** and **client-side**. Server-side components are processed on a server and sent to the client as static HTML, reducing the load on the browser. Client-side components still have all the capabilities of browser JavaScript but with one requirement: you need to use the use client directive at the beginning of the file.

To use server-side components in Next.js, you will need to create a new project. For routing, you still use files, but now, the main folder for the project is the app folder, and route names are based solely on folder names. Inside each route (folder), there should be files with names specified by the framework. Here are some of the key files:

- page.tsx: This file and its component will be used to display the page.
- loading.tsx: The component of this file will be sent to the client as a loading state while the component from the page.tsx file is executed and loaded.

- layout.tsx: This is equivalent to the _app.tsx file, but in this case, we can have multiple layouts that can be nested within each other in nested routes.
- route.tsx: This file is used to implement an API endpoint.

Now, let's refactor our website with posts using the new architecture based on the **App Router**. Let's start with the home page. Since our website didn't have any interactive elements, I suggest adding one. Let's create the simplest button with a counter and place it on the home page. Here's the code for such a button:

```
"use client";

import React from "react";

export const Counter = () => {
  const [count, setCount] = React.useState(0);

  return <button onClick={() => setCount(count + 1)}>{count}</button>;
};
```

This component renders a button with a counter inside. By clicking the button, we update the counter. To make this component work with App Router, we need to add the "use client" directive, which tells Next.js to include this component's code in the bundle and send it to the browser upon request.

Now, let's add this button to the home page, and here's what its code will look like:

```
export default function Home() {
  return (
    <main>
      <h1>Home Page</h1>
      <Counter />
    </main>
  );
}
```

Since the page is simple, it doesn't differ from what we saw in the Pages Router, except for the new button. Although, by default, the App Router considers all components as server ones, in this case, the page will be rendered during the build process and saved as a static page.

Now, let's move on to the About page. To create this page, we need to create a folder named about and create a file inside it named page.tsx, where we'll place the component. Here's the code for it:

```
export const dynamic = "force-dynamic";

export default async function About() {
  const res = await fetch("https://api.github.com/users/sakhnyuk");
  const user: GitHubUser = await res.json();

  return (
    <main>
      <Image src={user.avatar_url} alt={user.login} width="100"
height="100" />
      <h2>{user.name || user.login}</h2>
      <p>{user.bio}</p>
      <p>Location: {user.location || "Not specified"}</p>
      <p>Company: {user.company || "Not specified"}</p>
      <p>Followers: {user.followers}</p>
      <p>Following: {user.following}</p>
      <p>Public Repos: {user.public_repos}</p>
    </main>
  );
}
```

As you can see, the code for this page has become simpler compared to using the Pages Router. The About component has become asynchronous, allowing us to make a network request and wait for the result. Since, in our example, we wanted to use SSR and render the page on the server for each request, we needed to export the "dynamic" variable from the file with the force-dynamic value. This parameter explicitly tells Next.js that we want to generate a new page for each request. Otherwise, Next.js would have generated the page during the project build and saved the result as a static page (by using SSG).

However, it would be strange if the App Router simply repeated the previous functionality without offering anything new. If we create a loading.tsx file inside the about folder, when opening the About page, instead of waiting for the server to request information from GitHub and prepare the page, it will instantly serve the page with content from the loading file as a fallback. And as soon as the component from the page.tsx file is ready, the server will send it to the client to replace the loading component. This provides a significant performance advantage and improves the user experience.

Now, let's move on to the Posts page. Create a posts folder and a page.tsx file inside it. Here's how the updated code for the /posts page will look:

```
export default async function Posts() {
  const posts = ["1", "2", "3"];

  return (
    <main>
      <h1>Posts</h1>
      <ul>
        {posts.map((post) => (
          <li key={post}>
            <Link href={`/posts/${post}`}>Post {post}</Link>
          </li>
        ))}
      </ul>
    </main>
  );
}
```

Once again, the code has become very clean. Everything we needed to fetch before rendering the page can be obtained and created directly inside the component. In our example, we have hardcoded three pages that will be rendered as links.

To implement a Post page, inside the posts folder, you need to create a folder with the name [post] and create the page.tsx file inside it. Here's the code, which is now much cleaner and more readable:

```
export async function generateStaticParams() {
  return [{ post: "1" }, { post: "2" }, { post: "3" }];
}
```

Instead of using getStaticPaths, we provide Next.js with information about the list of static pages to generate during the project build using the generateStaticParams function. Then, we use props inside the component to display the page's content:

```
export const revalidate = 3600

export default async function Post({ params }: { params: { post: string }
}) {
```

```
  return (
    <main>
      <h1>Post - {params.post}</h1>
      <p>
        This is a dynamic route example. The value of the post parameter
is
        {params.post}.
      </p>
    </main>
  );
}
```

The content remains mostly unchanged. To activate ISR, all we need to do is export the `revalidate` variable from the file with the revalidation value in seconds.

In this example, we covered the fundamental approaches to building an application using React Server Components and the App Router in Next.js. The Page Router and App Router examples provided in this chapter do not cover all the possibilities of Next.js. For a deeper understanding of this framework, I recommend checking out the excellent documentation on its website: `https://nextjs.org/docs`.

Summary

In this chapter, we explored SSR in the context of React applications. We discussed approaches such as SSR, SSG, and ISR, learning the advantages and disadvantages of each approach.

Then, we learned how to apply these approaches in an application using Next.js and the Pages Router. Finally, we introduced a new technology called React Server Components and the updated Next.js architecture called the App Router.

In the next chapter, we will learn how to test our components and applications.

14

Unit Testing in React

Although testing is an integral part of the software development process, developers and companies often pay surprisingly little attention to it in reality, especially to automated testing. In this chapter, we will try to understand why it is important to pay attention to testing and what advantages it gives. We will also explore the basics of unit testing in ReactJS, including general testing theory, tools, and methods, as well as specific aspects of testing ReactJS components.

In this chapter, we will cover the following topics:

- Testing in general
- Unit testing
- Testing ReactJS

Technical requirements

You can find the code files of this chapter on GitHub at https://github.com/PacktPublishing/
React-and-React-Native-5E/tree/main/Chapter14.

Testing in general

Software testing is a process aimed at identifying errors and verifying the functionality of a product to ensure its quality. Testing also allows developers and testers to assess the system's behavior under various conditions and to ensure that new changes have not led to regression, meaning they have not disrupted existing functionality.

The testing process includes a series of actions conducted to detect and identify any aspects that do not meet requirements or expectations. One example of such an action could be **manual testing**, where a developer or tester manually checks the application. However, this approach is time-consuming and provides little guarantee that the application is secure and free of critical errors in operation.

To ensure a higher level of application reliability while saving time on testing, there are **automated tests.** They allow the functionality of the application to be verified without human intervention.

An automated test typically consists of a set of predefined tests and a software product, often referred to as a **runner,** which launches these tests and analyzes the results to determine the success or failure of each test. In addition to this, automated tests can be used to check performance, stability, security, availability, and compatibility, allowing you to write truly stable, large, and successful projects. That's why it's never a good idea to avoid tests; on the contrary, it's worth getting to know them better and trying to use them in all possible projects.

As developers, we are obviously more interested in automated testing than manual testing, so this chapter will focus on that. But before that, let's briefly look at the approaches to testing and the types of tests that exist.

Test types and approaches

Software testing can be classified by various criteria, including the level of testing and the objectives it pursues.

Typically, the following types of tests are distinguished:

- **Unit testing**: Testing individual modules or components of the program for correct operation. Unit tests are usually written and executed by developers to check specific functions or methods. Such tests are generally quick to write and can be executed quickly, but they do not test the final application for critical bugs, as the tested and stable components themselves may have problems when interacting with each other. An example of a unit test would be checking the functionality of a single function, React component, or Hook.

- **Integration testing**: Testing in which we check the interaction between various modules or system components. The goal is to detect defects in the interfaces and interactions between integrated components. This type of testing is usually conducted on the server side to ensure that all systems work smoothly together and that the business logic meets the specified requirements.

For example, an integration test would be one that checks that user registration works by making real calls to REST API endpoints and checking the returned data. Such a test depends less on the application's implementation and code and more on checking behavior and business logic.

- **End-to-end (E2E) testing**: Testing a complete and integrated software system to ensure that it meets specified requirements. E2E testing evaluates the program as a whole. This type of testing is the most reliable, as it completely abstracts from the application's implementation and checks the final behavior by interacting directly with the application itself. In the process of such testing, for example, in a web application, a real browser is launched in a special environment, in which a script performs real actions with the application like clicking buttons, filling out forms, and navigating through pages.

Although test types such as integration and E2E testing provide greater confidence in verifying the quality of an application, they come with drawbacks such as complexity and speed of test development, execution speed, and consequently, their costliness. Therefore, it is considered good practice to maintain a balance where preference is given to unit tests, as they are easier to maintain and faster to run. Then, all main business processes and logic are verified using integration tests, and E2E tests cover only the most critical business cases. This approach can be depicted in the form of a pyramid:

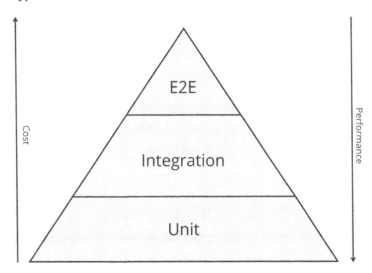

Figure 14.1: Test pyramid

The pyramid perfectly describes the approach we have discussed above. At its base lies **unit testing**, which should cover the application's source code as extensively as possible. It has the lowest cost of development and maintenance, as well as the highest test execution performance. In the middle are the **integration** tests, which are quite fast but more expensive to develop. At the very top, we have the **E2E** tests, which take the longest to execute and are the most expensive to develop, but they provide the maximum confidence in the quality of the product being tested.

Since integration and E2E tests abstract away from the implementation, and thus from the programming language or libraries used in the application, we are not going to cover those types of testing. Therefore, let's focus in more detail on unit testing.

Unit testing

We already know that unit testing is the process of verifying the correctness of individual "**units**" of code: namely, **functions** and **methods**. The goal of unit testing is to ensure that each separate unit performs its task correctly, which, in turn, increases confidence in the reliability of the entire application.

```
export function sum(a: number, b: number): number {
  return a + b;
}


test('adds 1 + 2 to equal 3', () => {
  expect(sum(1, 2)).toBe(3);
});
```

The above represents the most basic and simplest test of a function that adds two values. The test code itself is a function that calls a special method, expect, which takes a value and then has a series of methods allowing for the checking and comparing of results.

Looking at this code, the first question that might come to mind is, is it really necessary to write another three lines of tests for such a simple three-line function? And why test such a function at all? I would answer with a definitive *yes*. It often happens that a function can be covered by a test that is larger in volume than the function itself, and there is nothing wrong with that. Let's understand why.

Unit testing is most useful and effective when you are testing **pure functions**, which have no side effects and do not depend on external state. Conversely, unit testing is useless when the function being tested can change its behavior due to external factors or simply because that's how the function was designed. For example, functions for requesting data from the server, getting data from `localStorage`, or relying on global variables might return different results for the same input. From this, we can conclude that in an application development approach that requires code coverage with tests, you will automatically strive to write **testable code**, meaning more modular, independent, clean, and scalable code. This becomes especially noticeable on large projects. If tests were written from the start, such projects could continue to grow without the need for major refactoring or rewriting functionality from scratch. Also, in projects with tests, it is easier for newcomers to understand, as tests can serve as additional documentation for modules, reading which one can understand what the module is responsible for and what behavior it possesses.

For writing unit tests, there are entire concepts and methodologies. The main and most popular one is the traditional coverage of tests after code development. The advantage of this approach is the speed of development of the main functionality, as tests are usually dealt with later. Hence, the problem with this approach lies in delaying testing, which poses a risk of accumulating code that is not covered by tests. Later, when writing tests, it often becomes necessary to correct the main code, making it more modular and cleaner, which takes additional time.

There is also a methodology directly aimed at writing tests, called **test-driven development (TDD)**. This is a software development methodology in which tests are written before the code itself. The benefit of this approach is that your code will be immediately covered by tests, meaning it will be cleaner and more reliable. However, this approach may not be suitable for prototyping or for projects where requirements often change.

The choice between TDD and testing after development depends on many factors, including the team's culture, project requirements, and developers' preferences. It is important to understand that neither approach is a universal solution, and different choices may be justified in different situations. Most importantly, understand the importance of testing and that one should avoid an approach in work where tests are not written at all as, in most cases, such code is doomed to be rewritten from scratch.

Now that we understand what unit tests are and their importance, let's take a closer look at them. Before writing tests, we should set up the environment in which we will run our tests.

Setting up the test environment

The most popular framework for writing and running unit tests is **Jest**. However, we will look at its more performant alternative, which is fully compatible with **Vite**, called **Vitest**. To install Vitest in your project, you need to execute this command:

```
npm install -D vitest
```

For basic operation, Vitest does not require any configuration, as it is fully compatible with the Vite configuration file.

Next, to get started, we need to create a file with the extension `*.test.ts`. The location of the file is not critical; the main thing is that the file is inside your project. Usually, test files are associated with the files of the functions being tested and are placed in the same directory; for example, for the `sum` function located in the `sum.ts` file, a file with a test named `sum.test.ts` is created and located in the same folder.

To run the tests, we need to add a launch script to the `package.json` file:

```
{
  "scripts": {
    "test": "vitest"
  }
}
```

Then, to call it, just execute the command in the terminal:

```
npm run test
```

This command will start the Vitest process, which will scan the project for files with the `.test.` extension and then execute all the tests in each such file. Once all tests are completed, you will see the result in the terminal window, and then the process will wait for changes in the test files to rerun them. This is specifically designed as a mode for developing tests, where you do not need to constantly run the test command. For a one-time test run, you can add another command that will close the process upon completion of testing:

```
"test:run": "vitest run"
```

The `run` parameter is precisely for telling Vitest that you want to run the tests only once.

Vitest features

Let's now look at the main features of Vitest and the types of tests we can write. Let's start with a simple function, squared:

```
export const squared = (n: number) => n * n
```

This function returns the square of a number. Here is what the test for this function would look like:

```
import { expect, test } from 'vitest'

test('Squared', () => {
  expect(squared(2)).toBe(4)
  expect(squared(4)).toBe(16)
  expect(squared(25)).toBe(625)
})
```

The test and expect functions are part of the Vitest package. The test function takes the name of the test as its first argument and the test function itself as its second argument. The expect method serves as the basis for checking the expected result from the function being tested. Calling the expect method creates an object that contains a large number of methods, allowing for different ways to check the execution result. In our example, we explicitly compare the result of executing the squared function with the expected value.

By running this test, in the terminal window, we will see the following message:

```
✓ test/basic.test.ts (1)
   ✓ Squared

 Test Files  1 passed (1)
      Tests  1 passed (1)
   Start at  17:39:33
   Duration  1.14s
```

To check that the tests are working correctly, let's change the expected value from 4 and see what result we get:

```
FAIL  test/basic.test.ts > Squared
AssertionError: expected 4 to be 5 // Object.is equality

- Expected
```

```
+ Received


> eval test/basic.test.ts:13:22
    11|
    12| test('Squared', () => {
    13|    expect(squared(2)).toBe(5);
      |                        ^
    14|    expect(squared(4)).toBe(16);
    15|    expect(squared(25)).toBe(625);


  ──────────────────────────────────────────────

  ──────────────────────[1/1]─

 Test Files  1 failed (1)
      Tests  1 failed (1)
   Start at  17:41:45
   Duration  1.15s
```

When a test fails, we can see directly in the results where the error occurred, what result we received, and what we expected.

The toBe method is very useful for direct comparison of results, but what about objects and arrays? Let's consider this test example:

```
test('objects', () => {
  const obj1 = { a: 1 };
  const obj2 = { a: 1 };
  expect(obj1).not.toBe(obj2);
  expect(obj1).toEqual(obj2);
});
```

In this test, we created two identical objects, which will not be equal as variables. To expect the opposite assertion, we use the additional .not. key, which ultimately gives us the statement that the two variables are not equal to each other. If we still want to check that the objects have the same structure, there is a method called toEqual, which recursively compares objects. This method also works similarly with arrays.

For arrays, there are also additional methods that allow checking for the presence of an element, which is often very useful:

```
test('Array', () => {
  expect(['1', '2', '3']).toContain('3');
});
```

The toContain method can also work with strings and even DOM elements, checking for the presence of a class in classList.

The next big part of unit testing is working with functions. Vitest allows you to create **spyable fake functions**, which lets you check how and with what parameters this function was called. Let's look at an example function:

```
const selector = (onSelect: (value: string) => void) => {
  onSelect('1');
  onSelect('2');
  onSelect('3');
};
```

This function is created just for demonstration, but we can easily imagine some module or selector component that takes the onSelect callback, which will be called under some condition: in our case, three times in a row. Now let's see how we can test using observable functions:

```
test('selector', () => {
  const onSelect = vi.fn();

  selector(onSelect);

  expect(onSelect).toBeCalledTimes(3);
  expect(onSelect).toHaveBeenLastCalledWith('3');
});
```

In the test, we created the onSelect function using the vi module from the Vitest package. This function now allows us to check how many times it was called and with what arguments. For this, we used the methods toBeCalledTimes and toHaveBeenLastCalledWith. There is also a method called toHaveBeenCalledWith, which can step-by-step check which arguments were used on each call of the observed function. In our case, the valid checks would be these three lines:

```
expect(onSelect).toHaveBeenCalledWith('1');
expect(onSelect).toHaveBeenCalledWith('2');
expect(onSelect).toHaveBeenCalledWith('3');
```

Vitest also allows you to spy a real function, for which you need to use the `vi.spyOn` method. However, for this, the function must be accessible from an object. Let's look at an example of spying on a real function:

```
test('spyOn', () => {
  const cart = {
    getProducts: () => 10,
  };

  const spy = vi.spyOn(cart, 'getProducts');

  expect(cart.getProducts()).toBe(10);

  expect(spy).toHaveBeenCalled();
  expect(spy).toHaveReturnedWith(10);
});
```

To create an observation for a function, we call `vi.spyOn` and pass it the object as the first argument and the name of the method as the second. Then, we can work with the original function and, later, make the necessary checks working with the `spy` variable. In the example above, you can also notice the new method `toHaveReturnedWith`, which allows you to check what the observed function returned.

Mocking

Moving on, I'd like to mention one of the most challenging parts of unit testing: namely, working with functions that have side effects or depend on external data or libraries. Earlier, I mentioned that testing is useless in functions with side effects, like calling something under the hood. Actually, that's not entirely true. In some cases, it's simply impossible to write a pure function, but that doesn't mean it can't be tested. To write tests for such functions, we can use **mocking**: namely, emulating external behavior or simply replacing the implementation of some modules or libraries.

An example could be a function that depends on the system time of the computer, or a function that returns data from a server. In such cases, we can apply a fake instruction that can change the current date of the computer specifically for this test, to have a clean result that is easier to test. Similarly, it is possible to create a fake implementation of a network request, which will ultimately be executed locally with the return of predetermined values. Let's discuss some of these scenarios in this section.

Consider the example of testing and using **timers**. In the testing environment, we can avoid wait-ing for timers and manually control them to more thoroughly test the behavior of the function. Let's look at an example:

```
function executeInMinute(func: () => void) {
  setTimeout(func, 1000 * 60)
}

function executeEveryMinute(func: () => void) {
  setInterval(func, 1000 * 60)
}

const mock = vi.fn(() => console.log('done'))
```

We created the executeInMinute and executeEveryMinute functions for delaying the call of a function by one minute and for cyclic execution every minute, respectively. We also created a mock function that we will subsequently spy on. Here's what the test will look like:

```
describe('delayed execution', () => {
  beforeEach(() => {
    vi.useFakeTimers()
  })
  afterEach(() => {
    vi.restoreAllMocks()
  })


  it('should execute the function', () => {
    executeInMinute(mock)
    vi.runAllTimers()
    expect(mock).toHaveBeenCalledTimes(1)
  })

  it('should not execute the function', () => {
    executeInMinute(mock)
    vi.advanceTimersByTime(2)
    expect(mock).not.toHaveBeenCalled()
  })
```

```
  it('should execute every minute', () => {
    executeEveryMinute(mock)
    vi.advanceTimersToNextTimer()
    expect(mock).toHaveBeenCalledTimes(1)
    vi.advanceTimersToNextTimer()
    expect(mock).toHaveBeenCalledTimes(2)
  })
})
```

In this example, there's a lot to discuss but let's start with the fact that we didn't use the test function; instead, we used describe and it. The describe function allows us to create a test suite that can have its own context and lifecycle. In the test suite, we can set initial parameters or mock some behavior so that our test cases can reuse this context and these parameters later on. In our example, we use the beforeEach and afterEach methods, which set up fake timers before each test and then restore everything back to its original state after each test.

The it method is an alias for the test method and does not differ functionally from it. It's only there to make the test case more readable in the results. For example, describe with 'delayed execution' and it with 'should execute the function' in the results would look like this:

```
    delayed execution > should execute the function
```

However, using test, we would see the result as:

```
    delayed execution > if should execute the function
```

Now, let's look at the tests themselves. The first test uses the executeInMinute function, which, in reality, would call our observed method only after a minute, but in the test, we can control time. By using vi.runAllTimers(), we force the environment to start and skip all timers and immediately check the result. In the next test, we move time forward by 2 milliseconds using vi.advanceTimersByTime(2), which already allows us to ensure that the original function will not be called.

Next, let's discuss the executeEveryMinute method, which should start a timer with a call to an argument every minute. In this case, we can step through each iteration of this timer using advanceTimersToNextTimer, giving us precise control over time without having to wait in real time.

When writing unit tests, we will often encounter that the function being tested will depend on some library or even a package.

Most often, you will encounter this in React Native, if a library or some method uses the device's native functions. In such a case, to write a test, we need to create a mock version of this logic that will be called during the test.

Let's consider a simple example where we imagine that we have a package that can interact with the device and get the current number of steps. To obtain the steps, we'll use the getSteps function:

```
export function getSteps() {
  // SOME NATIVE LOGIC
  return 100;
}
```

As an example, the function itself will be very simple and will just return the value of 100. However, in reality, such a function would interact with a smartphone API, which would be impossible to invoke within the scope of testing. Next, let's look at what we can do when writing a test:

```
import { beforeAll, describe, expect, it, vi } from 'vitest';
import { getSteps } from './ios-health-kit';

describe('IOS Health Kit', () => {
  beforeAll(() => {
    vi.mock('./ios-health-kit', () => ({
      getSteps: vi.fn().mockImplementation(() => 2000),
    }));
  });

  it('should return steps', () => {
    expect(getSteps()).toBe(2000);
    expect(getSteps).toHaveBeenCalled();
  });
});
```

The test and the entire example are quite primitive but they will give you an understanding of how mocking works. At the beginning of the file, we import our original package, ios-health-kit, then using the beforeAll method, we call vi.mock, passing it the path to the package as the first argument and a function that will return the implementation of the original file: namely, creating an object with the getSteps method as a fake function with an implementation that will return the value of 2000. Then, in the test, we check that it indeed returns this value.

In this test, the `vi.mock` function creates a mock of the imported package and replaces the original import with it, which allows us to successfully test this functionality.

In fact, this example, in essence, does not test anything but merely demonstrates the possibility of mocking. In a real project, you will likely need to test functions that somewhere inside may use libraries that are important to mock. For this, it may be inconvenient to constantly manually write mocks before the actual test; to solve this, you can mock libraries and APIs at a global level. For this, you will need to create a configuration file or use `vi.stubGlobal`. I do not recommend diving so deeply right away without understanding and learning the basics, so let's move on.

 More information about dependency mocking via configuration can be found at https://vitest.dev/guide/mocking.

The last but not least important example I'd like to discuss is mocking **network requests**. Almost any application you'll be developing will work with data that needs to be fetched from a server. For a unit test, this can be a problem, as it's important to test the unit abstracted from the external environment. Therefore, in unit tests, you should always mock server requests and provide the data necessary for the current test case. There's a library called `Mock Service Worker` for mocking server requests. It allows you to mock REST and GraphQL requests very flexibly. Let's look at an example:

```
import { http, HttpResponse } from 'msw';
import { setupServer } from 'msw/node';
import { describe, it, expect, beforeAll, afterEach, afterAll } from
'vitest';

const server = setupServer(
  http.get('https://api.github.com/users', () => {
    return HttpResponse.json({
      firstName: 'Mikhail',
      lastName: 'Sakhniuk',
    });
  })
);

describe('Mocked fetch', () => {
  beforeAll(() => server.listen());
```

```
    afterEach(() => server.resetHandlers());
    afterAll(() => server.close());

    it('should returns test data', async () => {
      const response = await fetch('https://api.github.com/users');

      expect(response.status).toBe(200);
      expect(response.statusText).toBe('OK');
      expect(await response.json()).toEqual({
        firstName: 'Mikhail',
        lastName: 'Sakhniuk',
      });
    });
  });
});
```

In this test, we created a mock network request for the path `https://api.github.com/users`, which returns the data we need. For this, we used the `setupServer` function from the `Mock Service Worker` package. Next, in the lifecycle methods, we set up the mock server to listen to server requests and then implemented a standard test where data is requested using the regular Fetch API. As you can see in the results, we can check the status code and the returned data.

With such a mocking approach, we truly have vast possibilities for testing different logic depending on the data returned from the server, status codes, errors, and so on.

In this section, we've introduced the basics of unit tests: namely, what they are and why we need to write them. We've learned how to set up the testing environment and write basic tests for our future projects. Next, let's move on to the main topic of our chapter, testing ReactJS compaonents.

Testing ReactJS

We already know that unit testing involves checking small units, and most often, just functions, which perform some logic and return a result. To understand how testing in ReactJS works, the concept and idea remain the same. We know that at their core, React components are actually `createElement` functions that return a node, which, as a result of the render function, is displayed on the browser screen as HTML elements. In unit testing, we don't have a browser, but this is not a problem for us since we know that the render target in React can be almost anything. As you may have already guessed, in the unit tests of ReactJS components, we will be rendering components into a specially created **JSDOM** format, which is fully identical to the DOM, and the **React Testing Library** will help us with this.

This library contains a set of tools that allow rendering components, simulating events, and then checking the results in various ways.

Before we start, let's set up the environment for testing React components. To do this, in a fresh Vite project, execute this command:

```
npm install --save-dev \
  @testing-library/react \

  @testing-library/jest-dom \
  vitest \
  jsdom
```

This command will install all the dependencies we need. Next, we need to create a `tests/setup.ts` file to integrate Vitest and the React Testing Library:

```
import { expect, afterEach } from 'vitest';
import { cleanup } from '@testing-library/react';
import * as matchers from "@testing-library/jest-dom/matchers";

expect.extend(matchers);

afterEach(() => {
  cleanup();
});
```

Next, we need to update the `vite.config.ts` configuration file and add the following code there:

```
test: {
  globals: true,
  environment: "jsdom",
  setupFiles: "./tests/setup.ts",
},
```

These parameters tell Vitest to use an additional environment and execute our setup script before starting the tests.

The last step is to configure TypeScript typing, where we will specify that the expect function will now have additional methods to work with React components. To do this, we need to add the following code to the `src/vite-env.d.ts` file:

```
import type { TestingLibraryMatchers } from "@testing-library/jest-dom/
matchers";

declare global {
  namespace jest {
    interface Matchers<R = void>
      extends TestingLibraryMatchers<typeof expect.stringContaining, R> {}
  }
}
```

This construction adds types for all the new methods provided by the React Testing Library. With this, the environment setup is complete, and we can proceed to writing tests.

First, let's consider the most basic check that a component has successfully rendered and is present in the document. For this, we'll create an App component that returns a title with the Hello world text:

```
export function App() {
  return <h1>Hello world</h1>;
}
```

The test for such a component would look like this:

```
import { render, screen } from "@testing-library/react";
import { describe, it, expect } from "vitest";
import { App } from "./App";

describe("App", () => {
  it("should be in document ", () => {
    render(<App />);
    expect(screen.getByText("Hello world")).toBeInTheDocument();
  });
});
```

The structure of the test itself is the same as before and is already familiar to us. The main thing to note is that at the beginning of the test, we render the component using the render function from testing-library, and after that, we can perform checks. To work with the rendering result, we use the screen module. It allows us to interact with our virtual DOM tree, and search for necessary elements in various ways.

We will cover the main ones later, but in this example, we used the getByText method, which queries for an element containing the text "Hello World". To check whether this element is present in the document, we use the toBeInTheDocument method. This is how the output looks when you run the test:

```
✓ src/App.test.tsx (1)
  ✓ App (1)
    ✓ should be in document


Test Files  1 passed (1)
     Tests  1 passed (1)
  Start at  14:19:01
  Duration  198ms
```

Now let's consider a more complex example, where we need to check that clicking a button adds a new className property to the component:

```
export function ClassCheck() {
  const [clicked, setClicked] = useState(false);

  return (
    <button
      className={clicked ? "active" : ""}
      onClick={() => setClicked(true)}
    >
      Click me
    </button>
  );
}
```

By clicking the button, we update the state, which updates the component and adds an active class to it. Now, let's write a test for this component:

```
describe("ClassCheck", () => {
  it("should have class active when button was clicked", () => {
    render(<ClassCheck />);
    const button = screen.getByRole("button");

    expect(button).not.toHaveClass("active");
    fireEvent.click(button);
```

```
        expect(button).toHaveClass("active");
    });
});
```

In this test, you first render the `ClassCheck` component, then we need to find the button element, and for this, we use the `screen` module with the `getByRole` method. This is the next method that allows query elements in the document, but it's important to understand that if there is more than one `button` in the document, this test will produce an error. Therefore, it's necessary to apply suitable query methods in different situations. Now that the button is accessible, we first ensure that the component does not contain the `active` class using the `toHaveClass` method with the `not` prefix.

To click on this button, the React Testing Library provides the `fireEvent` module, which allows generating click events. After clicking the button, we check that the required class is present in the element.

With `fireEvent`, it's possible to generate all possible events such as click, drag, play, focus, blur, and many others. A very common event that is also important to test is the change event in an input element. Let's discuss this using the `Input` component as an example:

```
export function Input() {
    return <input type="text" data-testid="userName" />;
}
```

This component simply returns an `input` element, but in this example, I've also added a special attribute, `data-testid`. This is used for more convenient searching of elements in the document, as this attribute abstracts you from working with the content of the component or the role of the element. During the development of the project, you will often update your components, and the `data-testid` attribute will help you less frequently fix broken tests due to content updates or changes, say from `h1` to `h2` or `div` to a more semantic element.

Now let's write a test for this component:

```
describe("Input", () => {
    it("should handle change event", () => {
        render(<Input />);
        const input = screen.getByTestId<HTMLInputElement>("userName");
        fireEvent.change(input, { target: { value: "Mikhail" } });

        expect(input.value).toBe("Mikhail");
```

```
    });
  });
```

In this test, as usual, we render the component, and then we find our element using the more convenient method, getByTestId. Next, we simulate the change event on input using the fireEvent.
change method, which takes the event object, and at the end of the test, we assert the entered
value in the expected one. In this way, we can now test large forms with various logic for formatting, validation, and so on.

Just like testing components, the React Testing Library can also test Hooks. This allows testing
only the custom logic and abstracting away from the components. Let's write a small useCounter
Hook, which will return the current counter value and the increment and decrement functions:

```
export function useCounter(initialValue: number = 0) {
  const [count, setCount] = useState(initialValue);

  const increment = () => setCount((c) => c + 1);
  const decrement = () => setCount((c) => c - 1);

  return { count, increment, decrement };
}
```

In order to test this Hook, instead of using the render function, the React Testing Library has a
renderHook method. This is what a test of this Hook would look like:

```
test("useCounter", () => {
  const { result } = renderHook(() => useCounter());

  expect(result.current.count).toBe(0);

  act(() => {
    result.current.increment();
  });

  expect(result.current.count).toBe(1);

  act(() => {
    result.current.decrement();
  });
```

```
    expect(result.current.count).toBe(0);
});
```

Initially, we render the Hook itself and check that the initial value is zero. The renderHook method returns the result object, through which we can read the data returned from the Hook. Next, we need to test the increment and decrement methods. To do this, it is not enough to simply call them, as Hooks are not pure functions by nature and contain a lot of logic under the hood. Therefore, we need to call those methods wrapped in the act method, which will synchronously wait for the method to execute and the Hook to re-render. After that, we can assert the expectations in the usual way. The output will look the same as we saw in the previous example, but let's now try to update the test to make failed results. Updating the first assertion from .toBe(0) to .toBe(10) will look like:

```
AssertionError: expected +0 to be 10 // Object.is equality


 - Expected
 + Received


 - 10
 + 0


 ❯ src/useCounter.test.ts:8:32
      6|    const { result } = renderHook(() => useCounter());
      7|
      8|    expect(result.current.count).toBe(10);
       |                                 ^
      9|
     10|    act(() => {


 ───────────────────────────────────────────


 ────────────────[1/1]─


 Test Files  1 failed (1)
      Tests  1 failed (1)
   Start at  14:24:06
   Duration  200ms
```

You will notice how Vitest highlights the part of the code where we got a failed assertion.

In this section, we have learned how we can test components and Hooks using the React Testing Library.

Summary

In this chapter, we explored the broad and extensive topic of testing. We became acquainted with the concept itself, testing types, and various approaches. Then, we delved into unit testing and learned what it is, and what possibilities this type of testing offers. After that, we learned how to set up the environment and write tests for regular functions and logic. At the end of the chapter, we examined the basic capabilities of testing React components and Hooks.

With this chapter, we conclude our acquaintance with the amazing ReactJS library and will next dive deeper into the React ecosystem with the incredible opportunity to create mobile applications based on React Native.

Join us on Discord!

Read this book alongside other users and the authors themselves. Ask questions, provide solutions to other readers, chat with the authors, and more. Scan the QR code or visit the link to join the community.

https://packt.link/ReactAndReactNative5e

Part 2

React Native

In this part, we look at building mobile apps with the **React Native** library. We'll explore the basic API and some common approaches to help you develop solid and performant applications.

This part contains the following chapters:

15

Why React Native?

Meta (formerly Facebook) created React Native to build its mobile applications. It was started as a hackathon project in the summer of 2013 inside Facebook and open sourced for everyone in 2015. The motivation to do so originated from the fact that React for the web was so successful. So, if React is such a good tool for UI development, and you need a native application, then why fight it? Just make React work with native mobile OS UI elements! Therefore, in the same year, Facebook divided React into two independent libraries, React and ReactDOM, and since then, React had to work only with interfaces and not care about where these elements will be rendered.

In this chapter, you'll learn about the motivations for using React Native to build native mobile web applications. Here are the topics that we'll cover in this chapter:

- What is React Native?
- React and JSX are familiar
- The mobile browser experiences
- Android and iOS: different yet the same
- The case for mobile web apps

Technical requirements

There aren't any technical requirements for this chapter since it is a brief conceptual introduction to React Native.

What is React Native?

Earlier in this book, I introduced the notion of a render target, the thing that React components render to. The render target is abstract as far as the React programmer is concerned. For example, in React, the render target can be a string, or it could be the **Document Object Model (DOM)**. Therefore, your components never directly interface with the render target because you can never make assumptions about where the rendering is taking place.

A mobile platform has **UI widget libraries** that developers can leverage to build apps for that platform. On Android, developers implement apps using **Java** or **Kotlin**, while, on iOS, developers implement **Objective-C** or **Swift** apps. If you want a functional mobile app, you're going to have to pick one. However, you'll need to learn both languages, as supporting only one of two major platforms isn't realistic for success.

For React developers, this isn't a problem. The same React components that you build work all over the place, even on mobile browsers! Having to learn two more programming languages to build and ship a mobile application is cost- and time-intensive. The solution to this is to introduce a new React platform that supports a new render target: native mobile UI widgets.

React Native uses a technique that makes asynchronous calls to the underlying mobile OS, which calls the native widget APIs. There's a JavaScript engine, and the React API is mostly the same as React for the web. The difference is with the target; instead of a DOM, there are asynchronous API calls. The concept is visualized here:

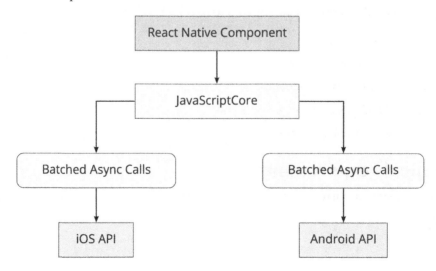

Figure 15.1: React Native workflow

This oversimplifies everything that's happening under the hood but the basic ideas are as follows:

- The same React library that's used on the web is used by **React Native** and runs in **JavaScriptCore**.

- Messages that are sent to native platform APIs are asynchronous and batched for performance purposes.

- React Native ships with components implemented for mobile platforms, instead of components that are HTML elements.

- React Native is just a way to render components via iOS and Android APIs. It can be replaced using the same concept with tvOS, Android TV, Windows, macOS, and even Web again. This is reachable by **forks** and add-ons for React Native. In this part of the book, we will learn how to write mobile apps for iOS and Android. More information about other possible platforms can be found here: `https://reactnative.dev/docs/out-of-tree-platforms`.

Much more on the history and mechanics of React Native can be found at `https://engineering.fb.com/2015/03/26/android/react-native-bringing-modern-web-techniques-to-mobile/`

React and JSX are familiar

Implementing a new render target for React is not straightforward. It's essentially the same thing as inventing a new DOM that runs on iOS and Android. So, why go through all the trouble?

First, there's a huge demand for mobile apps. The reason is that the mobile web browser user experience isn't as good as the native app experience. Second, JSX is a fantastic tool for building UIs. Rather than having to learn new technology, it's much easier to use what you know.

It's the latter point that's the most relevant to you. If you're reading this book, you're probably interested in using React for both web applications and native mobile applications. I can't put into words how valuable React is from a development-resource perspective. Instead of having a team that does web UIs, a team that does iOS, a team that does Android, and so on, there's just the UI team that understands React.

In the following section, you'll learn about the challenges of delivering good user experiences on mobile web browsers.

The mobile browser experiences

Mobile browsers lack many capabilities of mobile applications. This is because browsers cannot replicate the same native platform widgets as HTML elements. You can try to do this, but it's often better to just use the native widget rather than try to replicate it. This is partly because this requires less maintenance effort on your part, and partly because using widgets that are native to the platform means that they're consistent with the rest of the platform. For example, if a date picker in your application looks different from all the date pickers the user interacts with on their phone, this isn't a good thing. Familiarity is key and using native platform widgets makes familiarity possible.

User interactions on mobile devices are fundamentally different from the interactions that you typically design for the web. Web applications assume the presence of a mouse, for example, and that the click event on a button is just one phase. However, things become more complicated when the user uses their fingers to interact with the screen. Mobile platforms have what's called a **gesture system** to deal with this. React Native is a much better candidate for handling gestures than React for the web because it handles these types of things that you don't have to think about much in a web app.

As the mobile platform is updated, you want the components of your app to stay updated, too. This isn't a problem with React Native because the app uses actual components from the platform. Once again, consistency and familiarity are important for a good user experience. So, when the buttons in your app look and behave in the same way as the buttons in every other app on the device, your app feels like part of the device.

Now that you understand what makes developing UIs for mobile browsers difficult, it's time to look at how React Native can bridge the gap between the different native platforms.

Android and iOS: different yet the same

When I first heard about React Native, I automatically thought that it would be some cross-platform solution that lets you write a single React application that will run natively on any device. However, the reality is more nuanced. While React Native allows for a significant amount of code sharing between platforms, it's essential to understand that iOS and Android are different on many fundamental levels, and their user experience philosophies are different as well.

React Native's goal is to "learn once, write anywhere" rather than "write once, run anywhere." This means that, in some cases, you'll want your app to take advantage of platform-specific widgets to provide a better user experience.

That being said, there have been advancements in the React Native ecosystem that enable more seamless cross-platform development.

For instance, **Expo** now supports web development, allowing you to run your app on the web using **React Native for Web**. This means that you can develop apps that work on Android, iOS, and the web using a single code base. Additionally, the **Tamagui UI kit** offers 100% support for both web and mobile platforms, making it easier to create apps that run on multiple platforms without sacrificing user experience.

In light of these developments, it's important to recognize that while React Native may not provide a perfect "write once, run anywhere" solution, it has come a long way in enabling more efficient cross-platform development. With tools like Expo and Tamagui, developers can create apps that work across different platforms while still taking advantage of platform-specific features when necessary.

In the next section, we'll look at the case where mobile web apps that run in the browser might be a better fit for your users.

The case for mobile web apps

Not every one of your users is going to be willing to install an app, especially if you don't yet have a high download count and rating. The barrier to entry is much lower with web applications: the user only needs a browser.

Despite not being able to replicate everything that native platform UIs have to offer, you can still implement awesome things in a mobile web UI. Maybe having a good web UI is the first step toward getting those download counts and ratings up for your mobile app.

Ideally, what you should aim for is the following:

- Standard web (laptop/desktop browsers)
- Mobile web (phone/tablet browsers)
- Mobile apps (phone-/tablet-native platform)

Putting an equal amount of effort into all three of these spaces probably doesn't make much sense, as your users probably favor one area over another. Once you know, for example, that there's a high demand for your mobile app compared to the web versions, that's when you allocate more effort there.

Summary

In this chapter, you learned that React Native is an effort by Facebook to reuse React to create native mobile applications. React and JSX are good at declaring UI components, and since there's now a huge demand for mobile applications, it makes sense to use what you already know for the web.

The reason there's such a demand for mobile applications over mobile browsers is that they just feel better. Web applications lack the ability to handle mobile gestures the same way apps can, and they generally don't feel like part of the mobile experience from a look-and-feel perspective.

React Native has evolved significantly over the years, enabling developers to create more efficient cross-platform applications. While it's true that iOS and Android have fundamental differences, React Native has made strides in providing a more seamless development experience across platforms. However, it's important to remember that React Native's goal is to "learn once, write anywhere" rather than "write once, run anywhere." This means that developers can still take advantage of platform-specific features to provide a better user experience.

Now that you know what React Native is and what its strengths are, you'll learn how to get started with new React Native projects in the following chapter.

16

React Native under the Hood

The previous chapter briefly touched on what React Native is and the differences that users experience between the React Native UI and mobile browsers.

In this chapter, we will dig deeper into React Native, becoming well-versed on how it performs on mobile devices and what we should attain before commencing any efforts with this framework. We will also look at what options we can execute for the native functionality of JavaScript and what restrictions we will be up against.

We will cover the following topics:

- Exploring the React Native architecture
- Explaining JavaScript and Native modules
- Exploring React Native components and APIs

Exploring the React Native architecture

Before understanding how React Native works, let's revisit some historical points about the React architecture and the differences between web and native mobile apps.

The state of web and mobile apps in the past

Meta released **React** in 2013 as a monolith tool for creating apps, using a component approach and a **virtual DOM**. It gave us the opportunity to develop web applications without thinking about browser processes, such as parsing JS code, creating the DOM, and handling layers and rendering. We just had to create interfaces using state and props for data and CSS for styling, fetch data from the backend, save it in local storage, and so on.

React, together with browsers, allowed us to create a performance application in less time. At that time, the architecture of React looked like this:

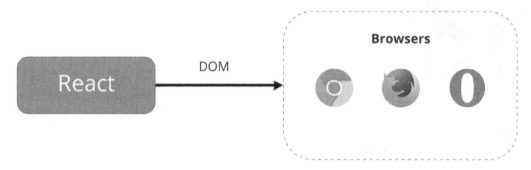

Figure 16.1: React architecture in 2013

The new declarative approach to developing interfaces became more favorable because of the fast development and the low threshold for novices. Additionally, if your backend is built with **Node.js**, you can benefit from the ease of support and development of the entire project using just one programming language.

At the same time, mobile apps require more complex techniques to create apps. For Android and iOS apps, companies should manage three different teams with unparalleled experience to support three major ecosystems:

- Web developers should know HTML, CSS, JS, and React.
- **Java** or **Kotlin** SDK experience is required for Android developers.
- The iOS developer should be familiar with **Objective-C** or **Swift** and **CocoaPods**.

Every step of developing an application, from prototyping to release, requires unique skills. Web and mobile app development before cross-platform solutions looked like this:

Figure 16.2: The state of web and mobile apps

Even if a corporation carries out a basic application, it can be faced with some major issues:

- Each of these teams implements the same business logic.
- There is no alternative to sharing code between teams.
- It is not conceivable to share resources between teams (Android developers can't write code for iOS applications, and vice versa).

As a result of these significant issues, we likewise have complications with having more testing resources, since there are more places to create bugs. The speed of development is also diverse because mobile apps take more time to deliver the same features. This all accumulates into a large, costly problem for the companies involved. Many of them came up with ideas on how to write a single code base or reuse a current one that can be used in multiple ecosystems. The simplest method would be to wrap a web app for mobile using a browser, but this has limitations in handling touch and gestures, as we explored in *Chapter 15, Why React Native?*.

In response to these issues, Meta started investing resources in developing a cross-platform framework and released the **React Native library** in 2015. Also, it divided React into two separate libraries. To render our app in the browser, we should now use the **ReactDOM** library.

In *Figure 16.3*, we can see how **React** works together with **ReactDOM** and **React Native** to render our apps:

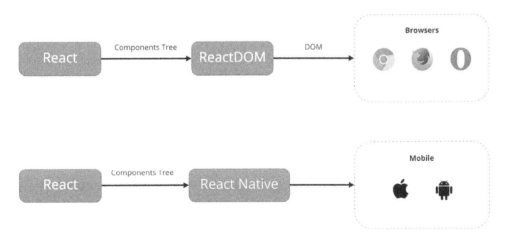

Figure 16.3: ReactDOM and React Native flow

Now, React only works to manage the components tree. This approach encapsulates any rendering APIs and hides a lot of platform-specific methods from us. We can concentrate solely on developing interfaces and cease speculating about how they would be rendered.

That's why React is frequently claimed as a renderer-agnostic library. Also, for web apps, we use ReactDOM, which forms elements and applies them right to the browser DOM. For mobile apps, React Native renders our interface directly on the mobile screen.

But how does React Native replace the whole browser API and allow us to write familiar code and run it on mobiles?

React Native current architecture

The React Native library allows you to create native applications with React and JS by utilizing native building blocks. For instance, the `<Image/>` component represents two other native components, `ImageView` on Android and `UIImageView` on iOS. This is viable because of the architecture of React Native, which includes two dedicated layers, represented by **JS** and **Native** threads:

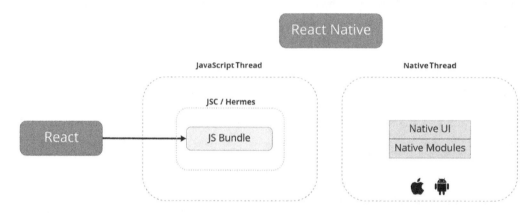

Figure 16.4: React Native threads

In the next sections, we will explore each thread and see how they can communicate, ensuring that JS is integrated into the native code.

JS as part of React Native

As the browser executes JS through **JS engines** such as **V8**, **SpiderMonkey**, and others, React Native also contains a **JS virtual machine**. There, our JS code is executed, API calls are made, touch events are processed, and many other processes occur.

Initially, React Native only supported Apple's **JavaScriptCore** virtual machine. With iOS devices, this virtual machine is built-in and available out of the box. In the case of Android, JavaScriptCore is bundled with React Native. This increases the size of the app.

Therefore, the *Hello World* application of React Native would consume approximately 3 to 4 MB on Android. From the 0.60 version, React Native started using the new **Hermes virtual machine**, and from 0.64, provided support for iOS as well.

The Hermes virtual machine introduced a lot of improvements for both platforms:

- Improvement of the app's startup time
- A size reduction of the downloaded app
- Decreased memory usage
- Built-in proxy support, enabling the use of **react-native-firebase** and **mobx**

Understanding the comparative benefits between the old and new architectures is a relatively common topic in interviews. More information about Hermes can be found here: `https://reactnative.dev/docs/hermes`.

JS in React Native, as in browsers, is implemented in a single thread. That thread is responsible for executing JS. The business logic we write is carried out in this thread. This means all our common code, such as components, state, Hooks, and REST API calls, will be handled in the JS part of the app.

Our entire application structure is packaged into a single file using the **Metro** bundler. It is also responsible for transpiling JSX code into JS. If we want to use TypeScript, **Babel** can support it. It works right out of the box, so there's no need to configure anything. In future chapters, we will learn how to start a ready-to-work project.

The "Native" part

Here is where native code is executed. React Native implements this part in native code for each platform: Java for Android and Objective-C for iOS. The **Native** layer is mainly composed of Native modules that communicate with the Android or iOS SDK and are supposed to provide native functionality for our apps, using a unified API. If we want to display an alert dialog, for instance, the **Native** layer presents a unified API for both platforms, which we will call from the JS thread using the single API.

This thread interacts with the JS thread when you need to update the interface or call the native functions. There are two parts to this thread:

- The first, the **React Native UI**, is responsible for using native interface shaping tools.
- The second is **Native Modules**, which allow applications to access the specific capabilities of the platform on which they run.

Communication between threads

As previously mentioned, each React Native layer implements a unique API for every native and UI feature in an application. The communication between layers is accomplished through the bridge. The module is written in C ++ and is based on an asynchronous queue. When the bridge receives data from one of the parties, it serializes it, converts it to a **JSON** string, and passes it through the queue. After arriving at its destination, the data is deserialized.

As shown in the alert example, the native part accepts the call from JS and displays the dialog. In reality, the JS method, upon being invoked, sends a message to the **bridge**, and upon receiving this message, the Native part executes the instruction. Native messages may also be forwarded to the **JS** layer. On clicking the button, for example, the **Native** layer sends a message to the **JS** one with an onClick event. It can be imagined as follows:

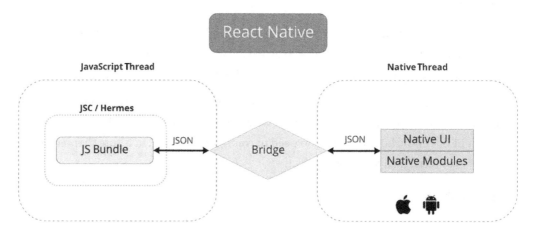

Figure 16.5: The bridge

JS and the Native part of this architecture, together with the bridge, resemble the server and client sides of web applications, where they communicate through the REST APIs. It does not matter to us in which language or how the Native part is implemented, since the code in JS is isolated. We simply send messages and receive responses from the bridge. This is both a significant advantage and a great disadvantage: first, it allows us to implement cross-platform apps with one code base, but it can be a bottleneck in our app when we have a lot of business logic in it. All events and actions in the application rely on asynchronous JSON-bridged messages. Each party sends these messages, expecting that sometime in the future, a response will be received from these messages (which is not guaranteed). With such a data exchange scheme, there is a risk of overloading the communication channel.

Here is an example commonly used to illustrate how such a communication scheme can cause performance problems for an application. Suppose a user of an application scrolls through a huge list. When the onScroll event occurs in the native environment, information is passed asynchronously to the JS environment. But native mechanisms do not wait until the JS part of the application does its job and reports to them about it. Because of this, there is a delay in the appearance of empty space in the list before displaying its contents. We can avoid a lot of usual problems using special approaches, such as using paginated FlatList on limitless lists. We will look at the main tricks in future chapters, but it is important to remember the limitations of the current architecture.

Styling

As we already understand the cross-platform concept, we can assume that each platform has its own technologies for creating and styling interfaces. In order to unify this, React Native has a **CSS-in-JS** syntax to style an app. Using **Flexbox**, components are able to specify the layout of their children. This ensures a consistent layout across different screen sizes. It is usually similar to how CSS works on the web, except the names are written in camel case, such as backgroundColor rather than background-color.

In JS, it is a plain object with style properties, and in native code, it is a separate thread called **Shadow**. It recalculates the layout of the application using the **Yoga** engine, which was developed by Meta. In this thread, the calculations related to the formation of the application interface are performed. The results of these calculations are sent to the Native UI thread responsible for displaying the interface.

With all the parts coming together, the final architecture of React Native is illustrated in this figure:

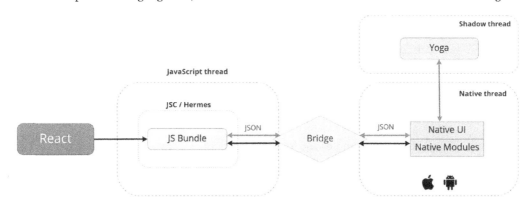

Figure 16.6: The current React Native architecture

The current architecture of React Native addresses major business problems: it is feasible to develop web and mobile applications within the same team, it is possible to reuse a large amount of business logic code, and even developers with no previous experience in mobile development can easily use React Native.

However, the current architecture is not ideal. Over the past few years, the React Native team has been working on a bridge bottleneck solution. The new architecture is designed to address this issue.

React Native future architecture

A series of significant improvements have been introduced to React Native that will streamline the development process and make it more convenient for everyone.

React Native's re-architecture will gradually deprecate the bridge and replace it with a new component called the **JS Interface (JSI)**. In addition, this element will enable new Fabric components and TurboModules.

The use of the JSI opens up many possibilities for improvement. In *Figure 16.7*, you can see the major updates to the React Native architecture:

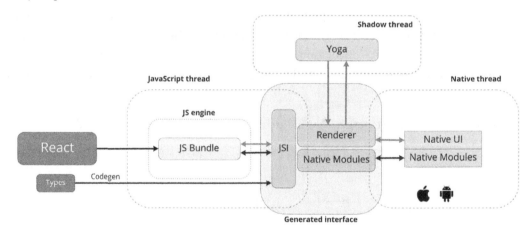

Figure 16.7: The new React Native architecture

The first change is that the JS bundle is no longer dependent on a **JavaScriptCore** virtual machine. It is actually part of the current architecture because, now, we can enable the new **Hermes JS engine** on both platforms. In other words, the JavaScriptCore engine can now easily be replaced with something else, quite possibly with better performance.

The second improvement is what lies at the heart of the new React Native architecture. The JSI allows JS to call native methods and functions directly. This was made possible by the HostObject C++ object, which stores references to native methods and properties. HostObject in JS binds native methods and props to a global object, so direct calls to JS functions will invoke Java or Objective-C APIs.

Another benefit of the new React Native is the ability to fully control native modules called TurboModules. Rather than starting them all at once, the application will only use them when they are needed.

Fabric is the new UI manager, called **Renderer** in *Figure 16.7*, which is expected to transform the rendering layer by eliminating the need for bridges. It is now possible to create a **Shadow Tree** directly in C++, which increases speed and reduces the number of steps to render a particular element.

In order to ensure smooth communication between React Native and Native parts, Meta is currently working on a tool called **CodeGen**. It is expected to automate the compatibility of strongly typed native code and dynamically typed JS to make them synchronize. With this upgrade, there will be no need to duplicate the code for both threads, thereby enabling smooth synchronization.

The new architecture could open the way for the development of new designs that are capable of things that were not available in old React Native applications. The fact is that we now have at our disposal the power of C++. This means that with React Native, it will now be possible to create many more varieties of applications than before.

Here, we discussed the fundamentals that explain how React Native works. It is important to understand the architecture of the tools we use. Having this knowledge allows you to avoid mistakes during planning and prototyping, as well as maximize the potential of your future applications. In the following section, we will briefly explore how to extend React Native with modules.

Explaining JS and Native modules

React Native does not cover all the native capabilities out of the box. It only provides the most common features that you will need in a basic application. Also, the Meta team itself has recently moved some functions into its own modules in an effort to reduce the size of the overall application. For example, AsyncStorage, for storing data on a device, was moved into a separate package and must be installed if you plan to use it.

However, React Native is an extendable framework. We can add our own native modules and expose the JS API using the same bridge or JSI. Our focus in this book will not be on developing native modules, since we need prior experience with Objective-C or Java. Also, it is not necessary, since the React community has created an enormous number of ready-to-use modules for all cases. We will learn how to install native packages in subsequent chapters.

The following are a few of the most popular native modules, without which most projects couldn't prosper.

React Navigation

React Navigation is one of the best React Native navigation libraries for creating navigation menus and screens for your app. It's a good tool for beginners because it's stable, fast, and less buggy. The documentation is really good, and it provides examples for all use cases.

We'll learn more about React Navigation in *Chapter 19, Navigating between Screens.*

UI component libraries

The UI component libraries enable you to quickly assemble an application layout without wasting time designing and coding atomic elements. In addition, such libraries are often more stable and consistent, which leads to better results both in terms of UI and UX.

These are some of the most popular libraries (we will explore a few of them in greater detail in future chapters):

- **NativeBase:** This is a component library that enables developers to build universal design systems. It is built on top of React Native, allowing you to develop apps for Android, iOS, and the web.
- **React Native Element:** This provides an all-in-one UI kit for creating apps in React Native.
- **UI Kitten:** This is a React Native implementation of the **Eva Design System**. The framework contains a set of general-purpose UI components styled in a similar way.
- **React-native-paper:** This is a collection of customizable and production-ready components for React Native, following Google's Material Design guidelines.
- **Tamagui:** This UI kit provides components that can run on mobiles and the web.

Splash screen

Adding a splash screen to your mobile app can be a tedious task, since this screen should appear before the JS thread begins. The **react-native-bootsplash** package allows you to create a fancy splash screen from the command line. The package will do all the work for you if you provide it with an image and a background color.

Icons

Icons are an integral part of the visualization of interfaces. Different approaches are used to display icons and other vector graphics on each platform. React Native unifies this for us but only with additional libraries such as **react-native-vector-icons**. Using **react-native-svg**, you can also render **scalable vector graphics (SVGs)** in a React Native app.

Handling errors

Usually, when we develop a web application, we are able to handle errors without any difficulty, since they do not reach beyond the scope of JS. As a result, we have more control and stability in the event of critical bugs because if the application does not start at all, we can easily see the reason and open the logs in **DevTools**.

There are even more complications with React Native applications, since we have a Native component in addition to the JS of the environment, which can also cause errors in application execution. Therefore, when an error occurs, our application will close immediately. It will be hard for us to figure out why.

`react-native-exception-handler` provides a simple technique for handling native and JS errors and providing feedback. To make it work, you need to install and link the module. Then, register your global handler for JS and native exceptions, as follows:

```
import { setJSExceptionHandler, setNativeExceptionHandler }
  from "react-native-exception-handler";

setJSExceptionHandler((error, isFatal) => {
  // …
});

const exceptionhandler = (exceptionString) => {
  // your exception handler code here
};
```

```
setNativeExceptionHandler(
  exceptionhandler,
  forceAppQuit,
  executeDefaultHandler
);
```

The `setJSExceptionHandler` and `setNativeExceptionHandler` methods are custom global error handlers. If a crash occurs, you can show an error message, use Google Analytics to track it, or use a custom API to inform the development team.

Push notifications

We live in a world where notifications are integral. We open dozens of apps every day just because we receive notifications from them.

Push notifications are often connected to a gateway provider that sends messages to users' devices. The following libraries can be used to add push notifications to your application:

- `react-native-onesignal`: A OneSignal provider for push notifications, email, and SMS
- `react-native-firebase`: Google Firebase
- `@aws-amplify/pushnotification`: AWS Amplify

Over-the-air updates

As part of a normal application update, when you build a new version and upload it to the app store, you can replace the JS package **over the air (OTA)**. As the bundle contains only one file, updating it is not complicated. You can update your application as often as you like without waiting for Apple or Google to verify your application. That is the real power of React Native.

We can use it due to the **CodePush** service made by Microsoft. You can find more information about CodePush here: `https://docs.microsoft.com/en-gb/appcenter/distribution/codepush/`.

Expo also supports OTA updates with the `expo-updates` package.

JS libraries

As for JS (non-native) modules, we have almost no restrictions, except for libraries that use unsupported APIs, such as the DOM and Node.js. We can use any packages written in JS: `Moment`, `Lodash`, `Axios`, `Redux`, `MobX`, and a thousand others.

We have barely scratched the surface of the possibilities to extend an application with various modules in this section. Because React Native has thousands of libraries, it makes little sense to go through them all. In order to find the required package you need, there is a project called **React Native Directory** that has collected and rated a huge list of packages. The project can be found here: `https://reactnative.directory/`.

We now know how React Native is organized internally and how we can expand its functionality. Our next step is to examine what API and components this framework offers.

Exploring React Native components and APIs

The main modules and components will be discussed in detail in each new chapter, but for now, let's familiarize ourselves with them. A number of core components are available in the React Native framework for use in an app.

Almost all apps use at least one of these components. These are the fundamental building blocks of React Native apps:

- `View`: The main brick of any app. This is the equivalent of `<div>`, and on mobiles, it is represented as `UIView` or `android.view`. Any `<View/>` component can nest inside another `<View/>` component and can have zero or many children of any type.

- `Text`: This is a React component for displaying text. As with `View`, `<Text/>` supports nesting, styling, and touch handling.

- `Image`: This displays images from a variety of sources, such as network images, static resources, temporary local images, and images from the camera roll.

- `TextInput`: This allows users to input text using a keyboard. Props enable a variety of features that can be configured, including auto-correction, auto-capitalization, placeholder text, and different keyboard types, such as a numeric keypad.

- `ScrollView`: This component is a generic container for scrolling multiple views and components. There can be both vertical and horizontal scrolling (by adjusting the horizontal property) for the scrollable items. If you need to render a huge or limitless list of items, you should use `FlatList`. This supports a set of special props such as **Pull to Refresh** and **Scroll loading** (lazy-loading). If your list needs to be divided into sections, then there is also a special component for this: `SectionList`.

- `Button`: React Native has advanced components that can be used to create custom buttons and other touchable components, such as `TouchableHighlight`, `TouchableOpacity`, and `TouchableWithoutFeedback`.

- `Pressable`: This gives more precise touch control with React Native version 0.63. Basically, it is a wrapper for detecting touch. It is a well-defined component that can be used instead of touchable components such as `TouchableOpacity` and `Button`.

- `Switch`: This component resembles a checkbox; however, it is presented in the form of a switch, which we are familiar with on mobile devices.

In the following chapters, we will delve deeper into common components and their properties, as well as explore new components that are rarely used. We'll also look at code examples that show how to combine components to create application interfaces.

Detailed information about all the available components can be found at `https://reactnative.dev/docs/components-and-apis`.

Summary

In this chapter, we looked at the history of the cross-platform framework React Native and what problems it solved for companies. With it, companies can use a single universal developer team to build one business logic and apply it to all platforms simultaneously, thus saving a lot of time and money. Considering, in detail, how React Native works under the hood allows us to identify potential issues at the planning stage and resolve them.

Additionally, we started to examine React Native's basic components, and with each new chapter, we will learn more about them.

In the next chapter, you'll learn how to get started with new React Native projects.

17

Kick-Starting React Native Projects

In this chapter, you'll get up and running with React Native. Thankfully, much of the boilerplate code involved in the creation of a new project is handled for you by the command-line tools. We will look at the different CLI tools for React Native apps and create our first simple app, which you will be able to upload and start right on your device.

In this chapter, we'll cover the following topics:

- Exploring React Native CLI tools
- Installing and using the Expo command-line tool
- Viewing your app on your phone
- Viewing your app on Expo Snack

Technical requirements

You can find the code files of this chapter on GitHub at `https://github.com/PacktPublishing/React-and-React-Native-5E/tree/main/Chapter17`.

Exploring React Native CLI tools

To simplify and speed up the development process, we use special command-line tools that install blank projects with application templates, dependencies, and other tools for starting, building, and testing. There are two major CLI approaches we can apply:

- The React Native CLI
- The Expo CLI

The **React Native CLI** is a tool created by Meta. The project is based on the original CLI tool and has three parts: native iOS and Android projects and a React Native JavaScript app. To get started, you will need either **Xcode** or **Android Studio**. One of the main advantages of the React Native CLI is its flexibility. You can connect any library with a Native module or directly write code to the native parts. However, all of this requires at least a basic understanding of mobile development.

The **Expo CLI** is just one part of the big ecosystem for developing React Native apps. **Expo** is a framework and a platform for universal React applications. Built around React Native and native platforms, it allows you to build, deploy, test, and rapidly iterate on iOS, Android, and web apps from a single JavaScript/TypeScript code base.

The Expo framework provides the following:

- The **Expo CLI**: A command-line tool that can create blank projects, then run, build, and update them.

- **Expo Go**: An Android and iOS app for running your projects directly on your device (without having to compile and sign native apps) and sharing them with your entire team.

- **Expo Snack**: The online playground that allows you to develop React Native apps in the browser.

- **Expo Application Services** (**EAS**): A set of deeply integrated cloud services for Expo and React Native applications. Apps can be compiled, signed, and uploaded to stores using EAS in the cloud.

Expo comes with a huge number of ready-to-use features. Previously, it imposed limitations on projects, as it did not support custom native modules. However, this limitation no longer exists. Expo now supports adding custom native code and customizing that native code (Android/Xcode projects) through Expo development builds. To use any custom native code, you can create a development build and config plugins.

Since Expo is useful for new developers without mobile development skills, we will use it to set up our first React Native project.

Installing and using the Expo command-line tool

The **Expo command-line tool** handles the creation of all of the scaffolding that your project needs to run a basic React Native application. Additionally, Expo has a couple of other tools that make running our app during development nice and straightforward. But first, we need to set up the environment and project:

1. Before we can use Expo, we need to install **Node.js**, **Git**, and **Watchman**. Watchman is a tool for watching files in our project to trigger actions like rebuilds when they change. All of the required tools and details can be found here: `https://docs.expo.dev/get-started/installation/#requirements`.

2. Once this installation is complete, we can start a new project by running the command:

```
npx create-expo-app --template
```

3. Next, the CLI will ask you questions about your future project. You should see something like this in your terminal:

```
? Choose a template: ' - Use arrow-keys. Return to submit.
    Blank
>   Blank (TypeScript) - blank app with TypeScript enabled
    Navigation (TypeScript)
    Blank (Bare)
```

   We'll choose the `Blank (TypeScript)` option.

4. Next, the process will ask you about a project name:

```
? What is your app named? ' my-project
```

   Let's call it `my-project`.

5. After installing all the dependencies, Expo will finish creating your project for you:

```
✓ Your project is ready!
```

Now that we have created a blank React Native project, you'll learn how to launch the Expo development server on your computer and view the app on one of your devices.

Viewing your app on your phone

In order to view your React Native project on your device during development, we need to start the Expo development server:

1. In the command-line terminal, make sure that you're in the project directory:

```
cd path/to/my-project
```

2. Once you're in `my-project`, you can run the following command to start the development server:

```
npm start
```

3. This will show you some information about the developer server in the terminal:

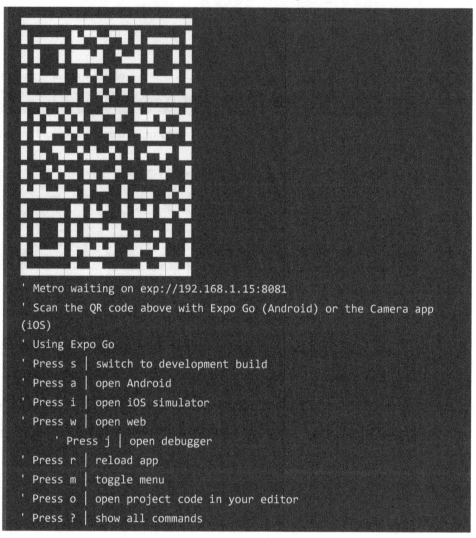

```
' Metro waiting on exp://192.168.1.15:8081
' Scan the QR code above with Expo Go (Android) or the Camera app
(iOS)
' Using Expo Go
' Press s │ switch to development build
' Press a │ open Android
' Press i │ open iOS simulator
' Press w │ open web
    ' Press j │ open debugger
' Press r │ reload app
' Press m │ toggle menu
' Press o │ open project code in your editor
' Press ? │ show all commands
```

4. In order to view the app on our devices, we need to install the **Expo Go** app. You can find it in the Play Store on Android devices or in the App Store on iOS devices. Once you have Expo installed, you scan the QR code using the native camera on your device:

Figure 17.1: Expo Go app

If you log in to Expo Go and the Expo CLI, you will be able to run the app without the QR code. In *Figure 17.1*, you can see the opened development session for my-project; if you click on it, the app will run.

5. Once the QR code is scanned or your opened session on Expo Go is clicked, you'll notice new logs and a new connected device in the terminal:

```
iOS Bundling complete 205ms
```

6.   Now you should see your app running:

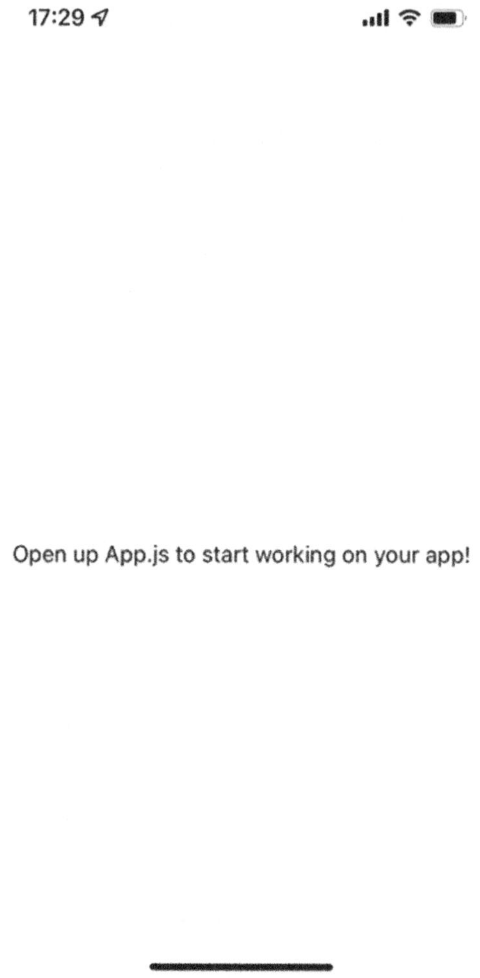

17:29 ✈   .ıll 🛜 🔋

Open up App.js to start working on your app!

Figure 17.2: Opened app in Expo Go

At this point, you're ready to start developing your app. In fact, you can repeat this same process
if you have several physical devices that you want to work with at the same time. The best part
of this Expo setup is that we get live reloading for free on our physical devices as we make code
updates on our computers. Let's try this now to make sure that everything works as expected:

1. Let's open up the App.ts file inside the my-project folder. There, you'll see the App component:

```
export default function App() {
  return (
    <View style={styles.container}>
      <Text>Open up App.tsx to start working on your app!</Text>
      <StatusBar style="auto" />
    </View>
  );
}
```

2. Now let's make a small style change to make the font bold:

```
export default function App() {
  return (
    <View style={styles.container}>
      <Text style={styles.text}>
        Open up App.tsx to start working on your app!
      </Text>
      <StatusBar style="auto" />
    </View>
  );
}

const styles = StyleSheet.create({
  container: {
    flex: 1,
    backgroundColor: "#fff",
    alignItems: "center",
    justifyContent: "center",
  },
  text: { fontWeight: "bold" },
});
```

3. We've added a new style called `text` and applied it to the `Text` component. If you save the file and return to your device, you'll immediately see the change applied:

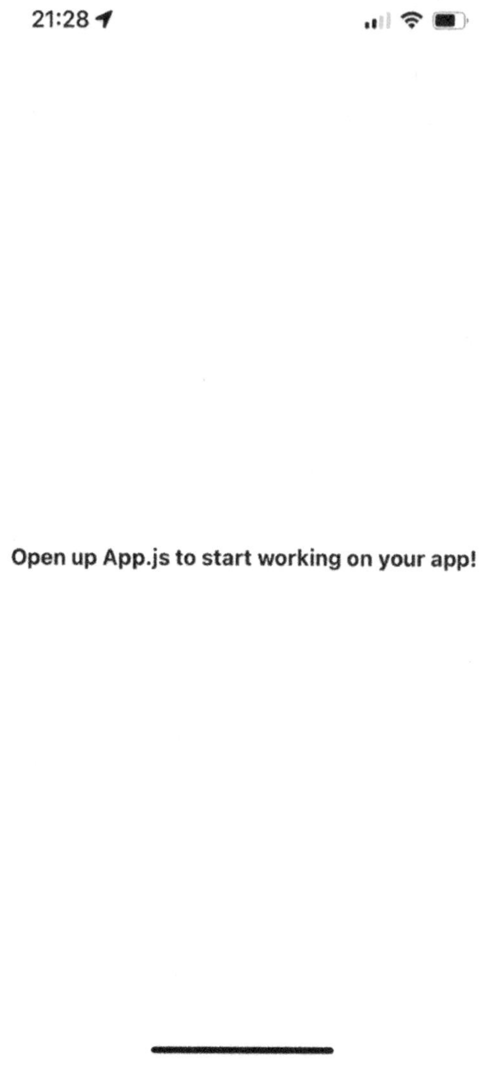

21:28 ✈   ⁝⁝ 🔋 ▇

Open up App.js to start working on your app!

_____

Figure 17.3: App with updates to style of text

Now that you're able to run your apps locally on your physical devices, it's time to look at running your React Native apps on a variety of virtual device emulators using the Expo Snack service.

Viewing your app on Expo Snack

The **Snack** service provided by Expo is a playground for your React Native code. It lets you organize your React Native project files just like you would locally on your computer. If you end up putting something together that is worth building on, you can export your Snack. You can also create an Expo account and save your Snacks to keep working on them or to share them with others. You can find Expo Snack with this link: `https://snack.expo.dev/`.

We can create a React Native app in Expo Snack from scratch, and it will be stored in an Expo account, or we can import existing projects from a Git repository. The nice thing about importing a repository is that when you push changes to Git, your Snack will also be updated. The Git URL for the example that we've worked on in this chapter looks like this: `https://github.com/PacktPublishing/React-and-React-Native-5E/tree/main/Chapter17/my-project`.

We can click on the **Import git repository** button in the Snack project menu and paste in this URL:

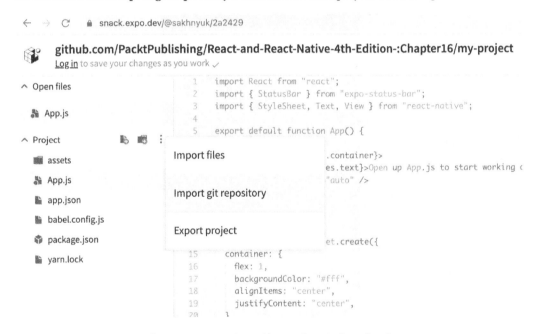

Figure 17.4: Importing a Git repository to Expo Snack

Once the repository is imported and the Snack is saved, you'll get an updated Snack URL that reflects the Git repository location. For example, the Snack URL from this chapter looks like this: `https://snack.expo.dev/@sakhnyuk/2a2429`.

If you open this URL, the Snack interface will load and you can make changes to the code to test things out before running them. The main advantage of Snack is the ability to easily run it on virtualized devices. The controls to run your app on a virtual device can be found on the right side of the UI and look like this:

Figure 17.5: Expo Snack emulator

The top control above the image of the phone controls which device type to emulate: **Android**, **iOS**, or **Web**. The **Tap to play** button will launch the selected virtual device. The **Run on your device** button allows you to run the app in Expo Go using the QR code approach.

Here's what our app looks like on a virtual iOS device:

Figure 17.6: Expo Snack iOS emulator

And here's what our app looks like on a virtual Android device:

Figure 17.7: Expo Snack Android emulator

This app only displays text and applies some styles to it, so it looks pretty much identical on different platforms. As we make our way through the React Native chapters in this book, you'll see how useful a tool such as Snack is for making comparisons between the two platforms to understand the differences between them.

Summary

In this chapter, you learned how to kick-start a React Native project using the Expo command-line tool. First, you learned how to install the Expo tool. Then, you learned how to initialize a new React Native project. Next, you started the Expo development server and learned about the various parts of the development server UI.

In particular, you learned how to connect the development server with the Expo app on any device that you want to test your app on. Expo also has the Snack service, which lets us experiment with snippets of code or entire Git repositories. You learned how to import a repository and run it on virtual iOS and Android devices.

In the next chapter, we'll look at how to build responsive layouts in our React Native apps.

18

Building Responsive Layouts with Flexbox

In this chapter, you'll get a feel for what it's like to lay components out on the screen of mobile devices. Thankfully, React Native polyfills many CSS properties that you might have used in the past to implement page layouts in web applications.

Before you dive into implementing layouts, you'll get a brief introduction to Flexbox and using CSS style properties in React Native apps: it's not quite what you're used to with regular CSS style sheets. Then, you'll implement several React Native layouts using Flexbox.

We will cover the following topics in this chapter:

- Introducing Flexbox
- Introducing React Native styles
- Using the Styled Components library
- Building Flexbox layouts

Technical requirements

You can find the code files present in this chapter on GitHub at https://github.com/PacktPublishing/React-and-React-Native-5E/tree/main/Chapter18.

Introducing Flexbox

Before the flexible box layout model was introduced to CSS, the various approaches used to build layouts were convoluted and prone to errors. For example, we used **floats**, which were originally intended for text wrapping around images, for table-based layouts. **Flexbox** solves this by abstracting many of the properties that you would normally have to provide in order to make the layout work.

In essence, the Flexbox model is what it probably sounds like to you: a box model that's flexible. That's the beauty of Flexbox: its simplicity. You have a box that acts as a container, and you have **child** elements within that box. Both the container and the **child** elements are flexible in how they're rendered on the screen, as illustrated here:

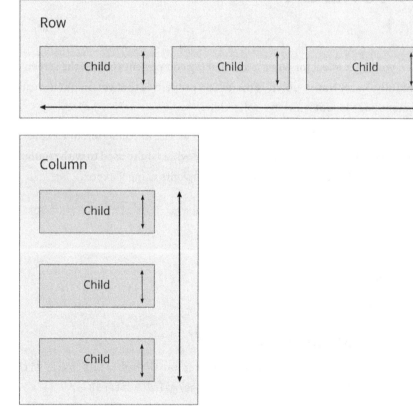

Figure 18.1: Flexbox elements

Flexbox containers have a direction, either column (up/down) or row (left/right). This actually confused me when I was first learning about Flexbox; my brain refused to believe that rows were organized beside each other from left to right. Rows are stacked on top of one another! The key thing to remember is that it's the direction in which the box flexes, not the direction in which boxes are placed on the screen.

 For a more in-depth treatment of Flexbox concepts, refer to https://css-tricks. com/snippets/css/a-guide-to-Flexbox.

Now that we've covered the basics of Flexbox layouts at a high level, it's time to learn how styles in React Native applications work.

Introducing React Native styles

It's time to implement your first React Native app, beyond the boilerplate that's generated by **Expo**. I want to make sure that you feel comfortable using React Native style sheets before you start implementing Flexbox layouts in the next section.

Here's what a React Native style sheet looks like:

```
import { Platform, StyleSheet, StatusBar } from "react-native";
export default StyleSheet.create({
  container: {
    flex: 1,
    justifyContent: "center",
    alignItems: "center",
    backgroundColor: "ghostwhite",
    ...Platform.select({
      ios: { paddingTop: 20 },
      android: { paddingTop: StatusBar.currentHeight },
    }),
  },
  box: {
    width: 100,
    height: 100,
    justifyContent: "center",
    alignItems: "center",
    backgroundColor: "lightgray",
```

```
    },
    boxText: {
        color: "darkslategray",
        fontWeight: "bold",
    },
});
```

This is a **JavaScript** module, not a CSS module. If you want to declare React Native styles, you need to use plain objects. Then, you call StyleSheet.create() and export this from the style module. Note that style names are pretty similar to the web CSS, except that they are written in camel case; for example, justifyContent rather than justify-content.

As you can see, this style sheet has three styles: container, box, and boxText. Within the container style, there's a call to Platform.select():

```
...Platform.select({
ios: { paddingTop: 20 },
android: { paddingTop: StatusBar.currentHeight }
})
```

This function will return different styles based on the platform of the mobile device. Here, you're handling the top padding of the top-level container view. You'll probably use this code in most of your apps to make sure that your React components don't render underneath the status bar of the device. Depending on the platform, the padding will require different values. If it's iOS, paddingTop is 20. If it's Android, paddingTop will be the value of StatusBar.currentHeight.

The preceding Platform.select() code is an example of a case where you need to implement a workaround for differences in the platform. For example, if StatusBar.currentHeight was available on iOS and Android, you wouldn't need to call Platform.select().

Let's see how these styles are imported and applied to React Native components:

```
import React from "react";
import { Text, View } from "react-native";
import styles from "./styles";
export default function App() {
  return (
    <View style={styles.container}>
```

```
        <View style={styles.box}>
          <Text style={styles.boxText}>I'm in a box</Text>
        </View>
      </View>
    );
  }
```

The styles are assigned to each component via the `style` property. You're trying to render a box with some text in the middle of the screen. Let's make sure that this looks as we expect it to.

Figure 18.2: Box in the middle of a screen

We have found out how to apply styles to components using a built-in module, but there is more than one way to define styles. We also have the option to write CSS in React Native. Let's quickly go through it.

Using the Styled Components library

Styled Components is a CSS-in-JS library that styles React Native components using plain CSS. With this approach, you don't need to define style classes via objects and provide style props. The CSS itself is determined via tagged template literals provided by `styled-components`.

To install `styled-components`, run this command in your project:

```
npm install --save styled-components
```

Let's try to rewrite components from the *Introducing React Native styles* section. This is what our Box component looks like:

```
import styled from "styled-components/native";
const Box = styled.View'
  width: 100px;
  height: 100px;
  justify-content: center;
  align-items: center;
  background-color: lightgray;
';
const BoxText = styled.Text'
  color: darkslategray;
  font-weight: bold;
';
```

In this example, we've got two components, Box and BoxText. Now we can use them as usual, but without any other additional styling props:

```
const App = () => {
  return (
    <Box>
      <BoxText>I'm in a box</BoxText>
    </Box>
  );
};
```

In further sections, I will use `StyleSheet` objects, but I will avoid `styled-components` for per-formance reasons. If you want to learn more about `styled-components`, you can read more here: `https://styled-components.com/`.

Perfect! Now that you have an idea of how to set styles on React Native elements, let's use Flexbox to start creating some screen layouts.

Building Flexbox layouts

In this section, you'll learn about several potential layouts that you can use in your React Native applications. I want to stay away from the idea that one layout is better than another. Instead, I'll show you how powerful the Flexbox layout model is for mobile screens so that you can design the kind of layout that best suits your application.

Simple three-column layout

To start things off, let's implement a simple layout with three sections that flex in the column direction (top to bottom). We'll look at the result we are aiming for first.

Figure 18.3: Simple three-column layout

The idea, in this example, is that you style and label the three screen sections so that they stand out. In other words, these components wouldn't necessarily have any styling in a real application since they're used to arrange other components on the screen.

Now, let's take a look at the components used to create this screen layout:

```
import React from "react";
import { Text, View } from "react-native";
import styles from "./styles";
export default function App() {
  return (
    <View style={styles.container}>
      <View style={styles.box}>
        <Text style={styles.boxText}>#1</Text>
      </View>
      <View style={styles.box}>
        <Text style={styles.boxText}>#2</Text>
      </View>
      <View style={styles.box}>
        <Text style={styles.boxText}>#3</Text>
      </View>
    </View>
  );
}
```

The container view (the outermost `<View>` component) is the column and the child views are the rows. The `<Text>` component is used to label each row. In terms of HTML elements, `<View>` is similar to a `<div>` element, while `<Text>` is similar to a `<p>` element.

Maybe this example could have been called a three-row layout since it has three rows. But, at the same time, the three layout sections are flexing in the direction of the column that they're in. Use the naming convention that makes the most conceptual sense to you.

Now, let's take a look at the styles used to create this layout:

```
import { Platform, StyleSheet, StatusBar } from "react-native";


export default StyleSheet.create({
  container: {
    flex: 1,
    flexDirection: "column",
    alignItems: "center",
    justifyContent: "space-around",
    backgroundColor: "ghostwhite",
    ...Platform.select({
      ios: { paddingTop: 20 },
      android: { paddingTop: StatusBar.currentHeight }
    })
  },
  box: {
    width: 300,
    height: 100,
    justifyContent: "center",
    alignItems: "center",
    backgroundColor: "lightgray",
    borderWidth: 1,
    borderStyle: "dashed",
    borderColor: "darkslategray"
  },
  boxText: {
    color: "darkslategray",
    fontWeight: "bold"
  }
});
```

The flex and flexDirection properties of container enable the layout of the rows to flow from top to bottom. The alignItems and justifyContent properties align the child elements to the center of the container and add space around them, respectively.

Let's see how this layout looks when you rotate the device from a portrait orientation to a landscape orientation:

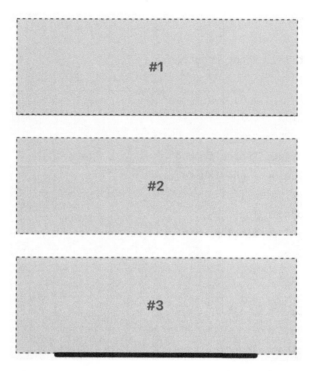

Figure 18.4: Landscape orientation

Flexbox automatically figured out how to preserve the layout for you. However, you can improve on this a little bit. For example, the landscape orientation now has a lot of wasted space to the left and right. You could create your own abstraction for the boxes that you're rendering. In the following section, we'll improve on this layout.

Improved three-column layout

There are a few things that I think you can improve on from the last example. Let's fix the styles so that the children of the Flexbox could stretch to take advantage of the available space. Do you remember, in the last example, when you rotated the device from a portrait orientation to a landscape orientation? There was a lot of wasted space. It would be nice to have the components automatically adjust themselves. Here's what the new style module looks like:

```
import { Platform, StyleSheet, StatusBar } from "react-native";

export default StyleSheet.create({
  container: {
    flex: 1,
    flexDirection: "column",
    backgroundColor: "ghostwhite",
    justifyContent: "space-around",
    ...Platform.select({
      ios: { paddingTop: 20 },
      android: { paddingTop: StatusBar.currentHeight },
    }),
  },
  box: {
    height: 100,
    justifyContent: "center",
    alignSelf: "stretch",
    alignItems: "center",
    backgroundColor: "lightgray",
    borderWidth: 1,
    borderStyle: "dashed",
    borderColor: "darkslategray",
  },
  boxText: {
    color: "darkslategray",
    fontWeight: "bold",
  },
});
```

The key change here is the alignSelf property. This tells elements with the box style to change their width or height (depending on the flexDirection of their container) to fill space. Also, the box style no longer defines a width property because this will be computed on the fly now.

Here's what the sections look like in portrait mode:

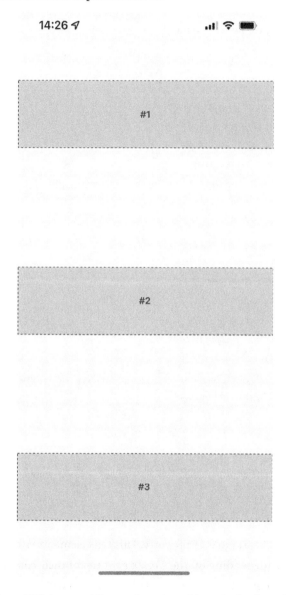

Figure 18.5: Improved three-column layout in portrait orientation

Now, each section takes the full width of the screen, which is exactly what you want to happen. The issue of wasted space was actually more prevalent in landscape orientation, so let's rotate the device and see what happens to these sections now.

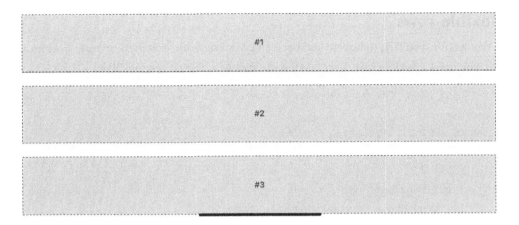

Figure 18.6: Improved three-column layout in landscape orientation

Now your layout is utilizing the entire width of the screen, regardless of orientation. Lastly, let's implement a proper Box component that can be used by App.js instead of having repetitive style properties in place. Here's what the Box component looks like:

```
import React from "react";
import { PropTypes } from "prop-types";
import { View, Text } from "react-native";
import styles from "./styles";
export default function Box({ children }) {
  return (
    <View style={styles.box}>
      <Text style={styles.boxText}>{children}</Text>
    </View>
  );
}
Box.propTypes = {
  children: PropTypes.node.isRequired,
};
```

You now have the beginnings of a nice layout. Next, you'll learn about flexing in the other direction: left to right.

Flexible rows

In this section, you'll learn how to make screen layout sections stretch from top to bottom. To do this, you need a **flexible row**. Here is what the styles for this screen look like:

```
import { Platform, StyleSheet, StatusBar } from "react-native";

export default StyleSheet.create({
  container: {
    flex: 1,
    flexDirection: "row",
    backgroundColor: "ghostwhite",
    alignItems: "center",
    justifyContent: "space-around",
    ...Platform.select({
      ios: { paddingTop: 20 },
      android: { paddingTop: StatusBar.currentHeight },
    }),
  },

  box: {
    width: 100,
    justifyContent: "center",
    alignSelf: "stretch",
    alignItems: "center",
    backgroundColor: "lightgray",
    borderWidth: 1,
    borderStyle: "dashed",
    borderColor: "darkslategray",
  },

  boxText: {
    color: "darkslategray",
    fontWeight: "bold",
  },
});
```

Here's the App component, using the same Box component that you implemented in the previous section:

```
import React from "react";
import { Text, View, StatusBar } from "react-native";
import styles from "./styles";
import Box from "./Box";
export default function App() {
  return (
    <View style={styles.container}>
      <Box>#1</Box>
      <Box>#2</Box>
    </View>
  );
}
```

Here's what the resulting screen looks like in portrait mode:

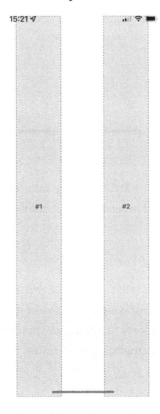

Figure 18.7: Flexible rows in portrait orientation

The two columns stretch all the way from the top of the screen to the bottom because of the alignSelf property, which doesn't actually specify which direction to stretch in. The two Box components stretch from top to bottom because they're displayed in a **flex row**. Note how the spacing between these two sections goes from left to right? This is because of the container's flexDirection property, which has a value of row.

Now, let's see how this flex direction impacts the layout when the screen is rotated to a landscape orientation.

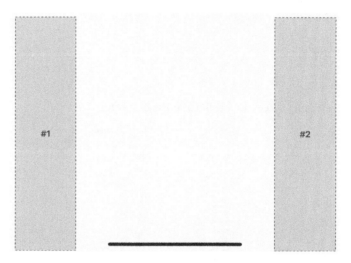

Figure 18.8: Flexible rows in landscape orientation

Since **Flexbox** has a justifyContent style property value of space-around, space is added proportionally to the left, the right, and in between the sections. In the following section, you'll learn about flexible grids.

Flexible grids

Sometimes, you need a screen layout that flows like a grid. For example, what if you have several sections that are the same width and height, but you're not sure how many of these sections will be rendered? Flexbox makes it easy to build a row that flows from left to right until the end of the screen is reached. Then, it automatically continues rendering elements from left to right on the next row.

Here's an example layout in portrait mode:

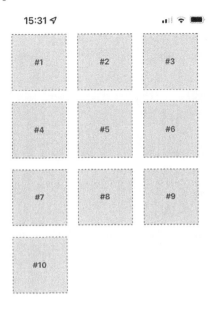

Figure 18.9: Flexible grids in portrait orientation

The beauty of this approach is that you don't need to know in advance how many columns are in a given row. The dimensions of each child determine what will fit in a given row.

To see the styles used to create this layout, you can follow this link: `https://github.com/` `PacktPublishing/React-and-React-Native-5E/tree/main/Chapter18/flexible-grids/` `styles.ts`.

Here's the App component that renders each section:

```
import React from "react";
import { View, StatusBar } from "react-native";
import styles from "./styles";
import Box from "./Box";
const boxes = new Array(10).fill(null).map((v, i) => i + 1);
export default function App() {
  return (
    <View style={styles.container}>
      <StatusBar hidden={false} />
      {boxes.map((i) => (
        <Box key={i}>#{i}</Box>
      ))}
    </View>
  );
}
```

Lastly, let's make sure that the landscape orientation works with this layout:

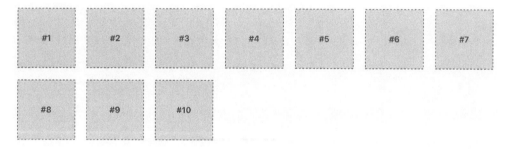

Figure 17.10: Flexible grids in landscape orientation

You may have noticed that there's some superfluous space on the right side. Remember, these sections are only visible in this book because we want them to be visible. In a real app, they're just grouping other React Native components. However, if the space to the right of the screen becomes an issue, play around with the margin and the width of the child components.

Now that you have an understanding of how **flexible grids** work, we'll look at flexible rows and columns next.

Flexible rows and columns

Let's learn how to combine rows and columns to create a sophisticated layout for your app. For example, sometimes, you need the ability to nest columns within rows or rows within columns. To see the App component of an application that nests columns within rows, you can follow this link: https://github.com/PacktPublishing/React-and-React-Native-5E/tree/main/Chapter18/flexible-rows-and-columns/App.tsx.

You've created abstractions for the layout pieces (<Row> and <Column>) and the content piece (<Box>). Let's see what this screen looks like:

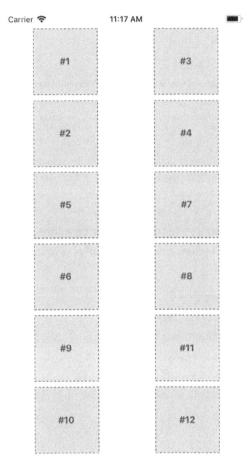

Figure 18.11: Flexible rows and columns

This layout probably looks familiar because you've done it in the *Flexible grids* section. The key difference as compared to *Figure 18.9* is in how these content sections are ordered.

For example, **#2** doesn't go to the right of **#1**, it goes below it. This is because we've placed **#1** and **#2** in `<Column>`. The same happens with **#3** and **#4**. These two columns are placed in a row. Then, the next row begins, and so on.

This is just one of many possible layouts that you can achieve by nesting row Flexboxes and column Flexboxes. Let's take a look at the Row component now:

```
import React from "react";
import PropTypes from "prop-types";
import { View, Text } from "react-native";
import styles from "./styles";
export default function Box({ children }) {
  return (
    <View style={styles.box}>
      <Text style={styles.boxText}>{children}</Text>
    </View>
  );
}
Box.propTypes = {
  children: PropTypes.node.isRequired,
};
```

This component applies the row style to the `<View>` component. The end result is cleaner JSX markup in the App component when creating a complex layout. Finally, let's look at the Column component:

```
import React from "react";
import PropTypes from "prop-types";
import { View } from "react-native";
import styles from "./styles";
export default function Column({ children }) {
  return <View style={styles.column}>{children}</View>;
}
Column.propTypes = {
  children: PropTypes.node.isRequired,
};
```

This looks just like the Row component, just with a different style applied to it. It also serves the same purpose as Row: to enable simpler JSX markup for layouts in other components.

Summary

This chapter introduced you to styles in React Native. Though you can use many of the same CSS style properties that you're used to, the CSS style sheets used in web applications look very different. Namely, they're composed of plain JavaScript objects.

Then, you learned how to work with the main React Native layout mechanism: **Flexbox**. This is the preferred way of laying out most web applications these days, so it makes sense to be able to reuse this approach in a Native app. You created several different layouts, and you saw how they looked in portrait and landscape orientation.

In the next chapter, you'll start implementing navigation for your app.

19

Navigating Between Screens

The focus of this chapter is on navigating between the screens that make up your React Native application. Navigation in native apps is slightly different than navigation on web apps: mainly because there isn't any notion of a URL that the user is aware of. In prior versions of React Native, there were primitive navigator components that you could use to control the navigation between screens. There were a number of challenges with these components that resulted in more code to accomplish basic navigation tasks. For example, initial navigation components, like `Navigator` and `NavigatorIOS`, were complex to implement and lacked features, leading to performance issues and inconsistency across platforms.

More recent versions of **React Native** encourage you to use the `react-navigation` package, which will be the focus of this chapter, even though there are several other options. You'll learn about navigation basics, passing parameters to screens, changing header content, using tab and drawer navigation, and handling state with navigation. Also, we'll take a look at a modern navigation approach called file-based navigation.

We'll cover the following topics in this chapter:

- The basics of navigation
- Route parameters
- The navigation header
- Tab and drawer navigation
- File-based navigation

Technical requirements

You can find the code files for this chapter on GitHub at https://github.com/PacktPublishing/
React-and-React-Native-5E/tree/main/Chapter19.

The basics of navigation

Navigation in React Native is crucial because it manages the transition between different screens
in an app. It improves user experience by organizing the app's flow logically, allowing users to
intuitively understand how to access features and information. Effective navigation makes an app
feel quick and responsive, reducing frustration and increasing user engagement. It also supports
the app's architecture, making it easier to scale and maintain by clearly defining how components
are linked and interact. Without proper navigation, an app can become confusing and difficult to
use, significantly impacting its success and user retention. This section will guide you through
setting up navigation in your app by creating a small app where you can navigate between screens.

Let's start off with the basics of moving from one page to another using the react-navigation
package.

Before starting, you should install the react-navigation package to a fresh project and some
additional dependencies related to the example:

```
npm install @react-navigation/native
```

Then, install native dependencies using expo:

```
npx expo install react-native-screens react-native-safe-area-context
```

The preceding installation steps will be required for each example in this chapter, but we need
to add one more package related to the stack navigator:

```
npm install @react-navigation/native-stack
```

Now, we are ready to develop navigation. Here's what the App component looks like:

```
import Home from "./Home";
import Settings from "./Settings";

const Stack = createNativeStackNavigator<RootStackParamList>();

export default function App() {
  return (
```

```
        <NavigationContainer>
          <Stack.Navigator>
            <Stack.Screen name="Home" component={Home} />
            <Stack.Screen name="Settings" component={Settings} />
          </Stack.Navigator>
        </NavigationContainer>
      );
    }
```

createNativeStackNavigator() is a function that sets up your navigation. It returns an object with two properties, the Screen and Navigator components, that are used for configuring the stack navigator.

The first argument to this function maps to the screen components that can be navigated. The second argument is for more general navigation options: in this case, you're telling the navigator that the homepage should be the default screen component that's rendered. The <NavigationContainer> component is necessary so that the screen components get all of the navigation properties that they need.

Here's what the Home component looks like:

```
    type Props = NativeStackScreenProps<RootStackParamList>;

    export default function Home({ navigation }: Props) {
      return (
        <View style={styles.container}>
          <StatusBar barStyle="dark-content" />
          <Text>Home Screen</Text>
          <Button
            title="Settings"
            onPress={() => navigation.navigate("Settings")}
          />
        </View>
      );
    }
```

This is your typical functional React component. You can use a class-based component here, but there's no need since there is no state or life cycle methods. It renders a View component where the container style is applied.

This is followed by a Text component that labels the screen followed by a Button component. A screen can be anything you want: it's just a regular React Native component. The navigator component handles the routing and the transitions between screens for you.

The onPress handler for this button navigates to the **Settings** screen when clicked. This is done by calling navigation.navigate('Settings'). The navigation property is passed to your screen component by react-navigation and contains all of the routing functionality you need. In contrast to working with URLs in React web apps, here you call navigator API functions and pass them the names of screens.

To get type safe environment in navigation, we need to define a type called RootStackParamList that contains all the information about our routes. We use it together with NativeStackScreenProps to define route Props. This is what RootStackParamList looks like:

```
export type RootStackParamList = {
  Home: undefined;
  Settings: undefined;
};
```

We pass undefined to each route because we don't have any parameters on routes. As a result, we can call navigation.navigate() only with Settings or Home.

Let's take a look at the Settings component:

```
type Props = NativeStackScreenProps<RootStackParamList>;

export default function Settings({ navigation }: Props) {
  return (
    <View style={styles.container}>
      <StatusBar barStyle="dark-content" />
      <Text>Settings Screen</Text>
      <Button title="Home" onPress={() => navigation.navigate("Home")} />
    </View>
  );
}
```

This component is just like the Home component, except with different text, and when the button is clicked, you're taken back to the **Home screen**.

This is what the **Home screen** looks like:

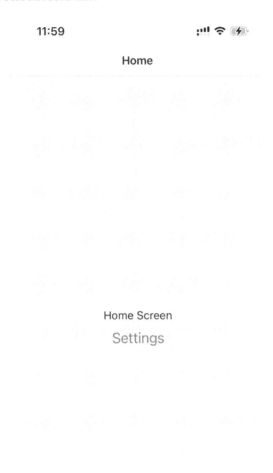

Figure 19.1: The Home screen

If you click the **Settings** button, you'll be taken to the **Settings screen**, which looks like this:

Figure 19.2: The Settings screen

This screen looks almost identical to the **Home screen**. It has different text and a different button that will take you back to the **Home screen** when clicked. However, there's another way to get back to the **Home screen**. Take a look at the top of the screen, where you'll notice a white navigation bar. On the left side of the navigation bar, there's a back arrow. This works just like the back button in a web browser and will take you back to the previous screen. What's nice about react-navigation is that it takes care of rendering this navigation bar for you.

> With this navigation bar in place, you don't have to worry about how your layout styles impact the status bar. You only need to worry about the layout of each of your screens.
>
> If you run this app on Android, you'll see the same back button in the navigation bar. But you can also use the standard back button found outside of the app on most Android devices.

In the next section, you'll learn how to pass parameters to your routes.

Route parameters

When you develop React web applications, some of your routes have **dynamic data** in them. For example, you can link to a details page, and within that URL, you'll have some sort of identifier. The component then has what it needs to render specific detailed information. The same concept exists within react-navigation. Instead of just specifying the name of the screen that you want to navigate to, you can pass along additional data.

Let's take a look at route parameters in action.

We'll start with the App component:

```
const Stack = createNativeStackNavigator<RootStackParamList>();

export default function App() {
  return (
    <NavigationContainer>
      <Stack.Navigator>
        <Stack.Screen name="Home" component={Home} />
        <Stack.Screen name="Details" component={Details} />
      </Stack.Navigator>
```

```
    </NavigationContainer>
  );
}
```

This looks just like the example in the *The basics of navigation* section, except instead of a Settings page, there's a Details page. This is the page that you want to pass data to dynamically so that it can render the appropriate information.

To enable TypeScript for our routes, need to define RootStackParamList:

```
export type RootStackParamList = {
  Home: undefined;
  Details: { title: string };
};
```

Next, let's take a look at the Home screen component:

```
type Props = NativeStackScreenProps<RootStackParamList, "Home">;

export default function Home({ navigation }: Props) {
  return (
    <View style={styles.container}>
      <StatusBar barStyle="dark-content" />
      <Text>Home Screen</Text>
      <Button
        title="First Item"
        onPress={() => navigation.navigate("Details", { title: "First
Item" })}
      />
      <Button
        title="Second Item"
        onPress={() => navigation.navigate("Details", { title: "Second
Item" })}
```

```
      />
      <Button
        title="Third Item"
        onPress={() => navigation.navigate("Details", { title: "Third
 Item" })}
      />
    </View>
  );
}
```

The Home screen has three Button components, and each navigates to the Details screen. Note that in the navigation.navigate() calls, in addition to the screen name, each has a second argument. These arguments are objects that contain specific data, which is passed to the Details screen.

Next, let's take a look at the Details screen and see how it consumes these route parameters:

```
type Props = NativeStackScreenProps<RootStackParamList, "Details">;

export default function ({ route }: Props) {
  const { title } = route.params;

  return (
    <View style={styles.container}>
      <StatusBar barStyle="dark-content" />
      <Text>{title}</Text>
    </View>
  );
}
```

Although this example is only passing one title parameter, you can pass as many parameters to the screen as you need to. You can access these parameters using the params value of the route prop to look up the value.

Here's what the **Home screen** looks like when rendered:

Figure 19.3: The Home screen

If you click on the **First Item** button, you'll be taken to the **Details** screen that is rendered using the route parameter data:

Figure 19.4: The Details screen

You can click the back button in the navigation bar to get back to the **Home** screen. If you click on any of the other buttons on the **Home screen**, you'll be taken back to the **Details** screen with updated data. Route parameters are necessary to avoid having to write duplicate components. You can think of passing parameters to `navigator.navigate()` as passing props to a React component.

In the following section, you'll learn how to populate navigation section headers with content.

The navigation header

The navigation bars that you've created so far in this chapter have been sort of plain. That's because you haven't configured them to do anything, so react-navigation will just render a plain bar with a back button. Each screen component that you create can configure specific navigation header content.

Let's build on the example discussed in the Route parameters section, which used buttons to navigate to a details page.

The App component has major updates, so let's take a look at it:

```
const Stack = createNativeStackNavigator<RoutesParams>();

export default function App() {
  return (
    <NavigationContainer>
      <Stack.Navigator>
        <Stack.Screen name="Home" component={Home} />
        <Stack.Screen
          name="Details"
          component={Details}
          options={({ route }) => ({
            headerRight: () => {
              return (
                <Button
                  title="Buy"
                  onPress={() => {}}
                  disabled={route.params.stock === 0}
                />
              );
            },
          })}
        />
      </Stack.Navigator>
    </NavigationContainer>
  );
}
```

The Screen component accepts the options prop as an object or function to provide additional screen properties.

The headerRight option is used to add a Button component to the right side of the navigation bar. This is where the stock parameter comes into play. If this value is 0 because there isn't anything in stock, you want to disable the Buy button.

In our case, we pass options as a function and read the stock screen params to disable the button. This is one of several ways to pass options to the Screen component. We'll apply another way to the Details component.

To understand how the stock props have been passed, take a look at the Home component here:

```
type Props = NativeStackScreenProps<RoutesParams, "Home">;


export default function Home({ navigation }: Props) {
  return (
    <View style={styles.container}>
      <StatusBar barStyle="dark-content" />
      <Button
        title="First Item"
        onPress={() =>
          navigation.navigate("Details", {
            title: "First Item",
            content: "First Item Content",
            stock: 1,
          })
        }
      />
      ...
    </View>
  );
}
```

The first thing to note is that each button is passing more route parameters to the Details component: content and stock. You'll see why in a moment.

Next, let's take a look at the Details component:

```
type Props = NativeStackScreenProps<RoutesParams, "Details">;
```

```
export default function Details({ route, navigation }: Props) {
  const { content, title } = route.params;

  React.useEffect(() => {
    navigation.setOptions({ title });
  }, []);

  return (
    <View style={styles.container}>
      <StatusBar barStyle="dark-content" />
      <Text>{content}</Text>
    </View>
  );
}
```

This time, the Details component renders the content route parameter. As with the App component, we add additional options to the screen. In this case, we update screen options using the navigation.setOptions() method. To customize the header, we can also add a title to that screen via the App component.

Let's see how all of this works now, starting with the **Home** screen:

Figure 19.5: The Home screen

Now there is header text in the navigation bar, which is set by the name property in the Screen component.

Next, try pressing the **First Item** button:

Figure 19.6: The First Item screen

The title in the navigation bar is set based on the `title` parameter that's passed to the `Details` component using the `navigation.setOptions()` method. The **Buy** button that's rendered on the right side of the navigation bar is rendered by the options property in the `Screen` component placed in the `App` component. It's enabled because the stock parameter value is 1.

Now, try returning to the **Home** screen and pressing the **Second Item** button:

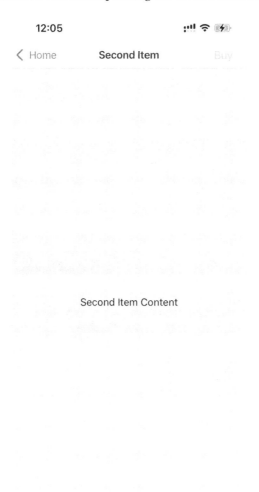

Figure 19.7: The Second Item screen

The title and the page content both reflect the new parameter values passed to Details, but so does the Buy button. It is in a disabled state because the stock parameter value was 0, meaning that it can't be bought.

Now that you've learned how to use navigation headers, in the next section, you'll learn about tab and drawer navigation.

Tab and drawer navigation

So far in this chapter, each example has used Button components to link to other screens in the app. You can use functions from react-navigation that will create **tab** or **drawer** navigation for you automatically based on the screen components that you give it.

Let's create an example that uses bottom tab navigation on iOS and drawer navigation on Android.

 You aren't limited to using tab navigation on iOS or drawer navigation on Android. I'm just picking these two to demonstrate how to use different modes of navigation based on the platform. You can use the exact same navigation mode on both platforms if you prefer.

For this example, we need to install a few other packages for tab and drawer navigators:

```
npm install @react-navigation/bottom-tabs @react-navigation/drawer
```

Also, the drawer navigator requires some native modules. Let's install them:

```
npx expo install react-native-gesture-handler react-native-reanimated
```

Then, add a plugin to the babel.config.js file. As a result, the file should look like the following:

```
module.exports = function (api) {
  api.cache(true);
  return {
    presets: ["babel-preset-expo"],
    plugins: ["react-native-reanimated/plugin"],
  };
};
```

Now, we are ready to continue coding. Here's what the App component looks like:

```
const Tab = createBottomTabNavigator<Routes>();
const Drawer = createDrawerNavigator<Routes>();

export default function App() {
  return (
    <NavigationContainer>
      {Platform.OS === "ios" && (
        <Tab.Navigator>
```

```
                <Tab.Screen name="Home" component={Home} />
                <Tab.Screen name="News" component={News} />
                <Tab.Screen name="Settings" component={Settings} />
              </Tab.Navigator>
          )}

          {Platform.OS == "android" && (
            <Drawer.Navigator>
              <Drawer.Screen name="Home" component={Home} />
              <Drawer.Screen name="News" component={News} />
              <Drawer.Screen name="Settings" component={Settings} />
            </Drawer.Navigator>
          )}
        </NavigationContainer>
    );
}
```

Instead of using the createNativeStackNavigator() function to create your navigator, you're importing the createBottomTabNavigator() and createDrawerNavigator() functions:

```
import { createDrawerNavigator } from "@react-navigation/drawer";
import { createBottomTabNavigator } from "@react-navigation/bottom-tabs";
```

Then, you're using the Platform utility from react-native to decide which navigator to use. The result, depending on the platform, is assigned to App. Each navigator contains the Navigator and Screen components, and you can pass them to your App. The resulting tab or drawer navigation will be created and rendered for you.

Next, let's take a look at the Home screen component:

```
export default function Home() {
  return (
    <View style={styles.container}>
      <Text>Home Content</Text>
    </View>
  );
}
```

The News and Settings components are essentially the same as Home. Here's what the bottom tab navigation looks like on iOS:

Figure 19.8: The tab navigator

The three screens that make up your app are listed at the bottom. The current screen is marked as active, and you can click on the other tabs to move around.

Now, let's see what the drawer layout looks like on Android:

Figure 19.9: The drawer navigator

To open the drawer, you need to swipe from the left side of the screen. Once it's open, you'll see buttons that will take you to the various screens of your app.

 Swiping the drawer open from the left side of the screen is the default mode. You can configure the drawer to swipe open from any direction.

Now, you've learned how to use tab and drawer navigation. Next, we'll explore the approach of how to define navigation based just on files.

File-based navigation

In this section, we will talk about **Expo Router**, a file-based router works in a similar way to routing in Next.js. To add a new screen, you just need to add a new file to the app folder. It's built on top of React Navigation, so the routes have the same options and parameters.

 For more information and details about Expo Router, take a look at this link:

https://docs.expo.dev/routing/introduction/

To try it out, we will install a fresh project using:

```
npx create-expo-app –template
```

To install the project with Expo Router ready, we just need to choose the Navigation (TypeScript) template:

```
    Blank
    Blank (TypeScript)
>   Navigation (TypeScript) - File-based routing with TypeScript enabled
    Blank (Bare)
```

When the installation is finished, you will find the app folder for the project. This folder will be used for all your screens. Let's try to replicate the example from the *The basics of navigation* section. First of all, we need to create _layout.tsx inside the app folder. That file is working as a root layer of our app. This is how it looks:

```
import { Stack } from "expo-router";

export default function RootLayout() {
  return <Stack />;
}
```

Then let's create the index.tsx files that will contain the Home screen. It has few differences compared to _layout.tsx, so let's take a look:

```
import { Link } from "expo-router";

export default function Home() {
  return (
    <View style={styles.container}>
      <StatusBar barStyle="dark-content" />
      <Text>Home Screen</Text>

      <Link href="/settings" asChild>
        <Button title="Settings" />
      </Link>
    </View>
  );
}
```

As you can see here, we don't use a navigation prop. We are instead using a Link component that accepts href props, just like a web page. Clicking on that button takes us to the Settings screen.

Let's create the settings.tsx file:

```
import { Link } from "expo-router";

export default function Settings() {
  return (
    <View style={styles.container}>
      <StatusBar barStyle="dark-content" />
      <Text>Settings Screen</Text>

      <Link href="/" asChild>
        <Button title="Home" />
      </Link>
    </View>
  );
}
```

Here, we use the same approach as the index.tsx files, but in Link, we set href to "/".

This is how easily we can define screens in a declarative way, and the URL approach to navigating between screens works out of the box. Also, one benefit we get here is that **deep linking** also works out of the box; with this method, we can open specific screens using app links.

Now you know how to use file-based routing, which can improve your experience of developing mobile apps, especially with a web-based mindset of URLs and linking.

Summary

In this chapter, you learned that mobile applications require navigation, just like web applications do. Although they are different, web application and mobile application navigation have enough conceptual similarities that mobile app routing and navigation don't have to be a nuisance.

Older versions of React Native attempted to provide components to help manage navigation within mobile apps, but they never really took hold. Instead, the React Native community has dominated this area. One example of this is the react-navigation library: the focus of this chapter.

You learned how basic navigation works with react-navigation. You then learned how to control header components within the navigation bar. Next, you learned about the tab and drawer navigation components. These two navigation components can automatically render the navigation buttons for your app based on the screen components. You also learned how to work with the file-based Expo Router.

In the next chapter, you'll learn how to render lists of data.

20

Rendering Item Lists

In this chapter, you'll learn how to work with item lists. Lists are a common web application component. While it's relatively straightforward to build lists using the `<ul>` and `<li>` elements, doing something similar on native mobile platforms is much more involved.

Thankfully, React Native provides an **item list** interface that hides all of the complexity. First, you'll get a feel for how item lists work by walking through an example. Then, you'll learn how to build controls that change the data displayed in lists. Lastly, you'll see a couple of examples that fetch items from the network.

We'll cover the following topics in this chapter:

- Rendering data collections
- Sorting and filtering lists
- Fetching list data
- Lazy list loading
- Implementing pull to refresh

Technical requirements

You can find the code files for this chapter on GitHub at https://github.com/PacktPublishing/React-and-React-Native-5E/tree/main/Chapter20.

Rendering data collections

Lists are the most common way to display a lot of information: for example, you can display your friend list, messages, and news. Many apps contain lists with data collections, and React Native provides the tools to create these components.

Let's start with an example. The React Native component you'll use to render lists is FlatList, which works the same way on iOS and Android. List views accept a data property, which is an array of objects. These objects can have any properties you like, but they do require a key property. If you don't have a key property, you can pass the keyExtractor prop to the Flatlist component and instruct what to use instead of key. The key property is similar to the requirement for rendering the <li> elements inside of a <ul> element. This helps the list to efficiently render when changes are made to list data.

Let's implement a basic list now. Here's the code to render a basic 100-item list:

```
const data = new Array(100)
  .fill(null)
  .map((v, i) => ({ key: i.toString(), value: `Item ${i}` }));

export default function App() {
  return (
    <View style={styles.container}>
      <FlatList
        data={data}
        renderItem={({ item }) => <Text style={styles.item}>{item.value}</
Text>}
      />
    </View>
  );
}
```

Let's walk through what's going on here, starting with the data constant. This has an array of 100 items in it. It is created by filling in a new array with 100 null values and then mapping this to a new array with the objects that you want to pass to <FlatList>. Each object has a key property because this is a requirement; anything else is optional. In this case, you've decided to add a value property that will be used later when the list is rendered.

Next, you render the <FlatList> component. It's within a <View> container because list views need height in order to make scrolling work correctly. The data and renderItem properties are passed to <FlatList>, which ultimately determines the rendered content.

At first glance, it seems like the FlatList component doesn't do too much. Do you have to figure out how the items look? Well, yes, the FlatList component is supposed to be generic. It's supposed to excel at handling updates and embeds scrolling capabilities into lists for us. Here are the styles that were used to render the list:

```
import { StyleSheet } from "react-native";

export default StyleSheet.create({
  container: {
    flex: 1,
    flexDirection: "column",
    paddingTop: 40,
  },

  item: {
    margin: 5,
    padding: 5,
    color: "slategrey",
    backgroundColor: "ghostwhite",
    textAlign: "center",
  },
});
```

Here, you're styling each item on your list. Otherwise, each item would be text-only, and it would be difficult to differentiate between other list items. The container style gives the list height by setting flex to 1.

Let's see what the list looks like now:

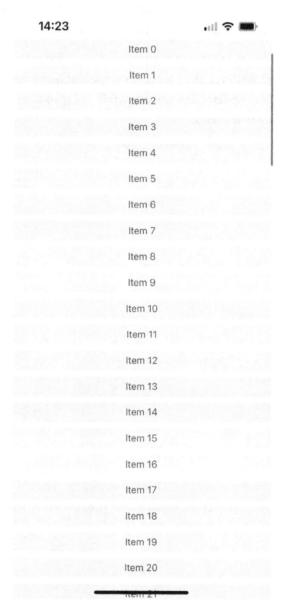

Figure 20.1: Rendering the data collection

If you're running this example in a simulator, you can click and hold down the mouse button anywhere on the screen, like a finger, and then scroll up and down through the items.

In the following section, you'll learn how to add controls for sorting and filtering lists.

Sorting and filtering lists

Now that you have learned the basics of the FlatList components, including how to pass data, let's add some controls to the list that you just implemented in the *Rendering data collections* section. The **FlatList** component can be rendered together with other components: for example, list controls. It helps you to manipulate the data source, which ultimately drives what's rendered on the screen.

Before implementing list control components, it might be helpful to review the high-level structure of these components so that the code has more context. Here's an illustration of the component structure that you're going to implement:

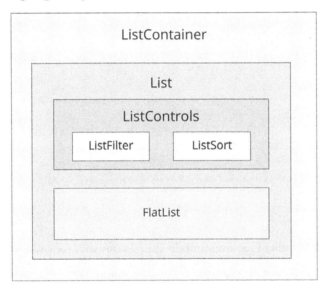

Figure 20.2: The component structure

Here's what each of these components is responsible for:

- ListContainer: The overall container for the list; it follows the familiar React container pattern
- List: A stateless component that passes the relevant pieces of state into ListControls and the React Native ListView component
- ListControls: A component that holds the various controls that change the state of the list
- ListFilter: A control for filtering the item list

- `ListSort`: A control for changing the sort order of the list
- `FlatList`: The actual React Native component that renders items

In some cases, splitting apart the implementation of a list like this is overhead. However, I think that if your list needs controls in the first place, you're probably implementing something that will stand to benefit from having a well-thought-out component architecture.

Now, let's drill down into the implementation of this list, starting with the **ListContainer** component:

```
function mapItems(items: string[]) {
  return items.map((value, i) => ({ key: i.toString(), value }));
}


const array = new Array(100).fill(null).map((v, i) => `Item ${i}`);

function filterAndSort(text: string, asc: boolean): string[] {
  return array
    .filter((i) => text.length === 0 || i.includes(text))
    .sort(
      asc
        ? (a, b) => (a > b ? 1 : a < b ? -1 : 0)
        : (a, b) => (b > a ? 1 : b < a ? -1 : 0)
    );
}
```

Here, we define a few utility functions and the initial array that we will use.

Then, we will define `asc` and `filter` for managing sorting and filtering the list, respectively, with the `data` variable implemented using the `useMemo` hook:

```
export default function ListContainer() {
  const [asc, setAsc] = useState(true);
  const [filter, setFilter] = useState("");

  const data = useMemo(() => {
    return filterAndSort(filter, asc);
  }, [filter, asc]);
```

It gives us an opportunity to avoid updating it manually because it will be recalculated automatically when the `filter` and `asc` dependencies are updated. It also helps us to avoid unnecessary recalculation when `filter` and `asc` are not changed.

This is how we apply this logic to the `List` component:

```
return (
  <List
    data={mapItems(data)}
    asc={asc}
    onFilter={(text) => {
      setFilter(text);
    }}
    onSort={() => {
      setAsc(!asc);
    }}
  />
);
```

If this seems like a bit much, it's because it is. This container component has a lot of state to handle. It also has some non-trivial behavior that it needs to make available to its children. If you look at it from the perspective of an encapsulating state, it will be more approachable. Its job is to populate the list with state data and provide functions that operate in this state.

In an ideal world, the child components of this container should be nice and simple, since they don't have to directly interface with the state. Let's take a look at the `List` component next:

```
export default function List({ data, ...props }: Props) {
  return (
    <FlatList
      data={data}
      ListHeaderComponent={<ListControls {...props}/>}
      renderItem={({ item }) => <Text style={styles.item}>{item.value}</
Text>}
    />
  );
}
```

This component takes the state from the ListContainer component as a property and renders a FlatList component. The main difference here from the previous example is the ListHeaderComponent property. This renders the controls for your List component. What's especially useful about this property is that it renders the controls outside the scrollable list content, ensuring that the controls are always visible. Let's take a look at the ListControls component next:

```
type Props = {
  onFilter: (text: string) => void;
  onSort: () => void;
  asc: boolean;
};


export default function ListControls({ onFilter, onSort, asc }: Props) {
  return (
    <View style={styles.controls}>
      <ListFilter onFilter={onFilter} />
      <ListSort onSort={onSort} asc={asc} />
    </View>
  );
}
```

This component brings together the ListFilter and ListSort controls. So, if you were to add another list control, you would add it here.

Let's take a look at the ListFilter implementation now:

```
type Props = {
  onFilter: (text: string) => void;
};
```

```
export default function ListFilter({ onFilter }: Props) {
  return (
    <View>
      <TextInput
        autoFocus
        placeholder="Search"
        style={styles.filter}
        onChangeText={onFilter}
      />
    </View>
  );
}
```

The filter control is a simple text input that filters the list of items by user type. The onFilter function that handles this comes from the ListContainer component.

Let's look at the ListSort component next:

```
const arrows = new Map([
  [true, "▼"],
  [false, "▲"],
]);

type Props = {
  onSort: () => void;
  asc: boolean;
};

export default function ListSort({ onSort, asc }: Props) {
  return <Text onPress={onSort}>{arrows.get(asc)}</Text>;
}
```

Here's a look at the resulting list:

Figure 20.3: The sorting and filtering list

By default, the entire list is rendered in ascending order. You can see the placeholder **Search** text when the user hasn't provided anything yet. Let's see how this looks when you enter a filter and change the sort order:

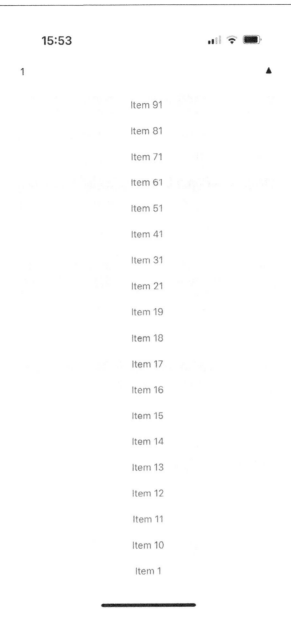

Figure 20.4: The list with a changed sort order and search value

This search includes items containing 1 and sorts the results in descending order. Note that you can either change the order first or enter the filter first. Both the filter and the sort order are part of the ListContainer state.

In the next section, you'll learn how to fetch list data from an API endpoint.

Fetching list data

Commonly, you'll fetch your list data from some API endpoint. In this section, you'll learn about making API requests from React Native components. The good news is that the `fetch()` API is polyfilled by React Native, so the networking code in your mobile applications should look and feel a lot like it does in your web applications.

To start things off, let's build a **mock API** for our list items using functions that return promises just like `fetch()` does:

```
const items = new Array(100).fill(null).map((v, i) => `Item ${i}`);

function filterAndSort(data: string[], text: string, asc: boolean) {
  return data
    .filter((i) => text.length === 0 || i.includes(text))
    .sort(
      asc
        ? (a, b) => (b > a ? -1 : a === b ? 0 : 1)
        : (a, b) => (a > b ? -1 : a === b ? 0 : 1)
    );
}

export function fetchItems(
  filter: string,
  asc: boolean
): Promise<{ json: () => Promise<{ items: string[] }> }> {
  return new Promise((resolve) => {
    resolve({
      json: () =>
        Promise.resolve({
          items: filterAndSort(items, filter, asc),
        }),
    });
  });
}
```

With the mock API function in place, let's make some changes to the ListContainer component. Instead of using local data sources, you can now use the fetchItems() function to load data from the mock API. Let's take a look and define the ListContainer component:

```
export default function ListContainer() {
  const [asc, setAsc] = useState(true);
  const [filter, setFilter] = useState("");
  const [data, setData] = useState<MappedList>([]);

  useEffect(() => {
    fetchItems(filter, asc)
      .then((resp) => resp.json())
      .then(({ items }) => {
        setData(mapItems(items));
      });
  }, []);
```

We've defined state variables using the useState and useEffect hooks to fetch initial list data.

Now, let's take a look at the usage of our new handlers in the List component:

```
return (
  <List
    data={data}
    asc={asc}
    onFilter={(text) => {
      fetchItems(text, asc)
        .then((resp) => resp.json())
        .then(({ items }) => {
          setFilter(text);
          setData(mapItems(items));
        });
    }}
    onSort={() => {
      fetchItems(filter, !asc)
        .then((resp) => resp.json())
        .then(({ items }) => {
          setAsc(!asc);
```

```
            setData(mapItems(items));
          });
        }}
      />
    );
}
```

Any action that modifies the state of the list needs to call `fetchItems()` and set the appropriate state once the promise resolves.

In the following section, you'll learn how list data can be loaded lazily.

Lazy list loading

In this section, you'll implement a different kind of list: one that scrolls infinitely. Sometimes, users don't actually know what they're looking for, so filtering or sorting isn't going to help. Think about the Facebook news feed you see when you log in to your account; it's the main feature of the application, and rarely are you looking for something specific. You need to see what's going on by scrolling through the list.

To do this using a `FlatList` component, you need to be able to fetch more API data when the user scrolls to the end of the list. To get an idea of how this works, you need a lot of API data to work with, and generators are great at this. So, let's modify the mock that you created in the *Fetching list data* section's example so that it just keeps responding with new data:

```
function* genItems() {
  let cnt = 0;

  while (true) {
    yield `Item ${cnt++}`;
  }
}

let items = genItems();

export function fetchItems({ refresh }: { refresh?: boolean }) {
  if (refresh) {
    items = genItems();
  }
```

```
      return Promise.resolve({
        json: () =>
          Promise.resolve({
            items: new Array(30).fill(null).map(() => items.next().value as
    string),

          }),
      });
    }
```

With fetchItems, you can now make an API request for new data every time the end of the list is reached. Eventually, this will fail when you run out of memory, but I'm just trying to show you in general terms the approach you can take to implement infinite scrolling in React Native. Now, let's take a look at what the ListContainer component looks like with fetchItems:

```
import React, { useState, useEffect } from "react";
import * as api from "./api";
import List from "./List";
export default function ListContainer() {
  const [data, setData] = useState([]);
  function fetchItems() {
    return api
      .fetchItems({})
      .then((resp) => resp.json())
      .then(({ items }) => {
        setData([
          ...data,
          ...items.map((value) => ({
            key: value,
            value,
          })),
        ]);
      });
  }
  useEffect(() => {
    fetchItems();
  }, []);
```

```
    return <List data={data} fetchItems={fetchItems} />;
}
```

Each time fetchItems() is called, the response is concatenated with the data array. This becomes the new list data source, instead of replacing it as you did in earlier examples.

Now, let's take a look at the List component to see how to respond to the end of the list being reached:

```
type Props = {
  data: { key: string; value: string }[];
  fetchItems: () => Promise<void>;
  refreshItems: () => Promise<void>;
  isRefreshing: boolean;
};

export default function List({
  data,
  fetchItems
}: Props) {
  return (
    <FlatList
      data={data}
      renderItem={({ item }) => <Text style={styles.item}>{item.value}</
Text>}
      onEndReached={fetchItems}
    />
  );
}
```

FlatList accepts the onEndReached handler prop, which will be invoked every time you reach the end of the list during scrolling.

If you run this example, you'll see that, as you approach the bottom of the screen while scrolling, the list just keeps growing.

Implementing pull to refresh

The **pull-to-refresh** gesture is a common action on mobile devices. It allows users to refresh the content of a view without having to lift a finger from the screen or manually reopen the app, just by pulling it down to trigger a page refresh. Loren Brichter, the creator of Tweetie (later Twitter for iPhone) and Letterpress, introduced this gesture in 2009. This gesture has become so popular that Apple integrated it into its SDKs as UIRefreshControl.

To use pull to refresh in the FlatList app, we just need to pass a few props and handlers. Let's take a look at our List component:

```
type Props = {
  data: { key: string; value: string }[];
  fetchItems: () => Promise<void>;
  refreshItems: () => Promise<void>;
  isRefreshing: boolean;
};




export default function List({
  data,
  fetchItems,
  refreshItems,
  isRefreshing,
}: Props) {
  return (
    <FlatList
      data={data}
      renderItem={({ item }) => <Text style={styles.item}>{item.value}</
Text>}
      onEndReached={fetchItems}
      onRefresh={refreshItems}
      refreshing={isRefreshing}
    />
  );
}
```

As we have provided the onRefresh and refreshing props, our FlatList component automatically enables the pull-to-refresh gesture. The onRefresh handler will be called when you pull the list, and the refreshing property will enable the loading spinner to reflect the loading state.

To apply defined props in the List component, let's implement the refreshItems function with the isRefreshing state in the ListContainer component:

```
const [isRefreshing, setIsRefreshing] = useState(false);

function fetchItems() {
  return api
    .fetchItems({})
    .then((resp) => resp.json())
    .then(({ items }) => {
      setData([
        ...data,
        ...items.map((value) => ({
          key: value,
          value,
        })),
      ]);
    });
}
```

In refreshItems, as well as in the fetchItems method, we get list items but save them as a new list. Also, note that before calling the API, we update the isRefreshing state to set it as a true value, and in the final block, we set it to false to provide information to FlatList that loading has ended.

Summary

In this chapter, you learned about the FlatList component in React Native. This component is general-purpose, as it doesn't impose any specific look on the items that get rendered. Instead, the appearance of the list is up to you, leaving the FlatList component to help with efficiently rendering a data source. The FlatList component also provides a scrollable region for the items it renders.

You implemented an example that took advantage of section headers in list views. This is a good place to render static content such as list controls. You then learned about making network calls in React Native; it's just like using `fetch()` in any other web application.

Finally, you implemented lazy lists that scroll infinitely by only loading new items after you've scrolled to the bottom of what's already been rendered. Also, we added a feature to refresh that list by means of a pull gesture.

In the next chapter, you'll learn how to show the progress of network calls, among other things.

21

Geolocation and Maps

In this chapter, you'll learn about the geolocation and mapping capabilities of React Native. You'll start the learning process with how to use the **Geolocation API**, and then you'll move on to using the MapView component to plot points of interest and regions. To do this, we'll use the react-native-maps package to implement maps.

The goal of this chapter is to go over what's available in React Native for geolocation and in react-native-maps for maps.

Here's a list of the topics that we'll cover in this chapter:

- Using the Geolocation API
- Rendering the map
- Annotating points of interest

Technical requirements

You can find the code file for this chapter on GitHub at https://github.com/PacktPublishing/React-and-React-Native-5E/tree/main/Chapter21.

Using the Geolocation API

The Geolocation API that web applications use to figure out where the user is located can also be used by React Native applications because the same API has been polyfilled. Other than maps, this API is useful for getting precise coordinates from the GPS on mobile devices. You can then use this information to display meaningful location data to the user.

Unfortunately, the data returned by the Geolocation API is of little use on its own. Your code must do the legwork to transform it into something useful. For example, latitude and longitude don't mean anything to the user, but you can use this data to look up something that is of use to the user. This might be as simple as displaying where the user is currently located.

Let's implement an example that uses the **Geolocation API** of React Native to look up coordinates and then use those coordinates to look up human-readable location information from the Google Maps API.

Before we start coding, let's create a project using `npx create-expo-app` and then add the location module:

```
npx expo install expo-location
```

Next, we need to configure location permissions in the app. Accessing a user's location in a mobile app requires explicit permission from the user. Later in this example, we will do that by calling the `Location.requestForegroundPermissionsAsync()` method. This will display a permission dialog to the user asking them to allow or deny location access. It's important to check the status returned to see if permission was granted before proceeding to use location methods. If permission is denied, you should gracefully handle it in your code and potentially prompt the user to grant permission in app settings if needed.

In real apps, before we can request permissions, we should first set those permissions up in the app configuration. We can do this by adding a plugin to the `app.json` file:

```
{
  "expo": {
    "plugins": [
      [
        "expo-location",
        {
          "locationAlwaysAndWhenInUsePermission": "Allow $(PRODUCT_NAME)
to use your location."
        }
      ]
    ]
  }
}
```

You should request location permission as early as possible, such as when your app first starts up or when the user first navigates to a screen that requires location. By requesting permission up-front and properly handling the user's choice, you can ensure your app works as expected while respecting the user's privacy preferences.

When you have a prepared project, let's have a look at the App component, which you can find here: https://github.com/PacktPublishing/React-and-React-Native-5E/tree/main/Chapter22/ where-am-i/App.tsx. The goal of this component is to render the properties returned by the Geolocation API on the screen, as well as looking up the user's specific location and displaying it.

To fetch a location from the app, we need to grant permissions. In App.tsx, we have called Location.requestForegroundPermissionsAsync() for that.

The setPosition() function is used as a callback in a couple of places, with its job being to set the state of your component. Firstly, setPosition() sets the latitude-longitude coordinates. Normally, you wouldn't display this data directly, but this is an example that shows the data that's available as part of the Geolocation API. And, secondly, it uses the latitude and longitude values to look up the name of where the user currently is, using the Google Maps API.

In the example, the API_KEY value is empty, and you can get it here: https://developers.google. com/maps/documentation/geocoding/start.

The setPosition() callback is used with getCurrentPosition(), which is only called once when the component is mounted. You're also using setPosition() with watchPosition(), which calls the callback any time the user's position changes.

 The iOS emulator and Android Studio let you change locations via menu options. You don't have to install your app on a physical device every time you want to test changing locations.

Let's see what this screen looks like once the location data has loaded:

12:28

Address: Camí de la Verneda, 30, Sant Martí, 08020
Barcelona, Spain

Latitude: 41.42500974177705

Longitude: 2.2070894112218014

Figure 21.1: Location data

The address information that was fetched is probably more useful in an application than latitude and longitude data. It works well for apps that need to find buildings around you or companies. Even better than physical address text is visualizing the user's physical location on a map; you'll learn how to do this in the next section.

Rendering the map

The MapView component from react-native-maps is the main tool you'll use to render maps in your React Native applications. It offers a wide range of tools for rendering maps, markers, polygons, heatmaps, and the like.

 You can find more information about react-native-maps on the website: https://github.com/react-native-maps/react-native-maps.

Let's now implement a basic MapView component to see what you get out of the box:

```
import { View, StatusBar } from "react-native";
import MapView from "react-native-maps";
import styles from "./styles";

StatusBar.setBarStyle("dark-content");

export default () => (
  <View style={styles.container}>
    <MapView style={styles.mapView} showsUserLocation followsUserLocation
/>
  </View>
);
```

The two Boolean properties that you've passed to MapView do a lot of work for you. The showsUserLocation property will activate the marker on the map, which denotes the physical location of the device running this application. The followsUserLocation property tells the map to update the location marker as the device moves around.

Here is the resulting map:

Figure 21.2: Current location

The current location of the device is clearly marked on the map. By default, points of interest are also rendered on the map. These are things close to the user so that they can see what's around them.

It's generally a good idea to use the `followsUserLocation` property whenever using `showsUserLocation`. This makes the map zoom to the region where the user is located.

In the following section, you'll learn how to annotate points of interest on your maps.

Annotating points of interest

Annotations are exactly what they sound like: additional information rendered on top of the basic map geography. You get annotations by default when you render MapView components. The MapView component can render the user's current location and points of interest around the user. The challenge here is that you probably want to show the points of interest relevant to your application instead of those rendered by default.

In this section, you'll learn how to render markers for specific locations on the map, as well as rendering regions on the map.

Plotting points

Let's plot some local breweries! Here's how you pass annotations to the MapView component:

```
<MapView
  style={styles.mapView}
  showsPointsOfInterest={false}
  showsUserLocation
  followsUserLocation
>
  <Marker
    title="Duff Brewery"
    description="Duff beer for me, Duff beer for you"
    coordinate={{
      latitude: 43.8418728,
      longitude: -79.086082,
    }}
  />
  {...}
</MapView>
```

In this example, we've opted out of this capability by setting the showsPointsOfInterest property to false. Let's see where these breweries are located:

Figure 21.3: Plotting points

The callout is displayed when you press the marker that shows the location of the brewery on the map. The title and description property values that you give to <Marker> are used to render this text.

Plotting overlays

In this last section of this chapter, you'll learn how to render region overlays. Think of a region as a connect-the-dots drawing of several points, and a point is a single `latitude`/`longitude` coordinate.

Regions can serve many purposes. In our example, we'll create a region that shows where we're more likely to find IPA drinkers versus stout drinkers. You can follow this link to see what the full code looks like: `https://github.com/PacktPublishing/React-and-React-Native-5E/tree/main/Chapter22/plotting-overlays/App.tsx`. Here is what the JSX part of the code looks like:

```
<View style={styles.container}>
  <View>
    <Text style={ipaStyles} onPress={onClickIpa}>
      IPA Fans
    </Text>
    <Text style={stoutStyles} onPress={onClickStout}>
      Stout Fans
    </Text>
  </View>
  <MapView
    style={styles.mapView}
    showsPointsOfInterest={false}
    initialRegion={{
      latitude: 43.8486744,
      longitude: -79.0695283,
      latitudeDelta: 0.002,
      longitudeDelta: 0.04,
    }}
  >
    {overlays.map((v, i) => (
      <Polygon
        key={i}
        coordinates={v.coordinates}
        strokeColor={v.strokeColor}
        strokeWidth={v.strokeWidth}
      />
    ))}
  </MapView>
</View>
```

The region data consists of several `latitude`/`longitude` coordinates that define the shape and location of the region. Regions are placed in the `overlays` state variable, which we map into `Polygon` components. The rest of this code is mostly about the handling state when the two text links are pressed.

By default, the IPA region is rendered as follows:

Figure 21.4: IPA Fans

When the **Stout Fans** button is pressed, the IPA overlay is removed from the map and the stout region is added:

Figure 21.5: Stout Fans

Overlays are useful when you need to highlight an area instead of a `latitude`/`longitude` point or an address. As an example, it might be an app for finding apartments for rent in the area or neighborhood you select.

Summary

In this chapter, you learned about geolocation and mapping in React Native. The Geolocation API works the same as its web counterpart. The only reliable way to use maps in React Native applications is to install the third-party `react-native-maps` package.

You saw the basic configuration `MapView` components and how they can track the user's location and show relevant points of interest. Then, you saw how to plot your own points of interest and regions of interest.

In the next chapter, you'll learn how to collect user input using React Native components that resemble HTML form controls.

22

Collecting User Input

In web applications, you can collect user input from standard HTML form elements that look and behave similarly on all browsers. With native UI platforms, collecting user input is more nuanced.

In this chapter, you'll learn how to work with the various React Native components that are used to collect user input. These include text input, selecting from a list of options, checkboxes, and date/time selectors. All of these are used in every app in cases of register or login flow, as well as the purchase form. The experience of creating such forms is very valuable and this chapter will help you to know how to create any form in your future apps. You'll learn the differences between iOS and Android and how to implement the appropriate abstractions for your app.

The following topics will be covered in this chapter:

- Collecting text input
- Selecting from a list of options
- Toggling between on and off
- Collecting date/time input

Technical requirements

You can find the code files for this chapter on GitHub at https://github.com/PacktPublishing/React-and-React-Native-5E/tree/main/Chapter22.

Collecting text input

It turns out that there's a lot to think about when it comes to implementing text inputs. For example, should it have placeholder text? Is this sensitive data that shouldn't be displayed on the screen? Should you process text as it's entered or when the user moves to another field?

In web apps, there is a special `<input>` HTML element that allows you to collect user inputs. In React Native, for that purpose, we use the `TextInput` component. Let's build an example that renders several instances of the `<TextInput>` component:

```
function Input(props: InputProps) {
  return (
    <View style={styles.textInputContainer}>
      <Text style={styles.textInputLabel}>{props.label}</Text>
      <TextInput style={styles.textInput} {...props} />
    </View>
  );
}
```

We have implemented the Input component that we will reuse several times. Let's take a look at a few use cases of text inputs:

```
export default function CollectingTextInput() {
  const [changedText, setChangedText] = useState("");
  const [submittedText, setSubmittedText] = useState("");
  return (
    <View style={styles.container}>
      <Input label="Basic Text Input:" />
      <Input label="Password Input:" secureTextEntry />
      <Input label="Return Key:" returnKeyType="search" />
      <Input label="Placeholder Text:" placeholder="Search" />
      <Input
        label="Input Events:"
        onChangeText={(e) => {
          setChangedText(e);
        }}
        onSubmitEditing={(e) => {
          setSubmittedText(e.nativeEvent.text);
        }}
```

```
        onFocus={() => {
          setChangedText("");
          setSubmittedText("");
        }}
      />
      <Text>Changed: {changedText}</Text>
      <Text>Submitted: {submittedText}</Text>
    </View>
  );
}
```

I won't go into depth about what each of these <TextInput> components is doing; there are labels in the Input components that explain this. Let's see what these components look like on the screen:

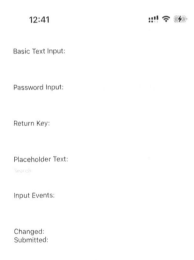

Figure 22.1: Text input variations

The plain text input shows the text that's been entered. The **Password Input** field doesn't reveal any characters. **Placeholder Text** is displayed when the input is empty. The **Changed** text state is also displayed. You can't see the **Submitted** text state because I didn't press the **Submitted** button on the virtual keyboard before I took the screenshot.

Let's take a look at the virtual keyboard for the input element where you changed the **Return Key** text via the returnKeyType prop:

Figure 22.2: Keyboard with changed Return key text

When the keyboard **Return key** reflects what's going to happen when the user presses it, the user feels more in tune with the application.

One more common use case is changing the keyboard type. By providing the keyboardType prop to the TextInput component, you will see different variations of keyboards. This is convenient when you need to enter a PIN code or email address. Here is an example of a numeric keyboard:

Figure 22.3: Numeric keyboard type

Now that you're familiar with collecting text input, it's time to learn how to select a value from a list of options.

Selecting from a list of options

In web applications, you typically use the <select> element to let the user choose from a list of options. React Native comes with a Picker component, which works on both iOS and Android, but in terms of reducing the React Native app size, the Meta team decided to delete it in future releases and extract Picker to its own package. To use that package, firstly, we install it in a clean project by running this command:

```
npx expo install @react-native-picker/picker
```

There is some trickery involved with styling this component based on which platform the user is on, so let's hide all of this inside a generic Select component. Here's the Select.ios.js module:

```
export default function Select(props: SelectProps) {
  return (
    <View style={styles.pickerHeight}>
      <View style={styles.pickerContainer}>
        <Text style={styles.pickerLabel}>{props.label}</Text>
        <Picker style={styles.picker} {...props}>
          {props.items.map((i) => (
            <Picker.Item key={i.label} {...i} />
          ))}
        </Picker>
      </View>
    </View>
  );
}
```

That's a lot of overhead for a simple Select component. It turns out that it's quite hard to style the React Native Picker component, because it looks completely different on iOS and Android. Despite that, we want to make it more cross-platform.

Here's the Select.android.js module:

```
export default function Select(props: SelectProps) {
  return (
    <View>
      <Text style={styles.pickerLabel}>{props.label}</Text>
      <Picker {...props}>
        {props.items.map((i) => (
```

```
            <Picker.Item key={i.label} {...i} />
        ))}
      </Picker>
    </View>
  );
}
```

This is what the styles look like:

```
container: {
    flex: 1,
    flexDirection: "column",
    backgroundColor: "ghostwhite",
    justifyContent: "center",
},

pickersBlock: {
    flex: 2,
    flexDirection: "row",
    justifyContent: "space-around",
    alignItems: "center",
},

pickerHeight: {
    height: 250,
},
```

As usual with the `container` and `pickersBlock` styles, we define the base layout of the screen.
Next, let's take a look at the styles of the `Select` component:

```
pickerContainer: {
    flex: 1,
    flexDirection: "column",
    alignItems: "center",
    backgroundColor: "white",
    padding: 6,
    height: 240,
},
```

```
  pickerLabel: {
    fontSize: 14,
    fontWeight: "bold",
  },

  picker: {
    width: 150,
    backgroundColor: "white",
  },

  selection: {
    flex: 1,
    textAlign: "center",
  },
```

Now, you can render your Select component. Here is what the App.js file looks like:

```
const sizes = [
  { label: "", value: null },
  { label: "S", value: "S" },
  { label: "M", value: "M" },
  { label: "L", value: "L" },
  { label: "XL", value: "XL" },
];

const garments = [
  { label: "", value: null, sizes: ["S", "M", "L", "XL"] },
  { label: "Socks", value: 1, sizes: ["S", "L"] },
  { label: "Shirt", value: 2, sizes: ["M", "XL"] },
  { label: "Pants", value: 3, sizes: ["S", "L"] },
  { label: "Hat", value: 4, sizes: ["M", "XL"] },
];
```

Here, we defined the default values for our Select component. Let's take a look at the final SelectingOptions component:

```
export default function SelectingOptions() {
```

```
  const [availableGarments, setAvailableGarments] = useState<typeof
garments>(
    []
  );
  const [selectedSize, setSelectedSize] = useState<string | null>(null);
  const [selectedGarment, setSelectedGarment] = useState<number |
null>(null);
```

With these hooks, we've implemented states of selectors. Next, we will use and pass them into components:

```
    <View style={styles.container}>
      <View style={styles.pickersBlock}>
        <Select
          label="Size"
          items={sizes}
          selectedValue={selectedSize}
          onValueChange={(size: string) => {
            setSelectedSize(size);
            setSelectedGarment(null);
            setAvailableGarments(
              garments.filter((i) => i.sizes.includes(size))
            );
          }}
        />
        <Select
          label="Garment"
          items={availableGarments}
          selectedValue={selectedGarment}
          onValueChange={(garment: number) => {
            setSelectedGarment(garment);
          }}
        />
      </View>
```

```
        <Text style={styles.selection}>{selectedSize && selectedGarment &&
    `${selectedSize} ${garments.find((i) => i.value === selectedGarment)?.
    label}`}</Text>
        </View>
```

The basic idea of this example is that the selected option in the first selector changes the available options in the second selector. When the second selector changes, the label shows `selectedSize` and `selectedGarment` as a string. Here's how the screen looks:

Figure 22.4: Selecting from the list of options

The **Size** selector is shown on the left-hand side of the screen. When the **Size** value changes, the available values in the **Garment** selector on the right-hand side of the screen change to reflect size availability. The current selection is displayed as a string after the two selectors.

This is how our app looks on an Android device:

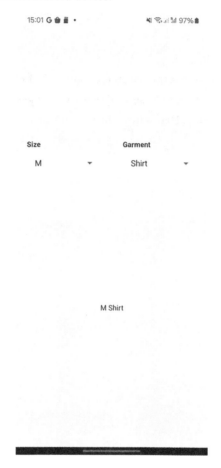

Figure 22.5: Selecting from the list of options on Android

When the iOS version of the `Picker` component renders a scrollable list of options, the Android one gives only buttons that open a dialog modal for selecting options.

In the following section, you'll learn about the buttons that toggle between on and off states.

Toggling between on and off

Another common element you'll see in web forms is checkboxes. For example, think of toggling Wi-Fi or Bluetooth on your device. React Native has a `Switch` component that works on both iOS and Android. Thankfully, this component is a little easier to style than the `Picker` component. Let's look at a simple abstraction you can implement to provide labels for your switches:

```
type CustomSwitchProps = SwitchProps & {
  label: string;
};


export default function CustomSwitch(props: CustomSwitchProps) {
  return (
    <View style={styles.customSwitch}>
      <Text>{props.label}</Text>
      <Switch {...props} />
    </View>
  );
}
```

Now, let's learn how we can use a couple of switches to control application state:

```
export default function TogglingOnAndOff() {
  const [first, setFirst] = useState(false);
  const [second, setSecond] = useState(false);

  return (
    <View style={styles.container}>
      <Switch
        label="Disable Next Switch"
        value={first}
        disabled={second}
        onValueChange={setFirst}
      />


      <Switch
        label="Disable Previous Switch"
        value={second}
        disabled={first}
        onValueChange={setSecond}
      />
    </View>
  );
}
```

These two switches toggle the disabled property of one another. When the first switch is toggled, the setFirst() function is called, which will update the value of the first state. Depending on the current value of first, it will either be set to true or false. The second switch works the same way, except it uses setSecond() and the second state value.

Turning on one switch will disable the other because we've set the disabled property value for each switch to the state of the other switch. For example, the second switch has disabled={first}, which means that it is disabled whenever the first switch is turned on. Here's what the screen looks like on iOS:

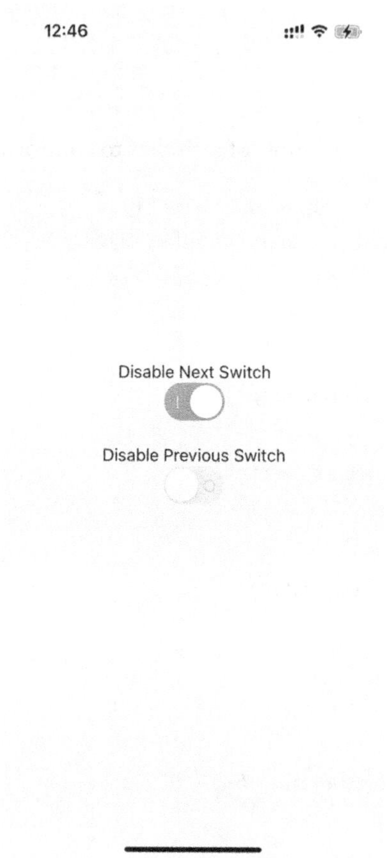

Figure 22.6: Switch toggles on iOS

Here's what the same screen looks like on Android:

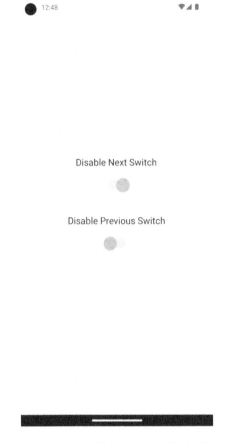

Figure 22.7: Switch toggles on Android

As you can see, our `CustomSwitch` component enables the same functionality on Android and iOS while using one component for both platforms. In the following section, you'll learn how to collect date/time input.

Collecting date/time input

In this final section of this chapter, you'll learn how to implement date/time pickers. React Native docs suggest using `@react-native-community/datetimepicker` independent date/time picker components for iOS and Android, which means that it is up to you to handle the cross-platform differences between the components.

To install datetimepicker, run the following command in the project:

```
npx expo install @react-native-community/datetimepicker
```

So, let's start with a DatePicker component for iOS:

```
export default function DatePicker(props: DatePickerProps) {
  return (
    <View style={styles.datePickerContainer}>
      <Text style={styles.datePickerLabel}>{props.label}</Text>
      <DateTimePicker
        mode="date"
        display="spinner"
        value={props.value}
        onChange={(event, date) => {
          if (date) {
            props.onChange(date);
          }
        }}
      />
    </View>
  );
}
```

There's not a lot to this component; it simply adds a label to the DateTimePicker component. The Android version works a bit differently; the better approach would be to use an **imperative API**. Let's take a look at the implementation:

```
export default function DatePicker({label, value, onChange }:
DatePickerProps) {
  return (
    <View style={styles.datePickerContainer}>
      <Text style={styles.datePickerLabel}>{label}</Text>
      <Text
        onPress={() => {
          DateTimePickerAndroid.open({
            value: value,
            mode: "date",
            onChange: (event, date) => {
              if (event.type === "set" && date) {
```

```
                onChange(date);
              }
            },
          });
        }}
      >
        {value.toLocaleDateString()}
      </Text>
    </View>
  );
}
```

The key difference between the two date pickers is that the Android version doesn't use a React Native component like DateTimePicker in iOS. Instead, we have to use the imperative DateTimePickerAndroid.open() API. This is triggered when the user presses the date text that our component renders and opens a date picker dialog. The good news is that this component of ours hides this API behind a declarative component.

 I've also implemented a time picker component that follows this exact pattern. So, rather than listing that code here, I suggest that you download the code for this book from https://github.com/PacktPublishing/React-and-React-Native-5E/tree/main/Chapter22 so that you can see the subtle differences and run the example.

Now, let's learn how to use our date and time picker components:

```
export default function CollectingDateTimeInput() {
  const [date, setDate] = useState(new Date());
  const [time, setTime] = useState(new Date());

  return (
    <View style={styles.container}>
      <DatePicker
        label="Pick a date, any date:"
        value={date}
        onChange={setDate}
      />
      <TimePicker
```

```
        label="Pick a time, any time:"
        value={time}
        onChange={setTime}
      />
    </View>
  );
}
```

Awesome! Now, we have DatePicker and TimePicker components that can help us select dates and times in our app. Also, they both work on iOS and Android. Let's see how the pickers look on iOS:

Figure 22.8: iOS date and time pickers

As you can see, the iOS date and time pickers use the Picker component that you learned about earlier in this chapter. The Android picker looks a lot different; let's look at it now:

Figure 22.9: Android date picker

The Android version follows a completely different approach from the iOS date/time picker, yet we can use the same DatePicker component that we've created on both platforms. This brings us to the end of the chapter.

Summary

In this chapter, we learned about the various React Native components that resemble the form elements from the web that we're used to. We started off by learning about text input and how each text input has its own virtual keyboard to take into consideration. Next, we learned about Picker components, which allow the user to select an item from a list of options. Then, we learned about the Switch component, which is kind of like a checkbox. With these components, you will be able to build a form of any complexity.

In the final section, we learned how to implement generic date/time pickers that work on both iOS and Android. In the next chapter, we'll learn about modal dialogs in React Native.

23

Responding to User Gestures

All of the examples that you've implemented so far in this book have relied on user gestures. In traditional web applications, you mostly deal with mouse events. However, touchscreens rely on the user manipulating elements with their fingers, which is fundamentally different from the mouse.

In this chapter, first, you'll learn about scrolling. This is probably the most common gesture, besides touch. Then, you'll learn about giving the user the appropriate level of feedback when they interact with your components. Finally, you'll implement components that can be swiped.

The goal of this chapter is to show you how the **gesture response system** inside React Native works and some of the ways in which this system is exposed via components.

In this chapter, we'll cover the following topics:

- Scrolling with your fingers
- Giving touch feedback
- Using Swipeable and cancellable components

Technical requirements

You can find the code files for this chapter on GitHub at https://github.com/PacktPublishing/React-and-React-Native-5E/tree/main/Chapter23.

Scrolling with your fingers

Scrolling in web applications is done by using the mouse pointer to drag the scrollbar back and forth or up and down, or by spinning the mouse wheel. This doesn't work on mobile devices because there's no mouse. Everything is controlled by gestures on the screen.

For example, if you want to scroll down, you use your thumb or index finger to pull the content up by physically moving your finger over the screen.

Scrolling like this is difficult to implement, but it gets more complicated. When you scroll on a mobile screen, the velocity of the dragging motion is taken into consideration. You drag the screen fast, then let go, and the screen continues to scroll based on how fast you moved your finger. You can also touch the screen while this is happening to stop it from scrolling.

Thankfully, you don't have to handle most of this stuff. The ScrollView component handles much of the scrolling complexity for you. In fact, you've already used the ScrollView component back in *Chapter 20, Rendering Item Lists*. The ListView component has ScrollView baked into it.

 You can adjust the low-level parts of user interactions by implementing gesture life cycle methods. You'll probably never need to do this, but if you're interested, you can read about it at https://reactnative.dev/docs/gesture-responder-system.

You can use ScrollView outside of ListView. For example, if you're just rendering arbitrary content such as text and other widgets: not a list, in other words: you can just wrap it in <ScrollView>. Here's an example:

```
export default function App() {
  return (
    <View style={styles.container}>
      <ScrollView style={styles.scroll}>
        {new Array(20).fill(null).map((v, i) => (
          <View key={i}>
            <Text style={[styles.scrollItem, styles.text]}>Some text</
Text>
            <ActivityIndicator style={styles.scrollItem} size="large" />
            <Switch style={styles.scrollItem} />
          </View>
        ))}
      </ScrollView>
    </View>
  );
}
```

The ScrollView component isn't of much use on its own: it's there to wrap other components. It needs height in order to function correctly. Here's what the scroll style looks like:

```
scroll: {
    height: 1,
    alignSelf: "stretch",
  },
```

The height property is set to 1, but the stretch value of alignSelf allows the items to display properly. Here's what the end result looks like:

Figure 23.1: ScrollView

There's a vertical scrollbar on the right-hand side of the screen as you drag the content down. If you run this example, you can play around with making various gestures, such as making content scroll on its own and then making it stop.

When the user scrolls through content on the screen, they receive visual feedback. Users should also receive visual feedback when they touch certain elements on the screen.

Giving touch feedback

The React Native examples you've worked with so far in this book have used plain text to act as buttons or links. In web applications, to make text look like something that can be clicked, you just wrap it with the appropriate link. There's no link component in React Native, so you can style your text to look like a button.

 The problem with trying to style text as links on mobile devices is that they're too hard to press. Buttons provide a bigger target for fingers, and they're easier to apply touch feedback on.

Let's style some text as a button. This is a great first step as it makes the text look touchable. But you also want to give visual feedback to the user when they start interacting with the button. React Native provides several components to help with this:

- `TouchableOpacity`
- `TouchableHighlight`
- `Pressable` API

But before diving into the code, let's take a look at what these components look like visually when users interact with them, starting with TouchableOpacity:

Figure 23.2: TouchableOpacity

There are three buttons being rendered here. The top one, labeled **Opacity**, is currently being pressed by the user. The opacity of the button is dimmed when pressed, which provides important visual feedback for the user.

Let's see what the **Highlight** button looks like when pressed:

Figure 23.3: TouchableHighlight

Instead of changing the opacity when pressed, the TouchableHighlight component adds a high-light layer over the button. In this case, it's highlighted using a more transparent version of the slate gray that's being used in the font and border colors.

The last example of a button is provided by the Pressable component. The Pressable API has been introduced as a core component wrapper and allows different stages of press interaction on any of its defined children. With such components, we can handle onPressIn, onPressOut (which we explore in the next chapter), and onLongPress callbacks and implement any touchable feedback that we want. Let's take a look at how PressableButton looks when we click on it:

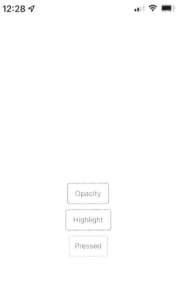

Figure 23.4: Pressable button

If we continue to keep our finger on this button, we get an `onLongPress` event and the button will update:

Figure 23.5: Long Pressed button

It doesn't really matter which approach you use. The important thing is that you provide the appropriate touch feedback for your users as they interact with your buttons. In fact, you might want to use all the approaches in the same app, but for different things.

Let's create an `OpacityButton` and `HighlightButton` component, which makes it easy to use the first two approaches:

```
type ButtonProps = {
  label: string;
  onPress: () => void;
```

```
};

export const OpacityButton = ({ label, onPress }: ButtonProps) => {
  return (
    <TouchableOpacity
      style={styles.button}
      onPress={onPress}
      activeOpacity={0.5}
    >
      <Text style={styles.buttonText}>{label}</Text>
    </TouchableOpacity>
  );
};

export const HighlightButton = ({ label, onPress }: ButtonProps) => {
  return (
    <TouchableHighlight
      style={styles.button}
      underlayColor="rgba(112,128,144,0.3)"
      onPress={onPress}
    >
      <Text style={styles.buttonText}>{label}</Text>
    </TouchableHighlight>
  );
};
```

Here are the styles that were used to create this button:

```
button: {
    padding: 10,
    margin: 5,
    backgroundColor: "azure",
    borderWidth: 1,
    borderRadius: 4,
    borderColor: "slategrey",
  },
  buttonText: {
    color: "slategrey",
  },
```

Now let's take a look at the button based on the Pressable API:

```
const PressableButton = () => {
  const [text, setText] = useState("Not Pressed");

  return (
    <Pressable
      onPressIn={() => setText("Pressed")}
      onPressOut={() => setText("Press")}
      onLongPress={() => {
        setText("Long Pressed");
      }}
      delayLongPress={500}
      style={({ pressed }) => [
        {
          opacity: pressed ? 0.5 : 1,
        },
        styles.button,
      ]}
    >
      <Text>{text}</Text>
    </Pressable>
  );
};
```

Here's how you can put those buttons into the main app module:

```
export default function App() {
  return (
    <View style={styles.container}>
      <OpacityButton onPress={() => {}} label="Opacity" />
      <HighlightButton onPress={() => {}} label="Highlight" />
      <PressableButton />
    </View>
  );
}
```

Note that the onPress callbacks don't actually do anything: we're passing them because they're a required property.

In the following section, you'll learn about providing feedback when the user swipes elements across the screen.

Using Swipeable and Cancellable components

Part of what makes native mobile applications easier to use than mobile web applications is that they feel more intuitive. Using gestures, you can quickly get a handle on how things work. For example, swiping an element across the screen with your finger is a common gesture, but the gesture has to be discoverable.

Let's say that you're using an app, and you're not exactly sure what something on the screen does. So, you press down with your finger and try dragging the element. It starts to move. Unsure of what will happen, you lift your finger up, and the element moves back into place. You've just discovered how part of this application works.

You'll use the Scrollable component to implement **swipeable** and **cancellable** behaviors like this. You can create a somewhat generic component that allows the user to swipe text off the screen and, when that happens, call a callback function. Let's look at the code that will render the swipeables before we look at the generic component itself:

```
export default function SwipableAndCancellable() {
  const [items, setItems] = useState(
    new Array(10).fill(null).map((v, id) => ({ id, name: "Swipe Me" }))
  );

  function onSwipe(id: number) {
    return () => {
      setItems(items.filter((item) => item.id !== id));
    };
  }

  return (
    <View style={styles.container}>
      {items.map((item) => (
        <Swipeable
          key={item.id}
          onSwipe={onSwipe(item.id)}
          name={item.name}
          width={200}
```

```
        />
      ))}
    </View>
  );
}
```

This will render 10 `<Swipeable>` components on the screen. Let's see what this looks like:

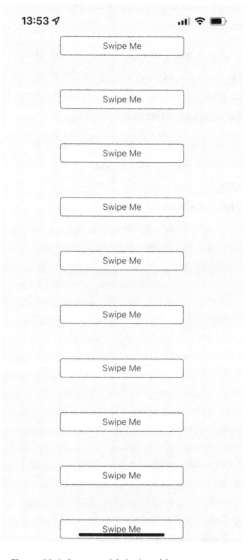

Figure 23.6: Screen with Swipeable components

Now, if you start to swipe one of these items to the left, it will move. Here's what this looks like:

Figure 23.7: Swiped component

If you don't swipe far enough, the gesture will be canceled and the item will move back into place, as expected. If you swipe it all the way, the item will be removed from the list completely and the items on the screen will fill the empty space.

Now, let's take a look at the Swipeable component itself:

```
type SwipeableProps = {
```

```
  name: string;
  width: number;
  onSwipe: () => void;
};

export default function Swipeable({ name, width, onSwipe }:
SwipeableProps) {
  function onScroll(e: NativeSyntheticEvent<NativeScrollEvent>) {
    console.log(e.nativeEvent.contentOffset.x);
    e.nativeEvent.contentOffset.x >= width && onSwipe();
  }

  return (
    <View style={styles.swipeContainer}>
      <ScrollView
        horizontal
        snapToInterval={width}
        showsHorizontalScrollIndicator={false}
        scrollEventThrottle={10}
        onScroll={onScroll}
      >
        <View style={[styles.swipeItem, { width }]}>
          <Text style={styles.swipeItemText}>{name}</Text>
        </View>

        <View style={[styles.swipeBlank, { width }]} />
      </ScrollView>
    </View>
  );
}
```

The component accepts the width property to specify the width itself, snapToInterval to create paging-like behavior with swipe canceling, and handling the distance where we can call the onSwipe callback to remove items from the list.

To enable swipe to the left, we need to add a blank component beside the component with text in it. Here are the styles that are used for this component:

```
  swipeContainer: {
```

```
    flex: 1,
    flexDirection: "row",
    width: 200,
    height: 30,
    marginTop: 50,
  },

  swipeItem: {
    height: 30,
    backgroundColor: "azure",
    justifyContent: "center",
    borderWidth: 1,
    borderRadius: 4,
    borderColor: "slategrey",
  },

  swipeItemText: {
    textAlign: "center",
    color: "slategrey",
  },

  swipeItemBlank: {
    height: 30,
  },
```

The `swipeItemBlank` style has the same height as `swipeItem`, but nothing else. It's invisible.

We have now covered all the topics in this chapter.

Summary

In this chapter, we were introduced to the idea that gestures on native platforms make a significant difference compared to mobile web platforms. We started off by looking at the `ScrollView` component, and how it makes life much simpler by providing native scrolling behavior for wrapped components.

Next, we spent some time implementing buttons with touch feedback. This is another area that's tricky to get right on the mobile web. We learned how to use the `TouchableOpacity`, `TouchableHighlight`, and `Pressable` API components to do this.

Finally, we implemented a generic `Swipeable` component. Swiping is a common mobile pattern, and it allows the user to discover how things work without feeling intimidated.

In the next chapter, we'll learn how to control animation using React Native.

24

Showing Progress

This chapter is all about communicating progress to the user. React Native has different components that are used to handle the different types of progress that you want to communicate. First, you'll learn why you need to communicate progress in the app. Then, you'll learn how to implement progress indicators and progress bars. And finally, you'll see specific examples that show you how to use progress indicators with navigation while data loads and progress bars to communicate the current position in a series of steps.

The following sections are covered in this chapter:

- Understanding progress and usability
- Indicating progress
- Measuring progress
- Exploring navigation indicators
- Step progress

Technical requirements

You can find the code files for this chapter on GitHub at https://github.com/PacktPublishing/React-and-React-Native-5E/tree/main/Chapter24.

Understanding progress and usability

Imagine that you have a microwave oven that has no window and makes no sound. The only way to interact with it is by pressing a button labeled "cook." As absurd as this device sounds, it's what many software users face: no indication of progress. Is the microwave cooking anything? If so, how do we know when it will be done?

One way to improve the microwave situation is to add a beep sound. This way, the user gets feedback after pressing the cook button. You've overcome one hurdle, but the user is still left asking, "When will my food be ready?" Before you go out of business, you had better add some sort of progress measurement display, such as a timer.

It's not that UI programmers don't understand the basic principles of this usability concern; it's just that they have stuff to do, and this sort of thing simply slips through the cracks in terms of priority. In React Native, there are components to give the user indeterminate progress feedback and precise progress measurements. It's always a good idea to make these things a top priority if you want a good user experience.

Now that you understand the role of progress in usability, it's time to learn how to indicate progress in your React Native UIs.

Indicating progress

In this section, you'll learn how to use the `ActivityIndicator` component. As its name suggests, you render this component when you need to indicate to the user that something is happening. The actual progress may be indeterminate, but at least you have a standardized way to show that something is happening, despite there being no results to display yet.

Let's create an example so that you can see what this component looks like. Here's the `App` component:

```
import React from "react";
import { View, ActivityIndicator } from "react-native";
import styles from "./styles";
export default function App() {
  return (
    <View style={styles.container}>
      <ActivityIndicator size="large" />
    </View>
  );
}
```

The <ActivityIndicator /> component is platform-agnostic. Here's how it looks on iOS:

Figure 24.1: An activity indicator on iOS

It renders an animated spinner in the middle of the screen. This is the large spinner, as specified in the size property. The ActivityIndicator spinner can also be small, which makes more sense if you're rendering it inside another smaller element.

Now, let's take a look at how this looks on an Android device:

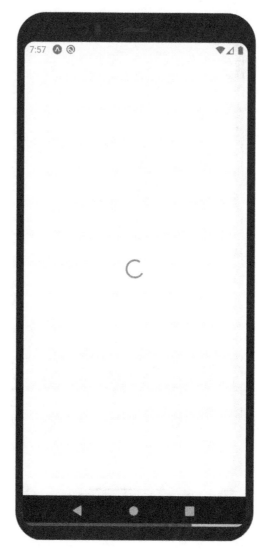

Figure 24.2: An activity indicator on Android

The spinner looks different, as it should, but your app conveys the same thing on both platforms: you're waiting for something.

This example spins forever. But don't worry: there's a more realistic progress indicator example coming up that shows you how to work with navigation and loading API data.

Exploring navigation indicators

Earlier in this chapter, you were introduced to the ActivityIndicator component. In this section, you'll learn how it can be used when navigating an application that loads data. For example, the user navigates from page or screen one to page two. However, page two needs to fetch data from the API that it can display to the user. So, while this network call is happening, it makes more sense to display a progress indicator instead of a screen devoid of useful information.

Doing this is actually kind of tricky because you have to make sure that the data that's required by the screen is fetched from the API each time the user navigates to the screen. Your goals should be as follows:

- Have the Navigator component automatically fetch API data for the scene that's about to be rendered.
- Use the promise that's returned by the API call as a means to display the spinner and hide it once the promise has been resolved.

Since your components probably don't care about whether a spinner is displayed or not, let's implement this as a generic Wrapper component:

```
export function LoadingWrapper({ children }: Props) {
  const [loading, setLoading] = useState(true);

  useEffect(() => {
    setTimeout(() => {
      setLoading(false);
    }, 1000);
  }, []);

  if (loading) {
    return (
      <View style={styles.container}>
        <ActivityIndicator size="large" />
      </View>
    );
  } else {
    return children;
  }
}
```

This `LoadingWrapper` component takes a `children` component and returns it (read renders) under a loading condition. It has a `useEffect()` hook with a timeout, and when it resolves, it changes the loading state to `false`. As you can see, the loading state determines whether the spinner or the `children` component is rendered.

With the `LoadingWrapper` component in place, let's take a look at the first screen component that you'll use with `react-navigation`:

```
const First = ({ navigation }: Props) => (
  <LoadingWrapper>
    <View style={styles.container}>
      <Button title="Second" onPress={() => navigation.navigate("Second")}
/>
      <Button title="Third" onPress={() => navigation.navigate("Third")}
/>
    </View>
  </LoadingWrapper>
);
```

This component renders a layout that's wrapped with the `LoadingWrapper` component we created earlier. It wraps the whole screen so that a spinner is displayed while the `setTimeout` method is pending. This is a useful approach to hiding extra logic in one place and reusing it on every page. Instead of the `setTimeout` method, in a real app, you can pass additional props to the `LoadingWrapper` and have full control of `loading` state from that screen itself.

Measuring progress

The downside of just indicating that progress is being made is that there's no end in sight for the user. This leads to a feeling of unease, like when you're waiting for food to cook in a microwave with no timer. When you know how much progress has been made and how much is left to go, you feel better. That is why it's always better to use a deterministic progress bar whenever possible.

Unlike the `ActivityIndicator` component, there's no platform-agnostic component in React Native for progress bars. So, we'll use the `react-native-progress` library for rendering progress bars.

 In the past, React-Native had special components for showing progress bars for iOS and Android, but due to React-Native size optimization, the Meta team is working on moving such components to separate packages. So, `ProgressViewIOS` and `ProgressBarAndroid` have been moved outside of the React-Native library.

Now, let's build the `ProgressBar` component that the application will use:

```
import * as Progress from "react-native-progress";

type ProgressBarProps = {
  progress: number;
};

export default function ProgressBar({ progress }: ProgressBarProps) {
  return (
    <View style={styles.progress}>
      <Text style={styles.progressText}>{Math.round(progress * 100)}%</
Text>
      <Progress.Bar width={200} useNativeDriver progress={progress} />
    </View>
  );
}
```

The `ProgressBar` component accepts the progress property and renders the label and progress bar. The `<Progress.Bar />` component accepts a set of props, but we need only width, progress, and `useNativeDriver` (for better animation). Now, let's put this component to use in the App component:

```
export default function MeasuringProgress() {
  const [progress, setProgress] = useState(0);

  useEffect(() => {
      let timeoutRef: NodeJS.Timeout | null = null;

    function updateProgress() {
        setProgress((currentProgress) => {
        if (currentProgress < 1) {
          return currentProgress + 0.01;
        } else {
          return 0;
        }
      });
      timeoutRef = setTimeout(updateProgress, 100);
```

```
    }

    updateProgress();

    return () => {
      timeoutRef && clearTimeout(timeoutRef);
    };
  }, []);

  return (
    <View style={styles.container}>
      <ProgressBar progress={progress} />
    </View>
  );
}
```

Initially, the `<ProgressBar>` component is rendered at 0%. In the `useEffect()` hook, the `updateProgress()` function uses a timer to simulate a real process that you want to show the progress of.

In the real world, you'll probably never use a simulation of timers. However, there are specific scenarios where this approach might be valuable, such as when displaying statistical data or monitoring the progress of file uploads to servers. In these situations, even though you're not relying on a direct timer, you will still have access to a current progress value that you can use.

Here's what the screen looks like:

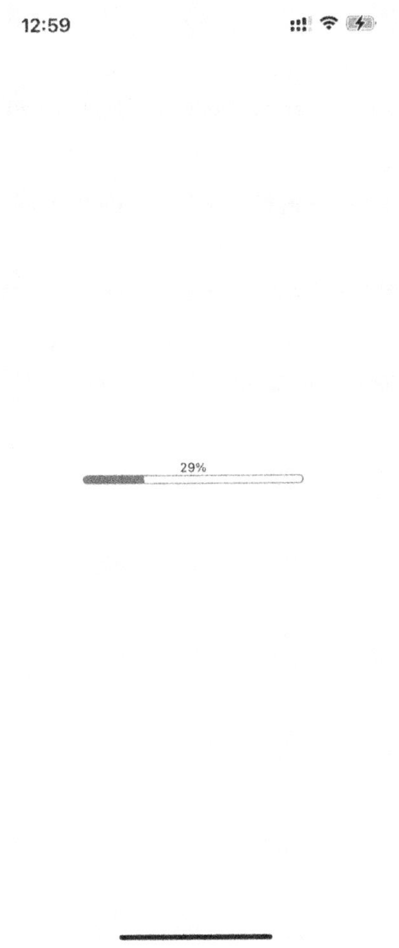

12:59   :::! 🛜 🔋

29%

Figure 24.3: The progress bar

Showing a quantitative measure of progress is important so that users can gauge how long something will take. In the next section, you'll learn how to use step progress bars to show the user where they are in terms of navigating screens.

Step progress

In this final example, you'll build an app that displays the user's progress through a predefined number of steps. For example, it might make sense to split a form into several logical sections and organize them in such a way that, as the user completes one section, they move to the next step. A progress bar would be helpful feedback for the user.

You'll insert a progress bar into the navigation bar, just below the title, so that the user knows how far they've gone and how far is left to go. You'll also reuse the ProgressBar component that you used earlier in this chapter.

Let's take a look at the result first. There are four screens in this app that the user can navigate. Here's what the **First** page (scene) looks like:

Figure 24.4: The first screen

The progress bar under the title reflects the fact that the user is 25% through the navigation. Let's see what the **Third** screen looks like:

Third Content

Figure 24.5: The third screen

The progress is updated to reflect where the user is in the route stack. Let's take a look at the App component here: `https://github.com/PacktPublishing/React-and-React-Native-5E/blob/main/Chapter21/step-progress-new/App.tsx`.

This app has four screens. The components that render each of these screens are stored in the `routes` constant, which is then used to configure the stack navigator using `createNativeStackNavigator()`. The reason for creating the `routes` array is so that it can be used by the `progress` parameter that is passed by `initialParams` to every route. To calculate the progress, we take the current route index as a value of the route's length.

For example, Second is in the number 2 position (an index of 1 + 1) and the length of the array is 4. This will set the progress bar to 50%.

Also, the **Next** and **Previous** buttons' calls to navigation.navigate() have to pass routeName, so we added the nextRouteName and prevRouteName variables to the screenOptions handler.

Summary

In this chapter, you learned how to show your users that something is happening behind the scenes. First, we discussed why showing progress is important for the usability of an application. Then, we implemented a basic screen that indicated progress was being made. After that, we implemented a ProgressBar component, which is used to measure specific progress amounts.

Indicators are good for indeterminate progress. We implemented navigation that showed progress indicators while network calls were pending. In the final section, we implemented a progress bar that showed the user where they were in a predefined number of steps.

In the next chapter, we'll look at React Native maps and geolocation data in action.

25

Displaying Modal Screens

The goal of this chapter is to show you how to present information to the user in ways that don't disrupt the current page. Pages use a View component and render it directly on the screen. There are times, however, when there's important information that the user needs to see but you don't necessarily want to kick them off the current page.

You'll start by learning how to display important information. By knowing what information is important and when to use it, you'll learn how to get user acknowledgment: both for error and success scenarios. Then, you'll implement passive notifications that show the user that something has happened. Finally, you'll implement **modal views** that show that something is happening in the background.

The following topics will be covered in this chapter:

- Terminology definitions
- Getting user confirmation
- Passive notifications
- Activity modals

Technical requirements

You can find the code files for this chapter on GitHub at https://github.com/PacktPublishing/ React-and-React-Native-5E/tree/main/Chapter25.

Terminology definitions

Before you dive into implementing alerts, notifications, and confirmations, let's take a few minutes and think about what each of these items means. I think this is important because if you end up passively notifying the user about an error, it can easily get missed. Here are my definitions of the types of information that you'll want to display:

- **Alert**: Something important just happened, and you need to ensure that the user sees what's going on. Possibly, the user needs to acknowledge the alert.

- **Confirmation**: This is part of an alert. For example, if the user has just performed an action and then wants to make sure that it was successful before carrying on, they would have to confirm that they've seen the information in order to close the modal. A confirmation can also exist within an alert, warning the user about an action that they're about to perform.

- **Notification**: Something happened but it's not important enough to completely block what the user is doing. These typically go away on their own.

The trick is to try to use notifications where the information is good to know but not critical. Use confirmations only when the workflow of the feature cannot continue without the user acknowledging what's going on. In the following sections, you'll see examples of alerts and notifications that are used for different purposes.

Getting user confirmation

In this section, you'll learn how to show modal views in order to get confirmation from the user. First, you'll learn how to implement a successful scenario, where an action generates a successful outcome that you want the user to be aware of. Then, you'll learn how to implement an error scenario where something went wrong and you don't want the user to move forward without acknowledging the issue.

Displaying a success confirmation

Let's start by implementing a modal view that's displayed as a result of the user successfully performing an action. Here's the Modal component, which is used to show the user a **confirmation modal**:

```
type Props = ModalProps & {
  onPressConfirm: () => void;
  onPressCancel: () => void;
};


export default function ConfirmationModal({
  onPressConfirm,
  onPressCancel,
  ...modalProps
}: Props) {
  return (
    <Modal transparent onRequestClose={() => {}} {...modalProps}>
      <View style={styles.modalContainer}>
        <View style={styles.modalInner}>
          <Text style={styles.modalText}>Dude, srsly?</Text>
          <Text style={styles.modalButton} onPress={onPressConfirm}>
            Yep
          </Text>
          <Text style={styles.modalButton} onPress={onPressCancel}>
            Nope
          </Text>
        </View>
      </View>
    </Modal>
  );
}
```

The properties that are passed to `ConfirmationModal` are forwarded to the React Native `Modal` component. You'll see why in a moment. First, let's see what this confirmation modal looks like:

Figure 25.1: The confirmation modal

The modal that's displayed once the user completes an action uses our own styling and confirmation message. It also has two actions, but it may only need one, depending on whether this confirmation is pre-action or post-action. Here are the styles that are being used for this modal:

```
modalContainer: {
    flex: 1,
    justifyContent: "center",
```

```
      alignItems: "center",
    },

    modalInner: {
      backgroundColor: "azure",
      padding: 20,
      borderWidth: 1,
      borderColor: "lightsteelblue",
      borderRadius: 2,
      alignItems: "center",
    },

    modalText: {
      fontSize: 16,
      margin: 5,
      color: "slategrey",
    },

    modalButton: {
      fontWeight: "bold",
      margin: 5,
      color: "slategrey",
    },
```

With the React Native Modal component, it's pretty much up to you how you want your confirmation modal view to look. Think of them as regular views, with the only difference being that they're rendered on top of other views.

A lot of the time, you might not care to style your own modal views. For example, in web browsers, you can simply call the alert() function, which shows text in a window that's styled by the browser. React Native has something similar: Alert.alert(). This is how we can open a native alert:

```
function toggleAlert() {
    Alert.alert("", "Failed to do the thing...", [
      {
        text: "Dismiss",
      },
    ]);
  }
```

Here's what the alert looks like on iOS:

Figure 25.2: A confirmation alert on iOS

In terms of functionality, there's nothing really different here. There is a title and text beneath it, but that's something that can easily be added to a modal view if you wanted. The real difference is that this modal looks like an iOS modal instead of something that's styled by the app. Let's see how this alert appears on Android:

Figure 25.3: A confirmation alert on Android

This modal looks like an Android modal, and you didn't have to style it. I think using alerts over modals is a better choice most of the time. It makes sense to have something styled to look like it's part of iOS or Android. However, there are times when you need more control over how the modal looks, such as when displaying error confirmations.

The approach to rendering modals is different from the approach to rendering alerts. However, they're both still declarative components that change based on the changing property values.

Error confirmation

All of the principles you learned about in the *Displaying a success confirmation* section are applicable when you need the user to acknowledge an error. If you need more control of the display, use a modal. For example, you might want the modal to be red and scary-looking, like this:

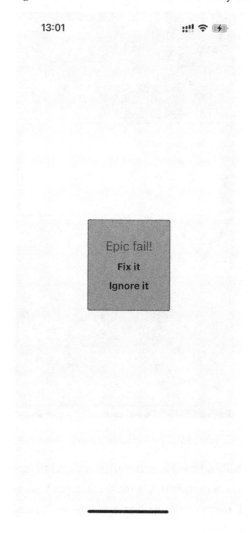

Figure 25.4: The error confirmation modal

Here are the styles that were used to create this look. Maybe you want something a bit more subtle, but the point is that you can make this look however you want:

```
modalInner: {
```

```
      backgroundColor: "azure",
      padding: 20,
      borderWidth: 1,
      borderColor: "lightsteelblue",
      borderRadius: 2,
      alignItems: "center",
   },
```

In the modalInner style property, we've defined screen styles. Next, we'll define modal styles:

```
   modalInnerError: {
      backgroundColor: "lightcoral",
      borderColor: "darkred",
   },

   modalText: {
      fontSize: 16,
      margin: 5,
      color: "slategrey",
   },

   modalTextError: {
      fontSize: 18,
      color: "darkred",
   },

   modalButton: {
      fontWeight: "bold",
      margin: 5,
      color: "slategrey",
   },

   modalButtonError: {
      color: "black",
   },
```

The same modal styles that you used for the success confirmations are still here. That's because the error confirmation modal needs many of the same style properties.

Here's how you apply both to the Modal component:

```
const innerViewStyle = [styles.modalInner, styles.modalInnerError];
const textStyle = [styles.modalText, styles.modalTextError];
const buttonStyle = [styles.modalButton, styles.modalButtonError];

type Props = ModalProps & {
  onPressConfirm: () => void;
  onPressCancel: () => void;
};

export default function ErrorModal({
  onPressConfirm,
  onPressCancel,
  ...modalProps
}: Props) {
  return (
    <Modal transparent onRequestClose={() => {}} {...modalProps}>
      <View style={styles.modalContainer}>
        <View style={innerViewStyle}>
          <Text style={textStyle}>Epic fail!</Text>
          <Text style={buttonStyle} onPress={onPressConfirm}>
            Fix it
          </Text>
          <Text style={buttonStyle} onPress={onPressCancel}>
            Ignore it
          </Text>
        </View>
      </View>
    </Modal>
  );
}
```

The styles are combined as arrays before they're passed to the style component property. The styles error always comes last, since conflicting style properties, such as backgroundColor, will be overridden by whatever comes later in the array.

In addition to styles in error confirmations, you can include whatever advanced controls you want. It really depends on how your application lets users cope with errors: for example, maybe there are several courses of action that can be taken.

However, the more common case is that something went wrong, and there's nothing you can do about it besides making sure that the user is aware of the situation. In these cases, you can probably get away with just displaying an alert:

Figure 25.5: An error alert

Now that you're able to display error notifications that require user engagement, it's time to learn about less aggressive notifications that don't disrupt what the user is currently doing.

Passive notifications

The notifications you've examined so far in this chapter all have required input from the user. This is by design because it's important information that you're forcing the user to look at. However, you don't want to overdo this. For notifications that are important but not life-altering if ignored, you can use **passive notifications**. These are displayed in a less obtrusive way than modals and don't require any user action to dismiss them.

In this section, you'll create an app that uses the **Toast API** provided by the react-native-root-toast library. It's called the Toast API because the information that's displayed looks like a piece of toast popping up. Toasts is a common component in Android to show some basic information that does not require user response. Since there is no Toast API for iOS, we will use a library that implements a similar API that works well on both platforms.

Here's what the App component looks like:

```
export default function PassiveNotifications() {
  return (
    <RootSiblingParent>
      <View style={styles.container}>
        <Text
          onPress={() => {
            Toast.show("Something happened!", {
              duration: Toast.durations.LONG,
            });
          }}
        >
          Show Notification
        </Text>
      </View>
    </RootSiblingParent>
  );
}
```

First we should wrap our app in the RootSiblingParent component and then we are ready to work with Toast API. To open a toast, we call the Toast.show method.

Here's what the Toast notification looks like:

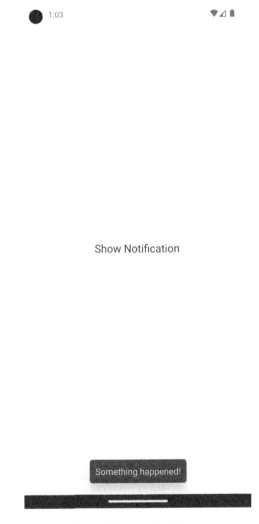

Figure 25.6: An Android toast

A notification stating **Something happened!** is displayed at the bottom of the screen and is removed after a short delay. The key is that the notification is unobtrusive.

Let's take a look at how the same toasts look on an iOS device:

Figure 25.7: An iOS notification

In the next section, you'll learn about activity modals, which show the user that something is happening.

Activity modals

In this final section of this chapter, you'll implement a modal that shows a progress indicator. The idea is to display the modal and then hide it when the promise resolves. Here's the code for the generic `Activity` component, which shows a modal with `ActivityIndicator`:

```
type ActivityProps = {
  visible: boolean;
  size?: "small" | "large";
};


export default function Activity({ visible, size = "large" }:
ActivityProps) {
  return (
    <Modal visible={visible} transparent>
      <View style={styles.modalContainer}>
        <ActivityIndicator size={size} />
      </View>
    </Modal>
  );
}
```

You might be tempted to pass the promise to the component so that it automatically hides when the promise resolves. I don't think this is a good idea because then you would have to introduce the state into this component. Furthermore, it would depend on a promise in order to function. With the way you've implemented this component, you can show or hide the modal based on the `visible` property alone.

Here's what the activity modal looks like on iOS:

Figure 25.8: An activity modal

There's a semi-transparent background on the modal that's placed over the main view with the **Fetch Stuff...** link. By clicking on this link, we will be shown the **activity loader**. Here's how this effect is created in styles.js:

```
modalContainer: {
    flex: 1,
    justifyContent: "center",
    alignItems: "center",
```

```
      backgroundColor: "rgba(0, 0, 0, 0.2)",
    },
```

Instead of setting the actual Modal component to transparent, you can set the transparency in backgroundColor, which gives the look of an overlay. Now, let's take a look at the code that controls this component:

```
export default function App() {

  const [fetching, setFetching] = useState(false);
  const [promise, setPromise] = useState(Promise.resolve());

  function onPress() {
    setPromise(
      new Promise((resolve) => setTimeout(resolve, 3000)).then(() => {
        setFetching(false);
      })
    );
    setFetching(true);
  }

  return (
    <View style={styles.container}>
      <Activity visible={fetching} />
      <Text onPress={onPress}>Fetch Stuff...</Text>
    </View>
  );
}
```

When the fetch link is pressed, a new promise is created that simulates asynchronous network activity. Then, when the promise resolves, you can change the fetching state back to false so that the activity dialog is hidden.

Summary

In this chapter, we learned about the need to show important information to mobile users. This sometimes involves explicit feedback from the user, even if that just means acknowledging the message. In other cases, passive notifications work better, since they're less obtrusive than confirmation modals.

There are two tools that we can use to display messages to users: modals and alerts. Modals are more flexible because they're just like regular views. Alerts are good for displaying plain text, and they take care of styling concerns for us. On Android, we have the `ToastAndroid` interface as well. We saw that it's also possible to do this on iOS, but it just requires more work.

In the next chapter, we'll dig deeper into the gesture response system inside React Native, which makes for a better mobile experience than browsers can provide.

26

Using Animations

Animations can be used to improve the user experience in mobile applications. They usually help users to quickly recognize that something has changed, or help them focus on what is important. They improve the user experience and user satisfaction. Also, animations are simply fun to look at. For example, the heartbeat reaction in the Instagram app when you like a post or the Snapchat ghost animation when refreshing a page.

There are a couple of different approaches to processing and controlling animations in React Native. Firstly, we will take a look at animation tools that we can use, discover their pros and cons, and compare them. Then, we will implement several examples to get to know APIs better.

We'll cover the following topics in this chapter:

- Using React Native Reanimated
- Animating layout components
- Animating component styles

Technical requirements

You can find the code files for this chapter on GitHub at https://github.com/PacktPublishing/React-and-React-Native-5E/tree/main/Chapter26.

Using React Native Reanimated

In the React Native world, we have a lot of libraries and approaches to animate our components, including the built-in **Animated API**. But in this chapter, I would like to opt for a library called **React Native Reanimated** and compare it with the Animated API to learn why it is the best choice.

The Animated API

The **Animated API** is the most common tool used to animate components in React Native. It has a set of methods that help you to create an animation object, control its state, and process it. The main benefit is that it can be used with any component, and not just animated components such as View or Text.

But, at the same time, this API has been implemented in the old architecture of React Native. Asynchronous communications between JavaScript and UI Native threads are used with the Animated API, delaying updates by at least one frame and lasting approximately 16 ms. Sometimes, the delay may last even longer if the JavaScript thread is running React's diff algorithm and comparing or processing network requests simultaneously. The problem of dropped or delayed frames can be solved with the React Native Reanimated library, which is based on the new architecture and processes all business logic from the JavaScript thread in the UI thread.

React Native Reanimated

React Native Reanimated can be utilized to provide a more exhaustive abstraction of the Animated API to use with React Native. It provides an imperative API with multistage animations and custom transitions, while at the same time providing a declarative API that can be used to describe simple animations and transitions in a similar way to how CSS transitions work. It's built on top of React Native Animated and reimplements it on the Native thread. This allows you to use the familiar JavaScript language while taking advantage of the most high performance and simple API.

Furthermore, React Native Reanimated defines worklets, which are JavaScript functions that can be synchronously executed within the UI thread. This allows instant animations without having to wait for a new frame. Let's take a look at what a simple worklet looks like:

```
function simpleWorklet() {
  "worklet";
  console.log("Hello from UI thread");
}
```

The only thing that is needed for the `simpleWorklet` function to get called inside the UI thread is to add the `worklet` directive at the top of the `function` block.

React Native Reanimated provides a variety of hooks and methods that help us handle animations:

- useSharedValue: This hook returns a SharedValue instance, which is the main stateful data object that lives in the UI thread context and has a similar concept to Animated. Value in the core Animated API. A Reanimated animation is triggered when SharedValue is changed. The key benefit is that updates to shared values can be synchronized across the React Native and UI threads without triggering a re-render. This enables complex animations to run smoothly at 60 FPS without blocking the JS thread.

- useDerivedValue: This hook creates a new shared value that automatically updates whenever the shared values used in its calculation change. It allows you to create shared values that depend on other shared values, while keeping them all reactive. useDerivedValue is used to create a **derived** state in a worklet that runs on the UI thread based on updates to the source shared values. This derived state can then drive animations or other side effects without triggering a re-render on the JS thread.

- useAnimatedStyle: The hook allows you to create a style object with the ability to animate its properties based on shared values. It maps shared value updates to the corresponding view properties. useAnimatedStyle is the main way to connect shared values to views and enable smooth animations running on the UI thread.

- withTiming, withSpring, withDecay: These are animation utility methods that update a shared value in a smooth, animated way using various curves and physics. They allow you to define animations declaratively by specifying the target value and animation configuration.

We have learned what React Native Reanimated is and how it is different from the Animated API. Next, let's try to install it and apply it to our app.

Installing the React Native Reanimated library

To install the React Native Reanimated library, run this command inside your Expo project:

```
expo install react-native-reanimated
```

After the installation is complete, we need to add the **Babel** plugin to babel.config.js:

```
module.exports = function(api) {
  api.cache(true);
  return {
    presets: ['babel-preset-expo'],
```

```
        plugins: ['react-native-reanimated/plugin'],
    };
};
```

The main purpose of that plugin is to convert our JavaScript worklet functions into functions that will work in the UI thread.

After you add the Babel plugin, restart your development server and clear the bundler cache:

```
expo start --clear
```

This section has introduced us to the React Native Reanimated library. We have found out why it is better than the built-in Animated API. In the next sections, we will use it in real examples.

Animating layout components

A common use case is animating the entering and exiting layouts of your components. This means that when your component renders for the first time and when you unmount your component, it appears animated. React Native Reanimated is an API that lets you animate layouts and add animations such as FadeIn, BounceIn, and ZoomIn.

React Native Reanimated also provides a special Animated component that is the same as the Animated component in the Animated API, but with additional props:

- entering: Accepts a predefined animation when the component mounts and renders
- exiting: Accepts the same animation object, but it will be called when the component unmounts

Let's create a simple to-do list with a button for creating tasks and a feature that allows us to delete tasks when we click on them.

 It's impossible to see animations in screenshots, so I suggest you open the code and try to implement the animations to see the results.

Firstly, let's take a look at the main screen of our to-do list app and how the items are rendering at the moment:

Figure 26.1: To-do list

This is a simple example with a list of task items and one button for adding new tasks. When we quickly press the **Add** button several times, the list items come from the left side of the screen with an animation:

Figure 26.2: To-do list with animated rendering

The magic is implemented in the TodoItem component. Let's take a look at it:

```
export const TodoItem = ({ id, title, onPress }) => {
  return (
    <Animated.View entering={SlideInLeft}
      exiting={SlideOutRight}>
      <TouchableOpacity onPress={() => onPress(id)}
        style={styles.todoItem}>
        <Text>{title}</Text>
      </TouchableOpacity>
    </Animated.View>
  );
};
```

As you can see, there is no complicated logic, and there isn't too much code. We just take the Animated component as the root of animation and pass predefined animations from the React Native Reanimated library to the entering and exiting props.

To see how the items disappear from the screen, we need to press the to-do items so the exiting animation will run. I've pressed a few items and tried to catch the result in the following screenshot:

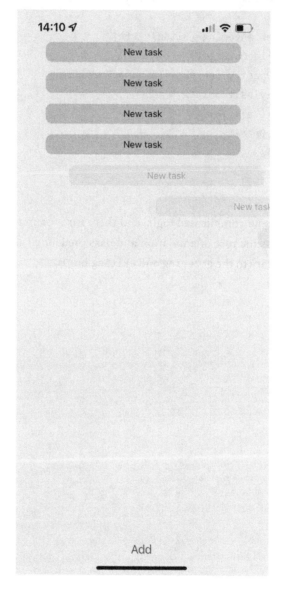

Figure 26.3: Deleting to-do items from the screen

Let's examine the App component to see the entire picture:

```
export default function App() {
  const [todoList, setTodoList] = useState([]);
```

```
    const addTask = () => {
      setTodoList([
        ...todoList,
        { id: String(new Date().getTime()), title: "New task"
          },
      ]);
    };
    const deleteTask = (id) => {
      setTodoList(todoList.filter((todo) => todo.id !== id));
    };
```

We have created a todoList state using the useState hook and handler functions for adding and deleting tasks. Next, let's take a look at how the animation will be applied to the layout:

```
    return (
      <View style={styles.container}>
        <View style={{ flex: 1 }}>
          {todoList.map(({ id, title }) => (
            <TodoItem key={id} id={id} title={title}
              onPress={deleteTask} />
          ))}
        </View>
        <Button onPress={addTask} title="Add" />
      </View>
    );
  }
```

In this example, we learned a simple way to apply animations to make our app look better. However, the React Native Reanimated library is a lot more powerful than we imagined. The next example illustrates how we can animate and create our own animations by applying them directly to the styles of our components.

Animating component styles

In a more complex example, I suggest creating a button with beautiful tappable feedback. This button will be built using the Pressable component that we learned about in *Chapter 23, Responding to User Gestures*. This component accepts the onPressIn, onLongPress, and onPressOut events. As a result of these events, we will be able to see how our touches will be reflected on the button.

Let's start by defining `SharedValue` and `AnimatedStyle`:

```
const radius = useSharedValue(30);
const opacity = useSharedValue(1);
const scale = useSharedValue(1);
const color = useSharedValue(0);

const backgroundColor = useDerivedValue(() => {
  return interpolateColor(color.value, [0, 1], ["orange",        "red"]);
   });

const animatedStyles = useAnimatedStyle(() => {
  return {
    opacity: opacity.value,
    borderRadius: radius.value,
    transform: [{ scale: scale.value }],
    backgroundColor: backgroundColor.value,
  };
}, []);
```

In order to animate style properties, we have created a `SharedValue` object using the `useSharedValue` hook. It takes default values as an argument. Next, we created the style object with the `useAnimatedStyle` hook. The hook accepts the callback that should return a style object. The `useAnimatedStyle` hook is similar to the `useMemo` hook, but all calculations are performed in the UI thread and all `SharedValue` changes will invoke the hook to recalculate the style object. The background color of the button was created using `useDerivedValue` by interpolating between orange and red to provide a smooth transition.

Next, let's create handler functions that will update the style properties in relation to the pressing state of the button:

```
const onPressIn = () => {
  radius.value = withSpring(20);
  opacity.value = withSpring(0.7);
  scale.value = withSpring(0.9);
};
const onLongPress = () => {
  scale.value = withSpring(0.8);
```

```
    color.value = withSpring(1);
  };
  const onPressOut = () => {
    radius.value = withSpring(30);
    opacity.value = withSpring(1);
    scale.value = withSpring(1, { damping: 50 });
    color.value = withSpring(0);
  };
```

The first handler, onPressIn, updates borderRadius, opacity, and scale from their default values. We also update these values using withSpring, which makes updating styles smoother. Like the first handler, other ones will also update the style of the button but in different ways. onLongPress turns the button red and makes it smaller. onPressOut resets all values to their default values.

We've implemented all necessary logic and can now apply it to the layout:

```
    <View style={styles.container}>
      <Animated.View style={[styles.buttonContainer,
        animatedStyles]}>
        <Pressable
          onPressIn={onPressIn}
          onPressOut={onPressOut}
          onLongPress={onLongPress}
          style={styles.button}
        >
          <Text style={styles.buttonText}>Press me</Text>
        </Pressable>
      </Animated.View>
    </View>
```

Finally, let's take a look at the result:

Figure 26.4: Button with default, pressed, and long-pressed styles

In *Figure 26.4*, you can see the three states of the button: default, pressed, and long-pressed.

Summary

In this chapter, we've learned how to use the React Native Reanimated library to add animations to the layout and components. We've gone through the basic principles of the library and found out how it works under the hood and how it executes code inside the UI thread without using Bridge to connect JavaScript and Native layers of the app.

We also went through two examples using the React Native Reanimated library. In the first example, we learned how to apply a layout animation using predefined declarative animations to get our component to appear and disappear beautifully. In the second example, we animated the button's styles with the `useSharedValue` and `useAnimatedStyle` hooks.

Skills to animate components and layout will help you make your app more beautiful and responsive. In the next chapter, we'll learn about controlling images in our apps.

27

Controlling Image Display

So far, the examples in this book haven't rendered any images on mobile screens. This doesn't reflect the reality of mobile applications. Web applications display lots of images. If anything, native mobile applications rely on images even more than web applications because images are a powerful tool when you have a limited amount of space.

In this chapter, you'll learn how to use the React Native Image component, starting with loading images from different sources. Then, you'll learn how you can use the Image component to resize images, and how you can set placeholders for lazily loaded images. Finally, you'll learn how to implement icons using the @expo/vector-icons package. These sections cover the most common use cases for using images and icons in apps.

We'll cover the following topics in this chapter:

- Loading images
- Resizing images
- Lazy image loading
- Rendering icons

Technical requirements

You can find the code and image files for this chapter on GitHub at https://github.com/PacktPublishing/React-and-React-Native-5E/tree/main/Chapter27.

Loading images

Let's get started by figuring out how to load images. You can render the `<Image>` component and pass its properties just like any other React component. But this particular component needs image blob data to be of any use. A **BLOB** (short for **Binary Large Object**) is a data type used to store large, unstructured binary data. BLOBs are commonly used to store multimedia files like images, audio, and video.

Let's look at some code:

```
const reactLogo = "https://reactnative.dev/docs/assets/favicon.png";
const relayLogo = require("./assets/relay.png");

export default function App() {
  return (
    <View style={styles.container}>
      <Image style={styles.image} source={{ uri: reactLogo }} />
      <Image style={styles.image} source={relayLogo} />
    </View>
  );
}
```

There are two ways to load the blob data into an `<Image>` component. The first approach loads the image data from the network. This is done by passing an object with a **URI** property to the source code. The second `<Image>` component in this example is using a local image file. It does this by calling `require()` and passing the result to the source code.

Now, let's see what the rendered result looks like:

Figure 27.1: Image loading

Here's the style that was used with these images:

```
image: {
  width: 100,
  height: 100,
  margin: 20,
},
```

Note that without the `width` and `height` style properties, images will not render. In the next section, you'll learn how image resizing works when the `width` and `height` values are set.

Resizing images

The `width` and `height` style properties of `Image` components determine the size of what's rendered on the screen. For example, you'll probably have to work with images at some point that have a larger resolution than you want to be displayed in your React Native application. Simply setting the `width` and `height` style properties on the `Image` is enough to properly scale the image.

Let's look at some code that lets you dynamically adjust the dimensions of an image using controls:

```
export default function App() {
  const source = require("./assets/flux.png");
  const [width, setWidth] = useState(100);
  const [height, setHeight] = useState(100);

  return (
    <View style={styles.container}>
      <Image source={source} style={{ width, height }} />
      <Text>Width: {width}</Text>
      <Text>Height: {height}</Text>
      <Slider
        style={styles.slider}
        minimumValue={50}
        maximumValue={150}
        value={width}
        onValueChange={(value) => {
          setWidth(value);
          setHeight(value);
        }}
      />
```

```
      </View>
   );
}
```

Here's what the image looks like if you're using the default 100 x 100 dimensions:

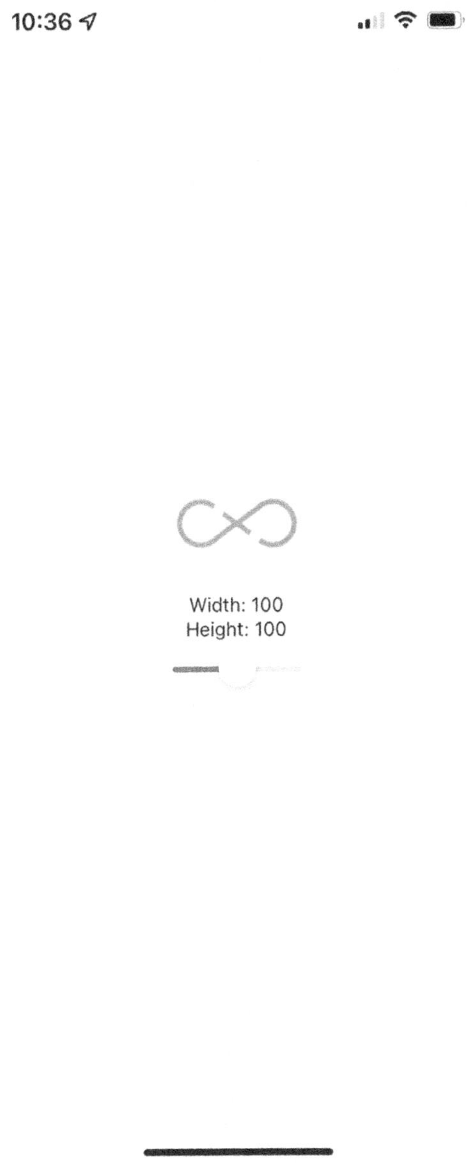

10:36 ✈   ⚬ 📶 🔋

Width: 100
Height: 100

Figure 27.2: 100 x 100 image

Here's a scaled-down version of the image:

Figure 27.3: 50 x 50 image

Lastly, here's a scaled-up version of the image:

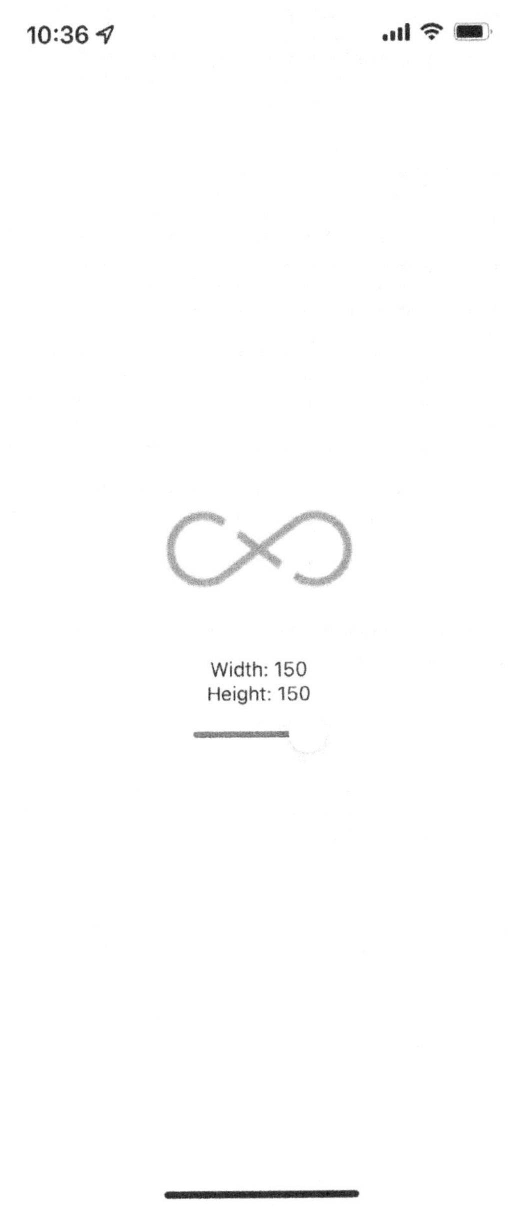

10:36 ✈

.ıl 🛜 🔋

Width: 150
Height: 150

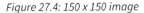

Figure 27.4: 150 x 150 image

 There's a `resizeMode` property that you can pass to `Image` components. This determines how the scaled image fits within the dimensions of the actual component. You'll see this property in action in the *Rendering icons* section of this chapter.

As you can see, the dimensions of the images are controlled by the `width` and `height` style properties. Images can even be resized while the app is running by changing these values. In the next section, you'll learn how to lazily load images.

Lazy image loading

Sometimes, you don't necessarily want an image to load at the exact moment that it's rendered; for example, you might be rendering something that's not visible on the screen yet. Most of the time, it's perfectly fine to fetch the image source from the network before it's actually visible. But if you're fine-tuning your application and discover that loading lots of images over the network causes performance issues, you can use the lazy loading strategy.

I think the more common use case in a mobile context is handling a scenario where you've rendered one or more images where they're visible, but the network is slow to respond. In this case, you will probably want to render a placeholder image so that the user sees something right away, rather than an empty space. So, let's get started.

Firstly, you can implement an abstraction that wraps the actual image that you want to show once it's loaded. Here's the code for this:

```
const placeholder = require("./assets/placeholder.png");
type PlaceholderProps = {
  loaded: boolean;
  style: StyleProp<ImageStyle>;
};

function Placeholder({ loaded, style }: PlaceholderProps) {
  if (loaded) {
    return null;
  } else {
    return <Image style={style} source={placeholder} />;
  }
}
```

Now, here, you can see the placeholder image will be rendered only while the original image isn't loaded:

```
type Props = {
  style: StyleProp<ImageStyle>;
  resizeMode: ImageProps["resizeMode"];
```

```
    source: ImageSourcePropType | null;
};

export default function LazyImage({ style, resizeMode, source }: Props) {
  const [loaded, setLoaded] = useState(false);

  return (
    <View style={style}>
      {!!source ? (
        <Image
          source={source}
          resizeMode={resizeMode}
          style={style}
          onLoad={() => {
            setLoaded(true);
          }}
        />
      ) : (
        <Placeholder loaded={loaded} style={style} />
      )}
    </View>
  );
}
```

This component renders a `View` component with two `Image` components inside it. It also has a loaded state, which is initially `false`. When `loaded` is `false`, the placeholder image is rendered. The loaded state is set to `true` when the `onLoad()` handler is called. This means that the placeholder image is removed and the main image is displayed.

Now, let's use the `LazyImage` component that we've just implemented. You'll render the image without a source, and the placeholder image should be displayed. Let's add a button that gives the lazy image a source. When it loads, the placeholder image should be replaced. Here's what the main app module looks like:

```
const remote = "https://reactnative.dev/docs/assets/favicon.png";

export default function LazyLoading() {
  const [source, setSource] = useState<ImageSourcePropType | null>(null);
```

```
    return (
      <View style={styles.container}>
        <LazyImage
          style={{ width: 200, height: 150 }}
          resizeMode="contain"
          source={source}
        />
        <Button
          label="Load Remote"
          onPress={() => {
            setSource({ uri: remote });
          }}
        />
      </View>
    );
}
```

This is what the screen looks like initially:

Figure 27.5: Initial state of the image

Then, click the **Load Remote** button to eventually see the image that we actually want:

Figure 27.6: Loaded image

You might notice that, depending on your network speed, the placeholder image remains visible, even after you click the **Load Remote** button. This is by design because you don't want to remove the placeholder image until you know for sure that the actual image is ready to be displayed. Now, let's render some icons in our React Native application.

Rendering icons

In the final section of this chapter, you'll learn how to render icons in React Native components. Using icons to indicate meaning makes web applications more usable. So, why should native mobile applications be any different?

We'll use the @expo/vector-icons package to pull various vector font packages into your React Native app. This package is already part of the Expo project that we're using as the base of the app, and now, you can import Icon components and render them. Let's implement an example that renders several **FontAwesome** icons based on a selected icon category:

```
export default function RenderingIcons() {
  const [selected, setSelected] = useState<IconsType>("web_app_icons");
  const [listSource, setListSource] = useState<IconName[]>([]);
  const categories = Object.keys(iconNames);

  function updateListSource(selected: IconsType) {
    const listSource = iconNames[selected] as any;
    setListSource(listSource);
    setSelected(selected);
  }

  useEffect(() => {
    updateListSource(selected);
  }, []);
```

Here, we have defined all necessary logic to store and update the icon data. Next, we will apply it to the layout:

```
return (
  <View style={styles.container}>
    <View style={styles.picker}>
```

```
          <Picker selectedValue={selected} onValueChange={updateListSource}>
            {categories.map((category) => (
              <Picker.Item key={category} label={category} value={category}
/>
            ))}
          </Picker>
        </View>
        <FlatList
          style={styles.icons}
          data={listSource.map((value, key) => ({ key: key.toString(), value
})))}
          renderItem={({ item }) => (
            <View style={styles.item}>
              <Icon name={item.value} style={styles.itemIcon} />
              <Text style={styles.itemText}>{item.value}</Text>
            </View>
          )}
        />
      </View>
    );
}
```

When you run this example, you should see something that looks like the following:

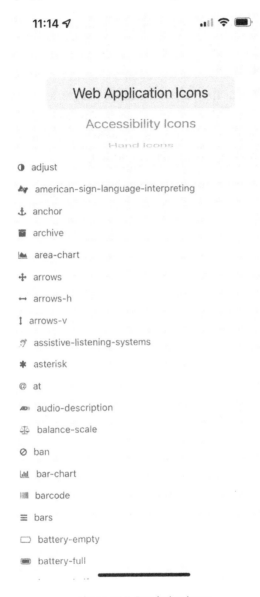

Figure 27.7: Rendering icons

Summary

In this chapter, we learned about handling images in our React Native applications. Images in a native application are just as important in a native mobile context as they are in a web context: they improve the user experience.

We learned about the different approaches to loading images, as well as how to resize them. We also learned how to implement a lazy image, which displays a placeholder image while the actual image is loading. Finally, we learned how to use icons in a React Native app. These skills will help you manage images and make your app more informative.

In the next chapter, we'll learn about local storage in React Native, which is handy when our app goes offline.

28

Going Offline

Users expect applications to operate seamlessly with unreliable network connections. If your mobile application can't cope with transient network issues, your users will use a different app. When there's no network, you have to persist data locally on the device. Alternatively, perhaps your app doesn't even require network access, in which case you'll still need to store data locally.

In this chapter, you'll learn how to do those three things with React Native. First, you'll learn how to detect the state of the network connection. Second, you'll learn how to store data locally. Lastly, you'll learn how to synchronize local data that's been stored due to network problems once it comes back online.

In this chapter, we'll cover the following topics:

- Detecting the state of the network
- Storing application data
- Synchronizing application data

Technical requirements

You can find the code files for this chapter on GitHub at https://github.com/PacktPublishing/ React-and-React-Native-5E/tree/main/Chapter28.

Detecting the state of the network

If your code tries to make a request over the network while disconnected using `fetch()`, for example an error will occur. You probably have error-handling code in place for these scenarios already, since the server could return some other type of error.

However, in the case of connectivity trouble, you might want to detect this issue before the user attempts to make network requests.

There are two potential reasons for proactively detecting the network state. The first one is to prevent the user from performing any network requests until you've detected that the app is back online. To do that, you can display a friendly message to the user stating that, since the network is disconnected, they can't do anything. The other possible benefit of early network state detection is that you can prepare to perform actions offline and sync the app state when the network is connected again.

Let's look at some code that uses the `NetInfo` utility from the `@react-native-community/netinfo` package to handle changes in network state:

```
const connectedMap = {
  none: "Disconnected",
  unknown: "Disconnected",
  cellular: "Connected",
  wifi: "Connected",
  bluetooth: "Connected",
  ethernet: "Connected",
  wimax: "Connected",
  vpn: "Connected",
  other: "Connected",
} as const;
```

connectedMap covers all connection states and will help us to render them on the screen. Let's now see the App component:

```
export default function App() {
  const [connected, setConnected] = useState("");

  useEffect(() => {
    function onNetworkChange(connection: NetInfoState) {
      const type = connection.type;
      setConnected(connectedMap[type]);
    }

    const unsubscribe = NetInfo.addEventListener(onNetworkChange);

    return () => {
      unsubscribe();
    };
  }, []);

  return (
    <View style={styles.container}>
      <Text>{connected}</Text>
    </View>
  );
}
```

This component will render the state of the network based on the string values in connectedMap. The onNetworkChange event of the NetInfo object will cause the connected state to change.

For example, when you run this app for the first time, the screen might look like this:

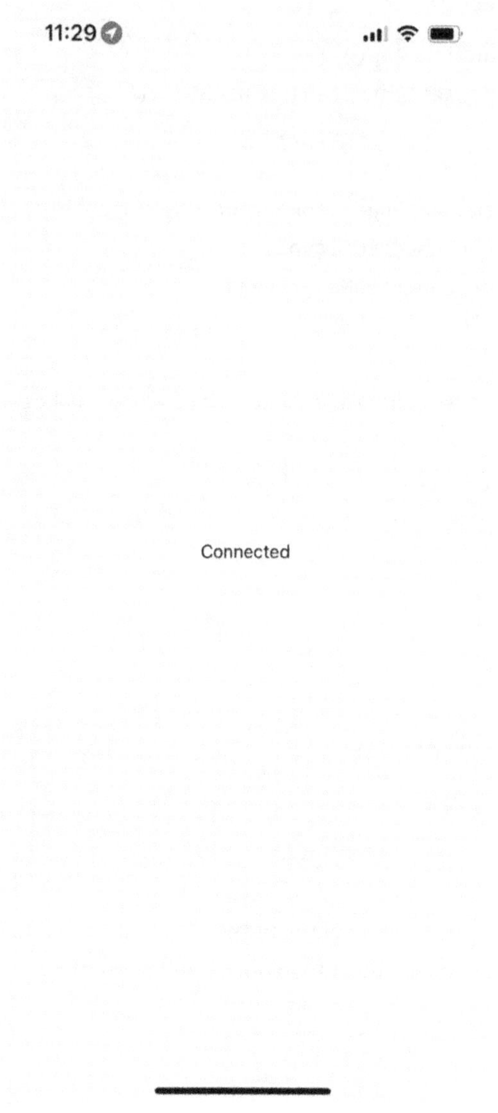

11:29 🧭   .ıll 🛜 🔋

Connected

Figure 28.1: Connected state

Then, if you turn off networking on your host machine, the network state will change on the emulated device as well, causing the state of our application to change, as follows:

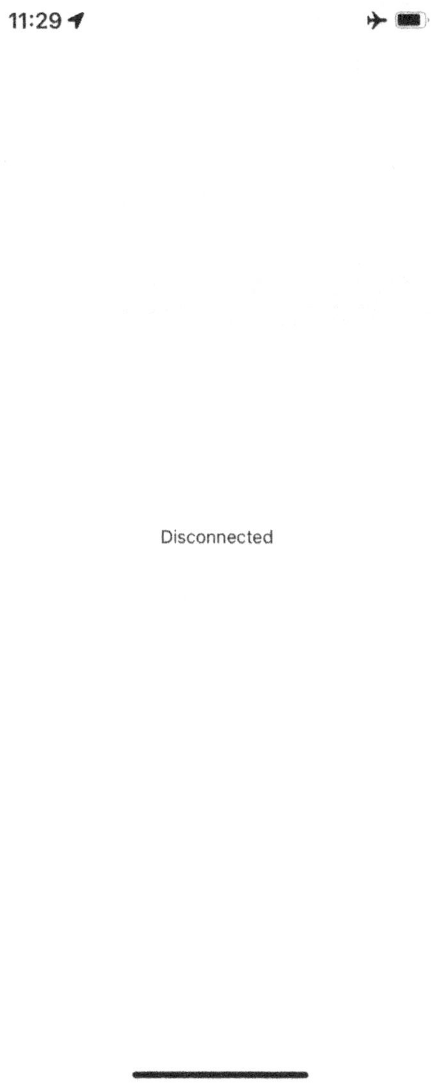

11:29 ✈ ➤ ▪ 🔋

Disconnected

——————

Figure 28.2: Disconnected state

This is how you can use network state detection in the app. As discussed, together with showing the message, you can use network state to prevent users from making API requests. Another valuable approach would be to save user inputs locally until the network gets back online. Let's explore it in the next section.

Storing application data

To store data on the device, there is a special cross-platform solution called AsyncStorage API. It works the same on both the iOS and Android platforms. You would use this API for applications that don't require any network connectivity in the first place or to store data that will eventually be synchronized using an API endpoint once a network becomes available.

To install the async-storage package, run the following command:

```
npx expo install @react-native-async-storage/async-storage
```

Let's look at some code that allows the user to enter a key and a value and then stores them:

```
export default function App() {
  const [key, setKey] = useState("");
  const [value, setValue] = useState("");
  const [source, setSource] = useState<KeyValuePair[]>([]);
```

The key, value, and source values will handle our state. To save it in AsyncStorage, we need to define functions:

```
function setItem() {
  return AsyncStorage.setItem(key, value)
    .then(() => {
      setKey("");
      setValue("");
    })
    .then(loadItems);
}

function clearItems() {
  return AsyncStorage.clear();
}

async function loadItems() {
  const keys = await AsyncStorage.getAllKeys();
  const values = await AsyncStorage.multiGet(keys);
  setSource([...values]);
}
```

```
  useEffect(() => {
    loadItems();
  }, []);
```

We've defined handlers to save values from the inputs, clear AsyncStorage, and load saved items when we start the app. Here's the markup that's rendered by the App component:

```
return (
  <View style={styles.container}>
    <Text>Key:</Text>
    <TextInput
      style={styles.input}
      value={key}
      onChangeText={(v) => {
        setKey(v);
      }}
    />
    <Text>Value:</Text>
    <TextInput
      style={styles.input}
      value={value}
      onChangeText={(v) => {
        setValue(v);
      }}
    />
    <View style={styles.controls}>
      <Button label="Add" onPress={setItem} />
      <Button label="Clear" onPress={clearItems} />
    </View>
```

The markup in the preceding code block is represented as inputs and buttons to create, save, and delete items. Next, we will render the list of items with the FlatList component:

```
    <View style={styles.list}>
      <FlatList
        data={source.map(([key, value]) => ({
          key: key.toString(),
          value,
```

```
      }))}
      renderItem={(({ item: { value, key } }) => (
        <Text>
          {value} ({key})
        </Text>
      )}
    />
  </View>
</View>
);
```

Before we walk through what this code is doing, let's take a look at the following screen, since it'll explain most of what we're going to cover when storing application data:

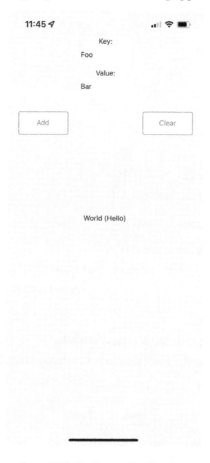

Figure 28.3: Storing application data

As you can see in *Figure 28.3*, there are two input fields and two buttons. The fields allow the user to enter a new key and value. The **Add** button allows the user to store this key-value pair locally on their device, while the **Clear** button clears any existing items that have been stored previously.

The AsyncStorage API works the same for both iOS and Android. Under the hood, AsyncStorage works very differently, depending on which platform it's running on. The reason React Native is able to expose the same storage API on both platforms is due to its simplicity: it's just key-value pairs. Anything more complex than that is left up to the application developer.

The abstractions that you've created around AsyncStorage in this example are minimal. The idea is to set and get items. However, even straightforward actions like this deserve an abstraction layer. For example, the setItem() method you've implemented here will make the asynchronous call to AsyncStorage and update the item's state once that has been completed. Loading items is even more complicated because you need to get the keys and values as two separate asynchronous operations.

The reason we do this is to keep the UI responsive. If there are pending screen repaints that need to happen while data is being written to disk, preventing those from happening by blocking them would lead to a suboptimal user experience.

In the next section, you'll learn how to synchronize data that's been stored locally while the device is offline with remote services once the device comes back online.

Synchronizing application data

So far in this chapter, you've learned how to detect the state of a network connection and how to store data locally in a React Native application. Now, it's time to combine these two concepts and implement an app that can detect network outages and continue to function.

The basic idea is to only make network requests when you know for sure that the device is online. If you know that it isn't, you can store any changes in the state locally. Then, when you're back online, you can synchronize those stored changes with the remote API.

Let's implement a simplified React Native app that does this. The first step is to implement an abstraction that sits between the React components and the network calls that store data. We'll call this module store.ts:

```
export function set(key: Key, value: boolean) {
  return new Promise((resolve, reject) => {
    if (connected) {
      fakeNetworkData[key] = value;
```

```
        resolve(true);
      } else {
        AsyncStorage.setItem(key, value.toString()).then(
          () => {

            unsynced.push(key);

            resolve(false);
          },
          (err) => reject(err)
        );
      }
    });
  }
```

The set method depends on the connected variable, and depending on whether there is an internet connection or not, it handles the different logic. Actually, the get method also follows the same approach:

```
export function get(key?: Key): Promise<boolean | typeof fakeNetworkData>
{
  return new Promise((resolve, reject) => {

    if (connected) {
      resolve(key ? fakeNetworkData[key] : fakeNetworkData);
    } else if (key) {
      AsyncStorage.getItem(key)
        .then((item) => resolve(item === "true"))
        .catch((err) => reject(err));
    } else {
      AsyncStorage.getAllKeys()
        .then((keys) =>
          AsyncStorage.multiGet(keys).then((items) =>
            resolve(Object.fromEntries(items) as any)
          )
        )
        .catch((err) => reject(err));
```

```
    }
  });
}
```

This module exports two functions, set() and get(). Their jobs are to set and get data, respectively. Since this is just a demonstration of how to sync between local storage and network endpoints, this module just mocks the actual network with the fakeNetworkData object.

Let's start by looking at the set() function. It's an asynchronous function that will always return a promise that resolves to a Boolean value. If it's true, it means that you're online and that the call over the network was successful. If it's false, it means that you're offline, and AsyncStorage was used to save the data.

The same approach is used with the get() function. It returns a promise that resolves a Boolean value that indicates the state of the network. If a key argument is provided, then the value for that key is looked up. Otherwise, all the values are returned, either from the network or from AsyncStorage.

In addition to these two functions, this module does two other things:

```
NetInfo.fetch().then(
  (connection) => {
    connected = ["wifi", "unknown"].includes(connection.type);
  },
  () => {
    connected = false;
  }
);
NetInfo.addEventListener((connection) => {
  connected = ["wifi", "unknown"].includes(connection.type);

  if (connected && unsynced.length) {
    AsyncStorage.multiGet(unsynced).then((items) => {
      items.forEach(([key, val]) => set(key as Key, val === "true"));
      unsynced.length = 0;
    });
  }
});
```

It uses NetInfo.fetch() to set the connected state. Then, it adds a listener to listen for changes in the network state. This is how items that were saved locally when you were offline become synced with the network when it's connected again.

Now, let's check out the main application that uses these functions:

```
export default function App() {
  const [message, setMessage] = useState<string | null>(null);
  const [first, setFirst] = useState(false);
  const [second, setSecond] = useState(false);
  const [third, setThird] = useState(false);
  const setters = new Map([
    ["first", setFirst],
    ["second", setSecond],
    ["third", setThird],
  ]);
```

Here, we have defined the state variables that we will use in the Switch components:

```
function save(key: Key) {
  return (value: boolean) => {
    set(key, value).then(
      (connected) => {
        setters.get(key)?.(value);
        setMessage(connected ? null : "Saved Offline");
      },
      (err) => {
        setMessage(err);
      }
    );
  };
}
```

The save() function helps us to reuse logic in a different Switch component. Next, we have the useEffect hook to get saved data when the page renders for the first time:

```
useEffect(() => {
  NetInfo.fetch().then(() =>
    get().then(
      (items) => {
```

```
            for (let [key, value] of Object.entries(items)) {
              setters.get(key)?.(value);
            }
          },
          (err) => {
            setMessage(err);
          }
        )
      );
    }, []);
```

Next, let's take a look at the final markup of the page:

```
    return (
      <View style={styles.container}>
        <Text>{message}</Text>
        <View>
          <Text>First</Text>
          <Switch value={first} onValueChange={save("first")} />
        </View>
        <View>
          <Text>Second</Text>
          <Switch value={second} onValueChange={save("second")} />
        </View>
        <View>
          <Text>Third</Text>
          <Switch value={third} onValueChange={save("third")} />
        </View>
      </View>
    );
```

The job of the App component is to save the state of three Switch components, which is difficult when you're providing the user with a seamless transition between online and offline modes. Thankfully, your set() and get() abstractions, which are implemented in another module, hide most of the details from the application's functionality.

Note, however, that you need to check the state of the network in this module before you attempt to load any items. If you don't do this, then the get() function will assume that you're offline, even if the connection is fine.

Here's what the app looks like:

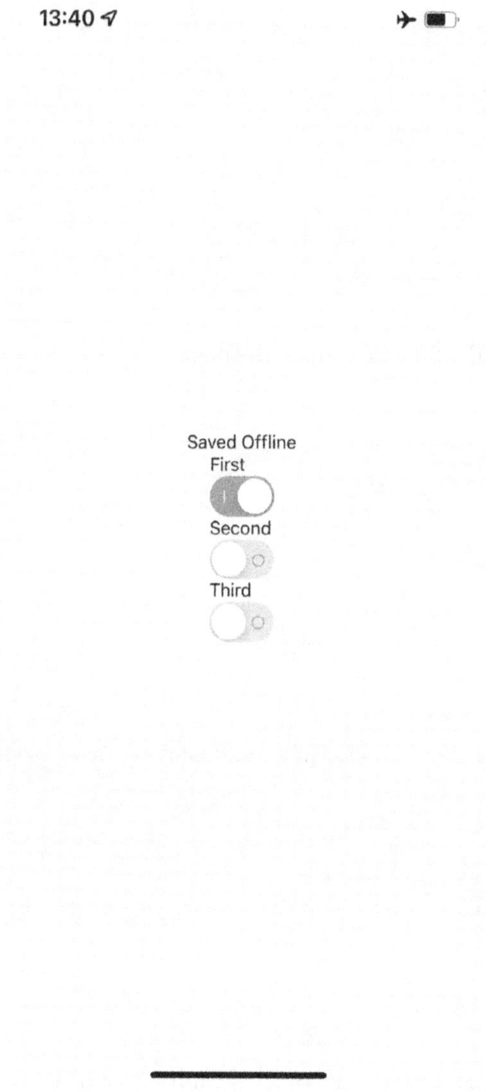

Figure 28.4: Synchronizing application data

Note that you won't actually see the **Saved Offline** message until you change something in the UI.

Summary

This chapter introduced us to storing data offline in React Native applications. The main reason we would want to store data locally is when the device goes offline and our app can't communicate with a remote API. However, not all applications require API calls, and AsyncStorage can be used as a general-purpose storage mechanism. We just need to implement the appropriate abstractions around it.

We also learned how to detect changes in the network state of React Native apps. It's important to know when the device has gone offline so that our storage layer doesn't make pointless attempts at network calls. Instead, we can let the user know that the device is offline and then synchronize the application state when a connection is available.

In the next chapter, we'll learn how to import and use UI components from the NativeBase library.

Join us on Discord!

Read this book alongside other users and the authors themselves. Ask questions, provide solutions to other readers, chat with the authors, and more. Scan the QR code or visit the link to join the community.

https://packt.link/ReactAndReactNative5e

Other Books You May Enjoy

If you enjoyed this book, you may be interested in these other books by Packt:

React 18 Design Patterns and Best Practices - Fourth Edition

Carlos Santana Roldán

ISBN: 9781803233109

- Get familiar with the new React 18 and Node 19 features
- Explore TypeScript's basic and advanced capabilities
- Make components communicate with each other by applying various patterns and techniques
- Dive into MonoRepo architecture

- Use server-side rendering to make applications load faster

- Write a comprehensive set of tests to create robust and maintainable code

- Build high-performing applications by styling and optimizing React components

React Key Concepts

Maximilian Schwarzmüller

ISBN: 9781803234502

- Build modern, user-friendly, and reactive web apps
- Create components and utilize props to pass data between them
- Handle events, perform state updates, and manage conditional content
- Apply styles dynamically and conditionally to create a modern UI
- Use advanced state management techniques such as React's context API
- Utilize React router to render different pages for different URLs
- Understand key best practices and optimization opportunities

Packt is searching for authors like you

If you're interested in becoming an author for Packt, please visit authors.packtpub.com and apply today. We have worked with thousands of developers and tech professionals, just like you, to help them share their insight with the global tech community. You can make a general application, apply for a specific hot topic that we are recruiting an author for, or submit your own idea.

Share your thoughts

Now you've finished *React and React Native, Fifth Edition*, we'd love to hear your thoughts! Scan the QR code below to go straight to the Amazon review page for this book and share your feedback or leave a review on the site that you purchased it from.

https://packt.link/r/1805127306

Your review is important to us and the tech community and will help us make sure we're delivering excellent quality content.

Index

Download a free PDF copy of this book

Thanks for purchasing this book!

Do you like to read on the go but are unable to carry your print books everywhere?

Is your eBook purchase not compatible with the device of your choice?

Don't worry, now with every Packt book you get a DRM-free PDF version of that book at no cost.

Read anywhere, any place, on any device. Search, copy, and paste code from your favorite technical books directly into your application.

The perks don't stop there, you can get exclusive access to discounts, newsletters, and great free content in your inbox daily.

Follow these simple steps to get the benefits:

1. Scan the QR code or visit the link below:

https://packt.link/free-ebook/9781805127307

2. Submit your proof of purchase.
3. That's it! We'll send your free PDF and other benefits to your email directly.

Made in the USA
Las Vegas, NV
07 July 2024

92011111R00280